the library
IN EAST AYRSHIRE

East Ayrshire
COUNCIL

Please return item by last date shown,
or contact library to renew

Published in the United Kingdom
by Eric Dobby Publishing Ltd
12 Warnford Rd, Orpington, Kent BR6 6LW, UK

A catalogue record is available for this book from the British Library.

ISBN: 1 85882 049 9

Printed by Sino Publishing House Ltd in Hong Kong.

Contents

'As, dangling in the wind, he hangs
A gibbet's tassle.'

- Robert Burns. 'To Colonel de Peyster'.

Acknowledgements

Although I particularly wish to thank Anne Escott and her staff in the Glasgow Room of the Mitchell Library, Glasgow, where my research was centred, this book would not have been possible without the assistance of the following individuals, librarians and archivists throughout Scotland and beyond.

Norman Adams, Banchory, Aberdeen
Sheena Andrews, Carnegie Library, Ayr
Andrew Bethune, Edinburgh Room, Central Library, Edinburgh
Audrey Brown, District Library, Kirkcaldy
Rosamund Brown, Principal Librarian, Selkirk
Patricia Burke, Central Library, Paisley
Stephen J Connelly, A K Bell Library, Perth
Ian C Copland, District Librarian, Cupar
Leslie Couperwhite, Watt Library, Greenock
Helen Darling, Library Headquarters, Selkirk
David Devereux, Library Services, Kirkcudbright
George A Dixon, Archive Services, Stirling
Alan R Fulton, Library Services, Aberdeen
Arthur F James, Local Studies Librarian, Dumbarton
Sheena McDougall, Edinburgh City Libraries
Jeff Parkes, Inveraray Jail
Marion Richardson, Local Studies Department, Dalkeith
Carol A Sneddon, District Library, Falkirk
Robert Steward, Archivist, Highland Council, Inverness
David Stockdale, McManus Galleries, Dundee
A T Wilson, City Archivist, Edinburgh
Graeme Wilson, Libraries Department, Elgin
The British Library, London
Bibliotheque Nationale, Paris

Illustrations

Introduction

Executions, especially when public and before the Capital Punishment Amendment Act of 1868, are part of our social history. Your forebears and mine, particularly if they lived in Edinburgh or one of the circuit towns, will have jostled for a place in the crowds around a gibbet or scaffold. Some may even have been the hapless culprit.

The subject has not been entirely ignored. The cases of Deacon Brodie and William Burke at Edinburgh are as renowned as William Pritchard and Peter Manuel at Glasgow, but generally attention has focused on the crime and not its expiation.

Due to the inherent dangers of 'Reminiscences', research for this book has come from contemporary newspapers - which in some instances, were going to press with the culprit still suspended. The dangers of secondary sources can be illustrated by the case of the murderer Matthew Clydesdale, executed at Glasgow on 4th November 1818. Peter McKenzie's book, *Reminiscences of Glasgow and the West of Scotland* (written and published in the 1860s), would have us believe that Clydesdale was restored to life during anatomical dissection, which contemporary writing shows to be nonsense.

What follows, of course, is only as good as surviving material. Some local authorities maintained better records than others - and preserved them - particularly Edinburgh in relation to its executioners, where each incumbent merits a mention in the council minutes. Glasgow, on the other hand, is poor in this respect.

The book has been compiled for reference, hence only a summary of each execution is given. But the cross references between 'Places of Execution', the Chronological Accounts of the Executions, the 'Capital Crimes and Culprits', along with the 'Alphabetic List of Culprits' should make an individual, or case, relatively easy to find.

A public hanging was a brutal affair, but no more so than the lives of many who watched. And at least the culprit could derive some support, or distraction, from the crowd. At private executions within prisons, from 1868 onwards, with no supporting crowd, the act became lonely and macabre.

1

The Gibbet, Gallows and Scaffold

By the eighteenth century, the freestanding gibbet or gallows structure had supplanted the trees, castle ramparts and cliffs of earlier times and from the widespread use of the prefix 'gallows' in place names - Gallowgate, Gallowhill and Gallows Knowe etc. - there must have been many of them across the country.

The Oxford English Dictionary defines each, as follows:

> **Gibbet;** *Hist*. Originally a gallows. Later an upright post with a projecting arm from which the bodies of criminals were hung after execution.

> **Gallows;** a structure usually consisting of two upright posts and a cross-piece, for the hanging of criminals.

The much later Scaffold, was a raised platform, upon which the gallows stood.

No gibbets have survived in Scotland, and the only known drawings come from Ayr and Inverness. Of several preserved in England, the best known is the Steng Cross Gibbet, or Winter's Gibbet in Northumbria, with its 18' upright post.

In 1768, Ayr Town Council commissioned a local surveyor, James Gregg, to draw, *A Map of the Common Grounds Belonging to Ayr*. The plan shows not only the gibbet, but the gibbeted body of David Edwards, executed in 1758. A diarist, writing in the 1790s, records that part of him was still there in 1778. It had cost 16s 10d to build.

George Penny, in his 1836 book *Traditions of Perth*, writes of the hazardous business carried on by executioners:

> 'The ancient practice was by means of a treble ladder which was set up

David Edwards on the Gibbet at Ayr (*Ayr Carnegie Library*)

'The Weird Gibbet Stone' engraving, Glasgow Cathedral (*Mitchell Library, Glasgow*)

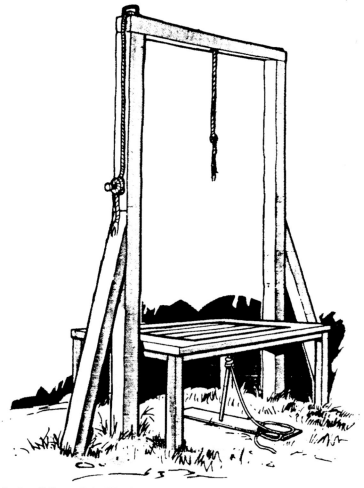

The Symington Gallows (John Worthington, 17th February, 1815)   (*Drawing, Christy Danielles*)

against the gallows; the criminal mounted on one side and the executioner the other, and when the signal was given, the hangman pushed the culprit off the ladder.'

Poor quality rope added to the problems. In May 1785, when Hislop and Wallace were thrown off at Jedburgh both ropes snapped; and three days later, the Magistrates of Ayr suffered the same embarrassment with Mossman, Means and Barns.

At a number of places, by way of an improvement on the ladder, the condemned stood on a cart, which was then driven away.

By the beginning of the nineteenth century, executions were coming into town centres, generally outside the tollbooth or prison. The days of the gibbet were gone.

With the scaffold, the culprit stood on a drop, i.e. a platform, which, through the activation of a lever, opened, leaving him suspended. As with the gibbet, death was by strangulation.

Robert Chambers in his book, *Traditions of Edinburgh*, retells the story of Deacon William Brodie's execution at Edinburgh on 1st October 1788:

'Brodie was the first who proved the excellence of an improvement he had

Nineteenth century Glasgow scaffold (*Mitchell Library, Glasgow*)

formerly made on the apparatus of the gibbet. This was the substitution of what is called the drop for the ancient practice of the double ladder. He inspected the thing with a professional air, and seemed to view the result of his ingenuity with a smile of satisfaction.'

Despite Chambers' recognised authority on the history of Edinburgh, there are problems with this romantic tale.

Reports of the execution of James and William Brodie and Jean Lindsay on 3rd November 1784 at Glasgow, where previously a cart had been used, relate that:

> "The Gibbet and Scaffold was constructed on the plan of the London Scaffold with springs ...'.

And at Aberdeen, in June 1788, James Grant was executed:

> '... in the way now used in England ... the place on which the criminal stood was made to fall down, and leave him suspended.'

A contemporary report of William Brodie's execution reads:

> 'Smith slowly ascended the steps, and was immediately followed by Brodie, who mounted with briskness and agility, and examined the dreadful apparatus with attention, and particularly the halter designed for himself.'

It is unlikely that the press would miss the irony of a man, particularly one as renowned as Deacon Brodie, being executed on a scaffold which he had designed.

The scaffold changed very little during the nineteenth century. When Montrose borrowed the Aberdeen scaffold to execute Andrew Brown in 1866, it was then 40 years old.

The report of Pritchard's execution in the *Edinburgh Evening Courant* of 29th July 1865, contains the following description of the Glasgow contraption:

> 'About two o'clock (am) the scaffold was brought from a shed in Clyde Street, a short distance from the jail, and its appearance caused great sensation.
>
> 'The erection of the scaffold, which has been in use during the last fifty years, was watched with much interest. On the rope being fastened to the beam, a thrill of horror ran through the crowd. The fitting up of the scaffold was concluded about half-past three.
>
> 'The scaffold is a large, black-painted box, the interior of which is about 12 feet square, the sides rising 3 feet above the platform. The height of the beam is about 8 or 9 feet, and the rope was placed so as to let the culprit fall between 3 and 4 feet.
>
> 'The frame of the scaffold is on wheels, and is put together for the most part with bolts. The platform is reached by a broad flight of steps. Underneath the platform, as usual, a coffin was placed. It was a plain, black shell, and certainly appeared scarcely long enough for the body it was to contain.' *(see page 3)*

Executions within prisons came with the Capital Punishment Amendment Act of 1868, and in some respects lost their dignity. Culprits were dropping into wells, pits and joiner shop basements.

For its first private execution - Docherty on 5th October 1875 - Glasgow had a new scaffold built. When two weeks later it was in Dumbarton to hang Wardlaw, The *Dumbarton Herald and County Advertiser*, due to the novelty of the occasion, described the contraption in their report:

> 'The scaffold was constructed to meet the requirements of Glasgow prison [Duke Street]. There, a window on the second storey has been broken out so as to form a doorway to the scaffold, and on leaving his cell the doomed man has merely to walk on to the scaffold without otherwise leaving the prison building at all ... It will be seen that the scaffold was about 10 feet or 10 feet six inches from the ground. It is almost square in its proportions, being fully six feet across each of the front, sides and the back. The fatal drop is of a novel construction. It is attached to the back part of the platform by strong hinges, and supported on the front by three small bolts, which come right through from the front and which are attached to a lever.
>
> This lever has a long handle immediately to the back of the prisoner and on the right hand side of the scaffold, which is held back by a small chain. Upon this being removed it allows the lever to work back, which withdraws the three bolts referred to, and the platform upon which the prisoner stands immediately drops down, and the one end falling against two pads of India rubber to prevent noise, is retained firmly there by two springs, and the unhappy victim is left hanging in mid air.'

The next change was the length of the drop. With the departure of William Calcraft and the arrival of Marwood and Berry, came science. Now the length of drop was adjusted according to the weight, build and apparent strength of the culprit. Instantaneous death had replaced agonising strangulation.

In the last change before the 'execution chamber', Glasgow led the way with, 'The New Scaffold', for the execution of George Paterson in Duke Street Prison in 1897.

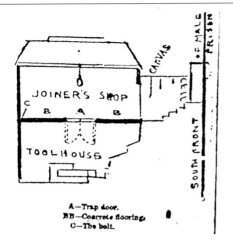

A—Trap door.
BB—Concrete flooring.
C—The bolt.

The Execution Shed', Duke Street Prison, Glasgow, 1890s
(*Mitchell Library, Glasgow*)

An Act for Better Preventing the Horrid Crime of Murder, 1752
The Anatomy Act, 1832

With a spiralling murder rate, particularly in London, which was 'contrary to the known humanity and natural Genius of the British Nation', Parliament in 1751 was forced to add 'a further Terror and peculiar Mark of Infamy to the Punishment of Death'.

With the implementation of, 'An Act for better preventing the horrid Crime of Murder', from the first day of the Easter Term 1752, the bodies of hanged murderers would either be gibbeted or given for anatomical dissection. What the surgeons had previously stolen, was now lawfully theirs.

The condemned cell was introduced. No longer would culprits await execution in the common rooms with other prisoners, which in the early days would have included debtors. In most prisons they were manacled to an iron bar set in the cell floor.

Their diet was to be bread and water. But as the last part of section 1 of the Act, which stated that culprits would be executed, 'on the Day next but one after Sentence passed, unless the same shall happen to be the Lord's Day, commonly called Sunday, and in that Case on the Monday following, was not implemented, it is doubtful whether this was enforced. It did however remain as part of the sentence of death.

Gibbeting, it was thought, would extend, 'a just Horror in the Mind of the Offender, and on the Minds of such as shall be present'. This early attempt at crime prevention, hoped that gibbeted bodies around the country would help the populace to mend its ways.

After execution, the murderer's body would be taken down, encased in an iron frame, and re-suspended.

In his epic poem, Robert Burns' intrepid hero, *Tam O'Shanter*, notes upon the holy table:

'A murderer's banes, in gibbet-airns

A description of 'gibbet irons', appears in an article in the *Elgin Courant and Courier*, of 3rd January 1868, and refers to the gibbeting of Kenneth Leal at Janet Innes's Cairn on 7th July 1773:

> In 1829 a number of workmen in the employment of Mr John Sellar, millwright, Longhill, were cutting timber in the Sleepieshill wood near "Kenny's

Reporting the execution, the *Evening Times* gave the following description of the scaffold:

'On the face of the brae opposite the entrance in the south front of the male prison is the joiner's shop, and underneath it, entering by a door from a stair leading down to the lower part of the prison, is a tool-house. The joiner's shop is lit from the roof.

'The floor is of cement, with the exception of a square in the centre, underneath the joiner's bench, which at ordinary times is filled in with wood.

'On the eve of the execution, as was done last week, this piece of wooden flooring is removed, and in its place is inserted the fatal trap, a couple of heavy hinged doors opening downward from the middle by the pulling of a bolt at the side.

'To the steel beam overhead supporting the roof is fixed the rope with the noose, and when the bolt is pulled the culprit, standing on the trap, drops down into the tool house, remaining suspended above his coffin.

These temporary structures survived until the 1940s, when they were replaced by the three storey death chamber.

Hillock", and in a frolic began poking up the ground with pointed sticks near where the gibbet had stood, when they discovered the body lying between two and three feet from the surface. The chain was first got hold of, and on pulling it up all the hoops attached to it and encircling the body were brought to light. The complete apparatus consisted of a ring round each ankle, from which a chain of ordinary make passed up either leg and was fastened to a band of strong hoop iron round the body; from this ring or band four straps of a similar construction passed over the shoulders to the ring that encircled the neck, the neck ring in its turn being attached to the head cap, which consisted of four straps passing up either side of the head and meeting at the top, where a strong swivel-link was riveted through them to allow it to turn with the wind.

The body was suspended from the gibbet by a chain rather more than two feet long and made of 3/8 inch round iron, the links being about three inches in diameter, in the form of a common chimney "crook".

The bones and the whole apparatus were again buried, with the exception of the head-piece and the chain to which it was riveted; these were carried as trophies to Longhill and hung dangling on the garden paling near Mr Sellar's workshop till the August flood of the same year, when the burn of Longhill carried off the paling and chain ... '

As with McLaughlane at Ayr in 1779 and others, it was not unknown for bodies to be stolen off the gibbet.

In Edinburgh, Aberdeen and Glasgow the medical schools had, so to speak, the gallows on their doorstep, but with executions elsewhere, it was the responsibility of the college or university to have someone on hand, with a cart, to take the body. In only two instances, Ayr in 1780, and Inveraray in 1807, did the body go to a local medical practitioner.

The Anatomy Act of 1832, in an attempt to fill the need for the supply of bodies to medical schools, brought more change. In its preamble, with reference to the activities of Burke and Hare, it says:

'And whereas, in order further to supply Human Bodies for such Purposes, divers great and grievous Crimes have been committed, and lately Murder, for the single object of selling for such purposes the Bodies of the Persons so murdered.'

By section 16 of the Act, the bodies of executed murderers would no longer be available for dissection, although they could still be hung in chains. The bodies would now be buried within the precincts of the prison in which they were last held.

Public to Private
The Capital Punishment Amendment Act, 1868

Following a report by a House of Commons Committee in 1866, Parliament debated the question of public executions. The ceremony, it was agreed, had fallen into disrepute:

'Through the scandalous and revolting scenes with which these spectacles were attended, the lawlessness and brutality of the crowd which they brought together, and the tendency of the exhibition rather to degrade and harden the minds of the spectators than to produce any ameliorating or deterrent effect.'

Mr Gathorne Hardy, the Home Secretary, introducing the bill, explained the proposed regulations and securities which would be adopted for assuring the public that the sentence had been carried into effect. Some feared difficulties affording evidence to satisfy the incredulous.

Passed by both Houses, the bill received the Royal Assent on 29th May 1868

The kernel of the Act, Section 2, reads:

'Judgement of Death [Sentence of Death in Scotland] to be executed on any prisoner sentenced after the passing of this Act on any Indictment or Inquisition for Murder shall be carried into effect within the Walls of the Prison in which the Offender is confined at the Time of Execution'.

To assist implementation of the Act the following 'rules' were printed and distributed:

'Rules made by Her Majesty's Principal Secretary of State for the Home Department, pursuant to the provisions of the Capital Punishment

Amendment Act 1868, for regulating the execution of Capital Sentences.

1)   For the sake of uniformity it is recommended that Executions should take place at the hour of 8 a.m. on the first Monday after the intervention of three Sundays from the day on which Sentence is passed.

2)   The mode of execution, and the ceremonial attending it, to be the same as heretofore in use.

3)   A Black flag to be hoisted at the moment of execution, upon a Staff placed on an elevated and conspicuous part of the Prison, and to remain displayed for one hour.

4)   The Bell of the Prison, or if arrangements can be made for that purpose, the Bell of the Parish or other neighbouring Church, to be tolled for 15 minutes before and 15 minutes after the execution.

By coincidence, both Scotland and England were to have their last public execution on the same day - 12th May 1868 - 17 days before the Act became law. At Dumfries, the Magistrates had to execute the murderer Robert Smith, whilst in London Michael Barrett was to be executed at Newgate.

With the new legislation so close, Dumfries petitioned the Home Secretary to have Smith hanged within the prison - but to no avail. It was a sordid and poorly attended affair.

A respite extended Barrett's life until the third day before the new act.

At Perth in October 1870, George Chalmers opened the new chapter, as the first Scottish culprit to be executed in private.

William Calcraft officiated at both Scottish executions.

Although the day of the vast crowd was past, there would always be a token crowd by the prison gate.

NOTICE

OF EXECUTION OF

SENTENCE OF DEATH

PASSED ON

ALBERT JAMES FRASER

AND

JAMES ROLLINS

BY THE RIGHT HONOURABLE LORD SANDS, AT GLASGOW, ON THE 5th DAY OF MAY, 1920,

Having been carried into effect within the walls of the Prison of Glasgow, between the hours of Eight and Ten o'clock a.m., on the 26th day of May, 1920.

(COPIES.)

We, the undersigned, hereby declare that SENTENCE OF DEATH was this day executed on ALBERT JAMES FRASER and JAMES ROLLINS in the Prison of Glasgow in our presence.

Dated this Twenty-sixth day of May, One Thousand Nine Hundred and Twenty.

WILLIAM NICOL, Magistrate.

T. W. SHEDDEN, Magistrate.

THOS. PICKEN, Depute Town-Clerk.

A. D. DRYSDALE, Governor, H.M. Prison, Glasgow.

GILBERT GARREY, Medical Officer, H.M. Prison, Glasgow.

R. WALKER MUIR, Chaplain, H.M. Prison, Glasgow.

J. V. STEVENSON, Chief Constable.

I, GILBERT GARREY, Medical Officer of the Prison of Glasgow, hereby certify that I this day examined the bodies of ALBERT JAMES FRASER and JAMES ROLLINS, on whom SENTENCE OF DEATH was this Day executed in the Prison of Glasgow, and, that, on that examination, I found that the said ALBERT JAMES FRASER and JAMES ROLLINS were dead.

Dated this Twenty-sixth day of May, One Thousand Nine Hundred and Twenty.

GILBERT GARREY, Medical Officer of the Prison of Glasgow.

I, DAVID JAMES MACKENZIE, Esquire, Advocate, Sheriff-Substitute of Lanarkshire, after public inquiry held before me within the Summary Court, County Buildings, Glasgow, this day, in terms of the Thirteenth Section of "The Capital Punishment Amendment Act, 1868," have found, and hereby report and declare, that the SENTENCE OF DEATH pronounced upon ALBERT JAMES FRASER and upon JAMES ROLLINS upon the Fifth day of May current, at Glasgow, by the Right Honourable Lord Sands, was this morning duly executed within the Prison of Glasgow.

Given under my hand at Glasgow, this Twenty-sixth day of May, Nineteen Hundred and Twenty.

DAVID J. MACKENZIE.

Printed by Robert Anderson, 142 West Nile Street, Glasgow

Notice of Sentence of Death (Rollins and Fraser, 26th May 1920) (*Mitchell Library, Glasgow*)

2
The Places of Execution

The Old Tolbooth, Aberdeen, 1806

Aberdeen

The Places of Execution

Standing at the head of the present Errol Street, Gallow Hill was in use from early times until 1776. Overlooking Pittodrie Stadium, its use by impecunious supporters of Aberdeen Football Club earned it the name 'Miser's Hillie'.

Coming to the city centre, the gallows occupied three sites in Castlegate or Castle Street. The first, put up for William Burnett in 1783, being a little east of the Tolbooth. The second, outside the Tolbooth, was chosen for James Grant in 1788. It was from the culprit's last view of the world at this spot that the colloquialism, 'facing down Marischal Street' arose. The third site, by the old Town House, made it possible to walk culprits out of an upper window and on to the scaffold.

Executions
Gallow Hill

26th January 1750	CHARLES GRANT	Wilful Fire-raising
25th June 1751	ALEXANDER GEDDES	Bestiality
24th November 1752	CHRISTIAN PHREN	Murder
	WILLIAM WAST	Murder
16th November 1753	JAMES MILLER	Theft by Housebreaking
28th June 1765	JOHN HUTCHEON	Theft by Housebreaking
29th June 1770	THOMAS STEWART	Murder
1st November 1776	ALEXANDER MORISON	Murder

Castlegate

31st October 1783	WILLIAM BURNETT	Theft
25th July 1784	JEAN CRAIG	Theft
14th January 1785	ELSPET REID	Theft
4th November 1785	JOHN McDONALD	Wilful Fire-raising
1st June 1787	WILLIAM WEBSTER	Theft
27th June 1788	JAMES GRANT	Theft
3rd July 1789	JOHN MONRO	Theft
29th October 1790	JAMES HENDERSON	Murder
11th December 1801	JOHN YOUNG	Murder
15th June 1810	ANDREW HOSACK	Robbery
5th June 1818	JAMES RITCHIE	Sheep Stealing
6th November 1818	JOHN BARNET	Theft by Housebreaking
16th November 1821	GEORGE THOM	Murder
31st May 1822	WILLIAM GORDON	Murder
	ROBERT McINTOSH	Murder
23rd May 1823	THOMAS DONALDSON & WILLIAM BUCHANAN	Stouthrief
	WILLIAM McLEOD	Stouthrief
27th August 1824	ALEXANDER MARTIN	Theft
10th February 1826	WILLIAM ALLEN	Murder
16th November 1827	MALCOLM GILLESPIE	Forgery
8th October 1830	CATHERINE DAVIDSON	Murder
22nd May 1849	JAMES BURNETT	Murder
16th October 1849	JAMES ROBB	Murder
13th January 1853	GEORGE CHRISTIE	Murder
21st October 1857	JOHN BOOTH	Murder

Craiginches Prison

15th August 1963	HENRY JOHN BURNETT	Murder

The Executioners

1773 - 1800/01	ROBERT WELSH
1803/4 - 1805	JOHN MCDONALD (died March 1805?)
1806 - 1818/19	JOHN MILNE

At their meeting on 27th January 1834 the City Council abolished the post.

Appin

The Place of Execution
James Stewart was hanged and gibbetted near the place where he allegedly murdered Colin Campbell, at the edge of Lettermore Wood on the south side of Loch Linnhe, west of Ballachullish. A monument stands at Ballachulish to his memory.

The Execution
8th November 1752   James Stewart   Murder

Executioner
The executioner, whose name in unknown, was reportedly brought from Glasgow.

The Tolbooth, Ayr, circa 1825

Ayr
The Places of Execution.
In June 1758, Ayr's Magistrates were without a gallows, the previous one, last used in 1749 and standing a few hundred yards north of the present railway station, had been lost to a new quarry.

The new gibbet would be on the Common, south of the town, and a plan drawn in 1768 shows not only the gibbet, but the gibbeted body of Edwards (*see page 1*). A diarist writing in 1792 records Edwards, or part of him, being there until 1778. Comparing this plan with current plans shows the gibbet to have stood on the boundary of the dwellinghouse 'The Knowe', Midton Road, and the 'Abbotsford Hotel' at 14 Corsehill Road.

This same gibbet served the town for the remainder of the eighteenth century.

The first execution of the new century, Dornan and Smith in 1809, brought executions to the Tolbooth at the head of New Bridge Street. The Gallows Knowe area on the Common had since been developed. The gallows would now be erected for its afternoon's work on the landing at the Tolbooth door - and laid away until the next occasion. Over the next eleven years, 14 culprits would end their days, 'at the head of the 'Nineteen Steps'.

When the Tolbooth was abandoned in 1825, its fabric was bought by John Robb of Blackburn, then developing Racecourse Road. In the frontage wall of 44 Racecourse Road, presently the Gartferry Hotel, can be seen two large rectangular stones with square centre holes, said to have supported the upper part of the gallows framework.

The new Prison and Courthouse, opened at the west end of Wellington Square in 1821, had the gallows sited at the south end of the west wall. The first to 'end up facing Arran', was the rapist James Burtnay, executed in December 1822. It was used until Ayr's final hanging in 1854. The prison was demolished in 1931 to rise as the present County Buildings.

Executions

The Town's Common

26th June 1758	DAVID EDWARDS	Murder.
25th June 1779	JAMES McLAUCHLANE	Murder.
13th October 1780	MATTHEW HAY	Murder
23rd November 1781	ROBERT DUN	Robbery.
20th May 1785	WILLIAM MOSSMAN	Theft by Housebreaking
	BERNARD MEANS &	Theft by Housebreaking
	JOHN BARNS	
19th October 1787	JAMES McNAB	Horse Stealing

The Tolbooth

20th May 1809	WILLIAM DORNAN &	Theft by Housebreaking
	ROBERT SMITH	
25th May 1810	JOHN McMILLAN	Murder
7th June 1811	GEORGE WATSON	Horsestealing
11th June 1813	JAMES MERRY	Forgery
27th May 1814	JOHN McMANUS	Murder
	ROBERT GIBSON	Robbery
31st May 1816	WILLIAM EVANS	Forgery
17th October 1817	MARGARET CROSSAN	Wilful Fire-Raising
	WILLIAM ROBERTSON &	Robbery
	JOSEPH CAIRNS	
28th May 1819	JOHN McNEIL	Theft by Housebreaking
10th March 1820	WILLIAM McGHEER &	Stouthrief
	CHARLES BRITTAN	

The Prison

20th December 1822	JAMES BURTNAY	Rape
12th December 1823	JAMES ANDERSON &	Murder
	DAVID GLEN	
19th January 1832	SAMUEL WAUGH	Murder
26th October 1848	JAMES McWHEELAN	Murder
11th May 1854	ALEXANDER CUNNINGHAM	Murder

Executioners.

1758 - 1759	Robert Jamieson
1785 - 1793	Peter Grant
1793 - 1793	Lauchlan Grant
1815 - 1815	John Chapman
1815 - 1823	James Aird
1823 - 1827	John Thomson

The post of executioner finally departed with Thomson on 24th October 1827.

Bishopbriggs

The Place of Execution
When condemning Doolan and Redding, the Lord Justice Clerk said the execution '... for an example to the country, should take place at or near to such place adjoining Crosshill, in the parish of Cadder, as the Sheriff shall adjudge'.

If he intended it as 'an example' to others working on the railway, his purpose failed, for few if any attended.

The *Glasgow Argus* reported:

> 'The scaffold was erected in a large field, a short distance from the bridge on which the murder was committed, and the two unhappy men had the fatal spot full in their view when they mounted the ladder.'

The Execution
14th May 1841	DENNIS DOOLAN & PATRICK REDDING	Murder

Executioner
Most probably John Murdoch of Glasgow.

Cupar

The Places of Execution
For Henderson's execution the scaffold was sited at the rear of the 1814 Jail (now Watts night club in Coal Road), where the rising ground in what is now Haugh Park formed a natural amphitheatre.

In 1843 a new County Prison was built in the north east of the town from where the Scanlane brothers were taken to Fluthers Green, which served as the town's common. The Green is now a car park.

McDonald was hanged within this same prison, closed in 1888, and now a Territorial Army barracks in Castlebank Road.

Executions
30th September 1830	JOHN HENDERSON	Murder
5th July 1852	MICHAEL SCANLANE & PETER SCANLANE	Murder
3rd October 1878	WILLIAM McDONALD	Murder

Executioners
There is no record of the town ever having employed an executioner.

Dalkeith

The Place of Execution
Brought from Edinburgh on the morning of his execution, Thomson was hanged on a scaffold erected in front of the Tolbooth on the south side of High Street. With a 1648 datestone, the two storey building with subterranean cells, is currently used as a hall by St Mary's Episcopal Church.

Execution
1st March 1827	WILLIAM THOMSON	Robbery

Executioners
No extant record of an executioner being employed by the town.

Dumbarton

The Places of Execution
Over the span of Dumbarton's three executions, two public and one private, three separate places were used.
  For the execution of Curry on 14th June 1754, the Magistrates and Council:

> '... appoint the Master of Works to take down the old gibbet as not fit for use, and order a stoop or post of a gibbet to [be taken to] the place where the gibbet now stands, on Monday next, at seven o'clock in the morning; and ordain the incorporation of hammermen to join the Master of Works in making and setting up the new gibbet in the same form as the last, in sufficient order, well supported with irons, and iron hooks for preventing any tumult or disorder on the day of the execution.'

Lunnay's execution was carried out in front of the County Buildings and Prison, built 1824, and probably on Glasgow's scaffold.
  The Glasgow scaffold was used to hang Wardlaw in October 1875, within the precincts of the prison. Newly constructed to execute Docherty at Glasgow two weeks before, the platform stood 10 feet from the ground, and had to be adapted.
  Erected against the back wall of the prison, the platform was reached by two gangways, each rising five feet, set at right angles to each other.

Executions
14th June 1754	MURDOCH CURRY	Theft by Housebreaking
18th January 1861	PATRICK LUNNAY	Murder
19th October 1875	DAVID WARDLAW	Murder

Executioners
There are no extant records of executioners employed by the council.

Dumfries

The Places of Execution
The surviving names Gallowsmuir and Gallowsloan suggest a place of execution in the area of the present Marchmount School, dating from the seventeenth and early eighteenth century, but it is unknown where the executions between 1753 and 1790 were carried out.
  From 1807, all executions were carried out in front of the new prison in Buccleuch Street. That of Robert Smith in May 1868 was the last public execution in Scotland.

Executions

31st October 1753	ROBERT McILYMONT	Horse Stealing
29th June 1763	THOMAS PRICE	Theft by Housebreaking
1st November 1780	WILLIAM JOHNSTON	Theft
30th June 1787	WILLIAM RICHARDSON	Murder
27th May 1789	JOHN CARMICHAEL	Theft by Housebreaking
9th June 1790	PATRICK FITZPATRICK	Theft by Housebreaking

Buccleuch Street

21st October 1807	MAITLAND SMITH	Murder
8th October 1820	EDWARD McRORY	Robbery
6th June 1821	JAMES GORDON	Murder
14th May 1823	JOHN McKANA &	Forgery
	JOSEPH RICHARDSON	
18th October 1826	JAMES McMANUS	Robbery
29th April 1862	MARY REID or TIMNEY	Murder
12th May 1868	ROBERT SMITH	Murder

Executioners

1758 - 1785	ROGER WILSON
1785 - 1808	JOSEPH TAIT

Dundee

The Places of Execution

Reporting Watt's execution, the *Edinburgh Advertiser* of 16th July 1801 said:

> 'John Watt or Wast, was executed at Dundee on Friday last, pursuant to his sentence at Perth for theft by housebreaking.
> A scene like this, at all times and all places awful and impressive, must be particularly so in Dundee, which has not witnessed any such thing of a similar nature for perhaps a century.
> 'We understand it is the intention of the Lords of Justiciary, that in future all criminals sentenced to die, shall be executed in the places where they committed the crimes. This is certainly a wise and salutary measure.'

It is unknown where Watt was hanged, but was probably, as in the cases of Balfour and Devlin who followed him, in front of the Town House, facing High Street.

With the scaffold built against the Town House, the culprits were brought out of the westmost window of the Guild Hall.

For Wood in 1839 and Leith in 1847, the scaffold was put up outside the newly built prison in Bell Street. The final execution, Bury in 1889, was carried out within the prison.

Executions

High Street

12th June 1801	JOHN WATT	Theft by Housebreaking
2nd June 1826	DAVID BALFOUR	Murder
30th May 1835	MARK DEVLIN	Rape

Bell Street

25th March 1839	ARTHUR WOOD	Murder
5th October 1847	THOMAS LEITH	Murder

Dundee Prison

24th April 1889	WILLIAM HENRY BURY	Murder

Executioners

There are no records of the city council having employed an executioner.

The Grassmarket and the West Bow, Edinburgh 1829   *(Edinburgh City Libraries)*

Edinburgh

The Places of Execution
Dating from an earlier period, the Gallowlee, 'on a hillock halfway between Edinburgh and Leith Walk at the present Shrubhill', was used for the executions of Normand Ross in January 1752 and Nicol Brown in April 1755, as both men were hanged and gibbetted.

Under the shadow of the Castle, the Grassmarket was used from the time of the Restoration up to 1784. The gallows site is marked by a memorial stone to the Covenanters.

William Mills, executed in 1785, was the first to suffer at the west end of the Tolbooth in High Street, at the head of Libberton Wynd. The final public execution in Edinburgh was George Bryce in June 1864.

Work began on Calton Jail in 1808, to replace the Old Tolbooth, and although it opened in 1817, It was not until the passing of the Capital Punishment Amendment Act 1868, that it was used for executions, starting with Eugene Marie Chantrelle in May 1878.

Philip Murray was the last culprit hanged in the jail, two years before its closure in 1925. In 1937 it was demolished to rise as St Andrews House, although the Governor's House remains.

The final three executions were carried out in Saughton Jail, which was built in 1924.

Executions
The Grassmarket

19th December 1750	JOHN YOUNG	Forgery
8th January 1752	JAMES WILSON & JOHN McDONALD	Theft

The Covenanters' Stone on the gallows site, Grassmarket, Edinburgh   (*Author's Collection*)

Gallowlee

10th January 1752	NORMAND ROSS	Murder

The Grassmarket

18th March 1752	HELEN TORRANCE & JEAN WALDIE	Murder

27th February 1754	RICHARD MUIR	Theft by Housebreaking
1st May 1754	HUGH LUNDIE	Robbery
18th September 1754	NICHOLAS COCKBURN	Murder

Gallowlee
23rd April 1755	NICOL BROWN	Murder

The Grassmarket
7th September 1756	AGNES CROCKAT	Murder
7th March 1759	ANN MORRISON	Murder
22nd April 1761	JANET HEATLY	Murder
13th January 1762	WILLIAM RIPLEY	Rape
13th November 1765	PATRICK OGILVIE	Murder
25th March 1767	ROBERT HAY	Robbery
24th February 1768	JOHN RAYBOULD	Forgery
25th April 1770	ANDREW McGHIE	Robbery
30th May 1770	WILLIAM HARRIS	Forgery
25th September 1771	WILLIAM PICKWITH	Robbery
15th September 1773	JAMES WILSON &	Murder
	JOHN BROWN	
2nd March 1774	MARGARET ADAMS	Murder
11th September 1776	ANNE MACKIE or MATHER	Murder
10th May 1780	DAVID DALGLEISH	Robbery
	WILLIAM DONALDSON	Theft by Housebreaking
11 September 1780	DAVID REID	Forgery
8th January 1782	JOHN McAFFEE	Forgery
4th February 1784	JAMES ANDREW	Robbery

Libberton's Wynd/West End of the Tolbooth
21st September 1785	WILLIAM MILLS	Theft by Housebreaking
22nd March 1786	JOHN HAUGH	Theft by Housebreaking
19th April 1786	WALTER ROSS	Theft
17th January 1787	DANIEL DAVOREN	Robbery
29th January 1787	CHARLES JAMIESON &	Theft
	JAMES JAMIESON	
21st March 1787	JOHN REID	Murder
4th July 1787	WILLIAM HAUGH	Theft by Housebreaking
2nd July 1788	PETER YOUNG	Theft by Housebreaking
1st October 1788	WILLIAM BRODIE &	Theft by Housebreaking
	GEORGE SMITH	
24th December 1788	JAMES FALCONER &	Theft by Housebreaking
	PETER BRUCE	
8th February 1790	BARTHOLOMEW COLLINS	Murder
23rd February 1791	WILLIAM GADESBY	Robbery
27th July 1791	JOHN PAUL &	Robbery
	JAMES STEWART	
12th October 1791	WILLIAM SMITH	Theft by Housebreaking
15th October 1794	ROBERT WATT	Treason
6th March 1799	JAMES STEWART	Theft
12th March 1800	GRIFFITH WILLIAMS	Murder
3rd September 1800	SAMUEL BELL	Forgery
11th February 1801	RICHARD BROXUP	Theft
7th April 1802	GEORGE LINDSAY	Murder
20th January 1804	JOHN COWIE	Murder

The Old Tolbooth, Edinburgh

7th January 1807	MARGARET CUNNINGHAM	Murder
21st January 1807	THOMAS SMITH &	Horse Stealing
	GEORGE STEPHENSON	
10th February 1808	BARBARA MALCOLM	Murder
22nd February 1809	ROBERT STEWART	Theft by Housebreaking
17th January 1810	JOHN ARMSTRONG	Theft by Housebreaking
27th March 1811	ADAM LYALL	Robbery

Stamp Office Close, High Street

22nd April 1812	HUGH McDONALD &	Robbery
	NEIL SUTHERLAND	
	HUGH McINTOSH	Murder

Corstorphine road

14th July 1813	JOHN McDONALD &	Murder
	JAMES WILLIAMSON BLACK	

West end of the Tolbooth

29th December 1813	CHRISTIAN SINCLAIR	Murder
10th August 1814	JAMES McDOUGALL	Forgery

Braid's Burn

25th January 1815	THOMAS KELLY & HENRY O'NEIL	Robbery

West end of the Tolbooth

29th March 1815	JOHN MURDOCH	Murder
13th March 1816	DAVID THOMSON	Theft by Housebreaking
11th December 1816	JOHN BLACK	Robbery
30th December 1818	ROBERT JOHNSTON	Robbery
14th April 1819	GEORGE WARDEN	Theft
5th January 1820	BRINE JUDD & THOMAS CLAPPERTON	Hamesucken
14th January 1821	JOHN DEMPSEY	Murder
17th January 1821	SAMUEL MAXWELL	Robbery
18th July 1821	DAVID HAGGART	Murder
26th February 1823	WILLIAM McINTYRE	Theft by Housebreaking
16th April 1823	MARY McKINNON	Murder
7th April 1824	CHARLES McEWEN	Murder
28th January 1829	WILLIAM BURKE	Murder
19th August 1829	JOHN STEWART & CATHERINE WRIGHT	Murder
6th January 1830	WILLIAM ADAMS	Robbery
17th March 1830	ROBERT EMOND	Murder
18th August 1830	JOHN THOMSON & DAVID DOBIE	Murder
11th August 1831	GEORGE GILCHRIST	Robbery
2nd December 1831	JAMES GOW	Murder
	THOMAS BEVERIDGE	Murder
19th December 1831	JOHN McCOURT	Murder
21st January 1832	JOHN HOWISON	Murder
13th July 1835	JAMES BELL	Murder
3rd August 1835	ELIZABETH BANKS	Murder
4th April 1836	CHARLES DONALDSON	Murder
16th April 1840	JAMES WEMYSS	Murder
3rd April 1844	JAMES BRYCE	Murder
16th August 1850	WILLIAM BENNISON	Murder
25th January 1854	WILLIAM CUMMING	Murder
21st June 1864	GEORGE BRYCE	Murder

Calton Jail

31st May 1878	EUGENE MARIE CHANTRELLE	Murder
31st March 1884	ROBERT FLOCKHART VICKERS WILLIAM INNES	Murder
11th March 1889	JESSIE KING	Murder
12th March 1898	JOHN HERDMAN	Murder
2nd October 1913	PATRICK HIGGINS	Murder
11th June 1923	JOHN HENRY SAVAGE	Murder
30th October 1923	PHILIP MURRAY	Murder

Calton Jail from Calton Hill, Edinburgh

Saughton Prison

13th August 1928	ALAN WALES	Murder
16th September 1951	ROBERT DOBIE SMITH	Murder
23rd April 1954	JOHN LYNCH	Murder
23rd June 1954	GEORGE ALEXANDER ROBERTSON	Murder

The Executioners

1749 - 1762	JAMES ALEXANDER
1762 - 1765	ISAAC GIBBS
1765 - 1767	JOHN LIDDLE
1767 - 1768	ANDREW BOYLE
1768 - 1776	EDWARD HAY
1776 - 1778	DONALD CAMERON
1778 - 1816	JOHN HIGH
1816 - 1819	JOHN SIMPSON
1819 - 1835	THOMAS WILLIAMS
1835 - 1835	JOHN WILLIAMS
1835 - 1847	JOHN SCOTT

The post of executioner in the city was abandoned with the death of John Scott in August 1835.

Elgin

The Places of Execution
Long after the drowning of witches in 'The Order Pot', Noble was the first and last to be executed in the town. Following the example of other burghs, the council erected the scaffold at the Tolbooth which had stood in High Street, at the west end of the Plainstanes, since 1717. It was demolished in 1843.

Executions
31st May 1834	WILLIAM NOBLE	Murder

Executioners
There are no records of an executioner having been employed by the town, although the post was advertised in the *Aberdeen Journal* in June 1789:

> ". . . He will have a free house, and about two acres of land, and a number of perquisites payable out of the commodities sold in town, and a considerable salary".

Falkirk

The Place of Execution
Although both McNair and Cockburn were executed by the Steeple or Tolbooth in High Street, there was no steeple in December 1811 - it having been demolished in 1803.

Work on the present 140 foot steeple of Brightons sandstone was begun in December 1812, and completed in June 1814. It contained 2 prison cells and a jailers room.

Executions
26th December 1811	THOMAS McNAIR	Robbery
8th May 1828	FRANCIS COCKBURN	Murder

Executioners
There are no records of an executioner being employed by the town.

Fans Farm

The Place of Execution
Condemned to be executed ' ... at such place as near to the farm steading or village of Fans as the sheriff-depute (of Berwickshire) or his substitute shall judge most convenient'.

The chosen place was in the field, east of Fans Farm steading, and on the north side of the minor road between the A6089 and the B6397, east of Earlston. The plantation of trees through which the road runs is still known as 'Rob Scott's Planting'.

Execution
23rd October 1823	ROBERT SCOTT	Murder

Forfar

The Places of Execution

In *Tales and Legends of Forfarshire*, Lowson writes of Low's journey to the gibbet:

> 'They strike off the Dundee Road a little above the toll, through the fields, still called the Gallowshade, and thence to the place of execution, where the gibbet was already erected, on the west hip of the Hill of Balmashanner'.

Both Wishart and Robertson were hanged in front of the east facing windows of the Town Hall, on gallows borrowed from Dundee.

Forfar Tolbooth

Executions
Balmashanner Hill

19th March 1785	ANDREW LOW	Theft by Housebreaking

The Townhouse

16th June 1827	MARGARET WISHART	Murder
19th May 1848	JAMES ROBERTSON	Murder

Executioners
The are no records of an executioner being employed by the town.

Glasgow

The Places of Execution

The city's earliest gallows was sited, not surprisingly, on the Gallowsmuir, and gave its name to the present Gallowgate, i.e. the way to the gallows. Robert Reid (Senex) writes in *Glasgow, Past and Present*:

> 'Old people in the last century [i.e. 18th century] recollected the gallows standing on the muir. The place was at the northwest end of the common, near the upper corner of what is now Barrack Street. At this point stood the hangman's house; and an adjoining declivity was long known as, and is still recognised by old people, as "the hangman's brae", opposite the mouth of Ladywell Street.'

Glasgow Tolbooth

In July 1765, Hugh Bilsland was the first of seven culprits to suffer at the Howgatehead. In the previous century Covenanters had paid for their beliefs on the site. In 1790 it too gave way to development, becoming a basin for the Monkland Canal.

The next move was to the other end of Howgate, later Castle Street, at Castleyard, under the shadow of the Cathedral, and amongst the ruins of the Bishop's Palace and Garden. Between 1784 and 1787, nine men and two women paid the penalty for dishonesty and one man for murder.

The 1788 execution of William McIntosh at the Cross finally brought Glasgow's executions into the city centre. Where High Street met the Saltmarket, and Trongate the Gallowgate, stood the Tolbooth and Courthouse. A tolbooth occupied the site from as early as 1454, with the last one built around 1627. 'A magnificent structure, being in length from E to W sixty-six foot, and from S to the N twenty four foot eight inches; it hath a stately staircase ascending to the justiciary hall ... In this great building are five rooms appointed for common prisoners'. The gallows would have been erected near the entrance. Only the steeple remains.

The Justiciary Buildings, Jail Square, Glasgow (*Mitchell Library, Glasgow*)

Duke Street Prison, Glasgow   (*Mitchell Library, Glasgow*)

In the book, *Glasghu Facies*, published in the late 1860s by Tweed of St Enoch Square, J F S Gordon writes, 'When the Gibbet was not in use, it was kept in the crypt of the Cathedral; and the Culprits were buried in the "Common Ground" on the North side of the Nave, to the west of the "Dripping Aisle".'

Between the executions of Muir and Moodie in November 1813 and Higgins and Harold eleven months later, the place moved to the front of the newly completed Justiciary Buildings, built at a cost of £34,000, and South Prison at the foot of the Saltmarket - Jail Square. With the square, and the Green beyond, Glasgow could boast a crowd of 80,000 at Pritchard's execution in 1865.

Ten years later, for the first private execution in Glasgow, Patrick Docherty was hanged in Duke Street Prison. In the 53 years to 1928, 18 murderers and one murderess were hanged. In the years before its closure in 1955, Duke Street served as a women's prison, all men having been transferred to Barlinnie Prison, 81 Lee Avenue.

Opened in 1882, Barlinnie was one of the first prisons to be entirely under the control of central government. Between 1946 and 1960, ten men were hanged behind its walls.

Executions
Howgatehead

10th July 1765	HUGH BILSLAND	Robbery
4th November 1767	AGNES DOUGAL	Murder
25th October 1769	ANDREW MARSHALL	Murder
17th November 1773	WILLIAM MITCHELL & CHRISTOPHER JARDYNE	Robbery
6th June 1781	ROBERT HISLOP	Theft by Housebreaking

Castleyard

7th July 1784	JAMES JACK	Robbery
3rd November 1784	JAMES BRODIE & WILLIAM BRODIE	Theft by Housebreaking
	JEAN SCOTT	Theft by Housebreaking
1st June 1785	NEIL McLEAN	Forgery
8th June 1785	DAVID STEVEN	Murder

Barlinnie Prison, Glasgow

9th November 1785	THOMAS VERNON	Robbery
7th June 1786	JAMES SPENCE	Theft by Housebreaking
25th October 1786	ELIZABETH PAUL	Theft by Housebreaking
23rd May 1787	JOHN McAULAY & THOMAS VEITCH	Robbery
	THOMAS GENTLES	Theft

The Cross

22nd October 1788	WILLIAM McINTOSH	Robbery
3rd December 1788	WILLIAM SCOTT	Theft by Housebreaking
9th June 1790	JOHN BROWN	Forgery
20th October 1790	JAMES DAY	Murder
11th January 1792	JAMES PLUNKET	Robbery
16th May 1792	JAMES DICK	Murder
7th November 1792	MORTIMER COLLINS	Murder
22nd May 1793	AGNES WHITE	Murder
	JAMES McKENZIE	Robbery
25th January 1797	JAMES McKEAN	Murder
16th May 1798	JOHN McMILLAN	Murder
11th June 1800	PETER GRAY	Hamesucken
8th June 1803	WILLIAM CUNNINGHAM	Theft
5th June 1805	DAVID SCOTT & HUGH ADAMSON	Forgery
10th June 1807	ADAM COX	Murder
20th July 1808	JAMES GILCHRIST	Murder
8th November 1809	JOHN GORDON McINTOSH & GEORGE STEWART	Theft by Housebreaking
26th May 1813	JAMES FERGUSON	Robbery
18th November 1813	WILLIAM MUIR & WILLIAM MOODIE	Robbery

Jail Square

19th October 1814	WILLIAM HIGGINS & THOMAS HAROLD	Robbery
1st November 1815	JOHN SHERRY	Robbery
28th May 1817	WILLIAM McKAY	Forgery
29th October 1817	FREEBAIRN WHITEHILL	Robbery
	WILLIAM McKECHNIE & JAMES McCORMICK	Theft by Housebreaking
3rd June 1818	WILLIAM BAIRD & WALTER BLAIR	Robbery

'Where Murdereres Sleep', Courtyard of the South Prison, Glasgow (*Mitchell Library, Glasgow*)

4th November 1818	MATTHEW CLYDESDALE	Murder
	SIMON ROSS	Theft by Housebreaking
7th April 1819	ALEXANDER ROBERTSON	Theft by Housebreaking
3rd November 1819	ROBERT McKINLAY &	Theft by Housebreaking
	WILLIAM BUCHANAN	
	ROBERT GUTHRIE &	Theft byHousebreaking
	ALEXANDER FORBES	
17th November 1819	JOHN BUCHANAN	Murder
21st May 1820	RICHARD SMITH	Theft by Housebreaking
30th August 1820	JAMES WILSON	Treason
8th November 1820	DANIEL GRANT	Robbery
	PETER CROSBIE	
	JOHN CONNOR &	
	THOMAS McCOLGAN	
16th May 1821	WILLIAM LEONARD SWAN	Forgery
25th October 1821	MICHAEL McINTYRE &	Theft by Housebreaking
	WILLIAM PATERSON	
	WARDROP DYER	Theft by Housebreaking
29th May 1822	WILLIAM CAMPBELL	Theft by Housebreaking
5th June 1822	THOMAS DONACHY	Theft by Housebreaking
4th June 1823	JOHN McDONALD	Theft by Housebreaking
	JAMES WILSON	Theft by Housebreaking
29th October 1823	FRANCIS CAIN	Robbery
	GEORGE LAIDLAW	Theft
12th November 1823	DAVID WYLIE	Theft by Housebreaking
19th May 1824	WILLIAM McTEAGUE	Forgery
2nd June 1824	JOHN McCREEVIE	Stouthrief
21st July 1824	WILLIAM DEVAN	Murder
1st June 1925	JAMES STEVENSON	Robbery
7th June 1825	JAMES DOLLAN	Robbery
1st November 1826	ANDREW STEWART	Robbery
	EDWARD KELLY	Robbery
12th December 1827	JAMES GLEN	Murder
22nd October 1828	THOMAS CONNOR &	Robbery
	ISABELLA McMENEMY	
20th May 1829	EDWARD MOORE	Murder
12th May 1830	JOHN HILL &	Robbery
	WILLIAM PORTER	
29th September 1830	WILLIAM McFEAT	Murder
27th January 1831	DAVID LITTLE	Stouthrief
16th May 1831	JAMES CAMPBELL	Theft by Housebreaking
6th October 1831	JAMES BYERS &	Murder
	MARY STEEL	
20th October 1831	WILLIAM HEATH	Theft by Housebreaking
18th January 1832	WILLIAM LINDSAY	Murder
7th November 1832	GEORGE DOFFY	Murder
7th February 1833	HENRY BURNETT	Robbery
20th January 1834	HUGH KENNEDY	Attempt to Murder
29th September 1835	GEORGE CAMPBELL	Murder
21st May 1838	ELIZABETH JEFFREY	Murder
27th May 1840	THOMAS TEMPLETON	Murder
18th May 1843	CHARLES MACKAY	Murder
31st January 1850	MARGARET LENNOX or HAMILTON	Murder
24th October 1851	ARCHIBALD HARE	Murder

11th August 1853	HANS SMITH McFARLANE &	Murder
	HELEN BLACKWOOD	
23rd May 1855	ALEXANDER STEWART	Murder
16th May 1864	JOHN RILEY	Murder
28th July 1865	EDWARD WILLIAM PRITCHARD	Murder

Duke Street Prison

5th October 1875	PATRICK DOCHERTY	Murder
31st May 1876	THOMAS BARR	Murder
23rd May 1883	HENRY MULLEN &	Murder
	MARTIN SCOTT	
23rd September 1890	HENRY DEVLIN	Murder
18th January 1893	WILLIAM McKEOWN	Murder
7th June 1897	GEORGE PATERSON	Murder
12th November 1902	PATRICK LEGGETT	Murder
26th July 1904	THOMAS GUNNING	Murder
14th November 1905	PASHA LIFFEY	Murder
16th May 1917	THOMAS McGUINNESS	Murder
11th November 1919	JAMES ADAMS	Murder
26th May 1920	ALBERT JAMES FRASER &	Murder
	JAMES ROLLINS	
21st February 1922	JAMES HARKNESS	Murder
10th October 1923	SUSAN McALLISTER	Murder
	or NEWELL	
24th September 1925	JOHN KEEN	Murder
24th January 1928	JAMES McKAY	Murder
3rd August 1928	GEORGE REYNOLDS	Murder

Barlinnie Prison

8th February 1946	JOHN LYON	Murder
6th April 1946	PATRICK CARRAHER	Murder
10th August 1946	JOHN CALDWELL	Murder
30th October 1950	PAUL CHRISTOPHER HARRIS	Murder
16th December 1950	JAMES RONALD ROBERTSON	Murder
12th April 1952	JAMES SMITH	Murder
29th May 1952	PETER GALLAGHER DEVENEY	Murder
26th January 1953	GEORGE FRANCIS SHAW	Murder
11th July 1958	PETER THOMAS ANTHONY MANUEL	Murder
22nd December 1960	ANTHONY JOSEPH MILLER	Murder

Executioners.

Glasgow City records are almost silent regarding the city's executioners, with the exception of Thomas Young, whose indenture is extant.

? - 1803	JOHN SUTHERLAND
1803 - 1813	ARCHEY McARTHUR
1814 - 1837	THOMAS YOUNG
1837 - 1856	JOHN MURDOCH

The post died with Thomas Young in 1837, for although Murdoch continued, he was not employed by the city.

Greenlaw

The Place of Execution

Berwickshire's county town until 1853, both Swiney and Williams were executed on the Green surrounding the 1829 Town Hall, on the north side of High Street. The prison dated from 1824.

Tod's *Scots Black Kalendar* gives the place of execution, in both instances, as 'in front of the County Hall', i.e. the Town Hall, whilst McLeish's *Death in the Borders* gives it as 'in front of the Castle Hotel', at that time the Castle Inn, on the opposite side of the street.

Executions
2nd April 1834	MANNES SWINEY	Robbery
14th March 1853	JOHN WILLIAMS	Murder

Executioners
There are no extant records of an executioner being employed by the town.

Greenock

The Places of the Execution

For the execution of Moses McDonald, the town's first, the magistrates chose Cathcart Square, close to the Mid Church, where a horseshoe set into the cobbles marks the spot of the gallows.

Storey was hanged within the 70 cell prison in Bank Street, opened in 1870.

Executions
Cathcart Square
5th June 1812	MOSES McDONALD	Theft by Housebreaking
10th October 1817	BERNARD McILVOGUE & HUGH McILVOGUE PATRICK McCRYSTAL	Stouthrief
6th June 1827	JOHN KERR	Murder
23rd October 1834	JOHN BOYD	Murder

Greenock Prison
11th January 1892	FREDERICK THOMAS STOREY	Murder

Executioners
There are no records of an executioner having been employed by Greenock Town Council.

Hawick

The Place of Execution

For Hawick's single execution, a spot near the old Tollhouse in the Common Haugh was chosen. The site is now occupied by Thornwood Motors at 4-8 Commercial Road.

Execution
12th May 1814	JOHN GIBSON	Murder

Executioners
There are no extant records of an executioner having been employed by the town.

Inveraray

The Places of Execution
It is unknown where Campbell and Graham were hanged, and although unsubstantiated, McDougall's execution is said to have taken place at the Crags, about one mile from Inverary.

Executions

2nd November 1753	ANNE CAMPBELL	Theft
	SARAH GRAHAM	Theft
28th November 1807	PETER McDOUGALL	Murder

Executioners
Although a circuit town, executioners, when required, appear to have been brought from Glasgow.

Inverness

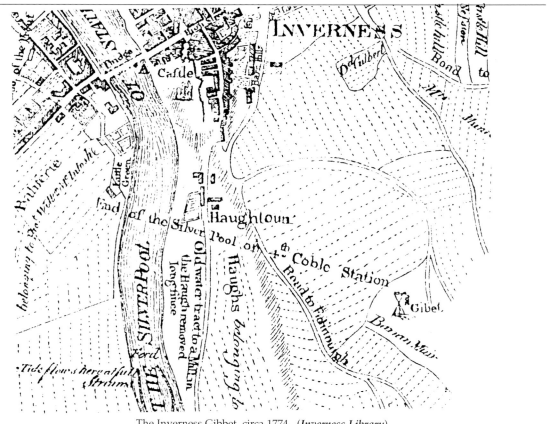

The Inverness Gibbet, circa 1774   (*Inverness Library*)

The Places of Execution
The ministers who contributed to Sinclair's Statistical Account of 1790-98 were understandably reticent when writing on the downside of their parish - except the minister at Inverness, who included the following list of prisoners in their Tolbooth:

'30 - horse stealing; 8 - petty theft; 4 - threatening expressions; 1 for alleged wilful fire-raising; 1 - scandal and defamation; 3 for deserting their apprenticeships; a boy for alleged murder, liberated on investigation; 3 for violent assaults; 3 for child murder; 1 for selling spiritous liquors without a licence; 2 women of bad fame; 5 men from Campbelltown for breach of the peace; 1 deserter; 17 civil debt'.

The reverend gentleman makes no mention of executions.

John Hume's 1774 map of Inverness shows an 'occupied' gibbet on the town's common, by the Edinburgh road, which was used from early times until 1812.

For McLeod in 1831 and Adam in 1835, the Longman, an area on the shores of the Moray Firth was used, and finally for Hume, Porterfield Prison which was opened in 1902.

Executions
The Common
9th July 1750	KENNETH DOW KENNEDY	Cattle Stealing
25th October 1751	EWAN McPHERSON & DUNCAN KENNEDY	Robbery
6th December 1751	HUGH FRASER	Cattle Stealing
22nd October 1757	WILLIAM STEWART	Murder
	DONALD McILROY	Murder
2nd November 1764	CHRISTIAN McKENZIE	Murder
	MARGARET DOUGLAS	Murder
11th July 1766	JAMES TAYLOR	Robbery
17th October 1788	WILLIAM CORMACK	Theft by Housebreaking
13th November 1812	ROBERT FERGUSON	Murder

The Longman
24th October 1831	HUGH McLEOD	Murder
10th October 1835	JOHN ADAM	Murder

Porterfield Prison
5th March 1908	JOSEPH HUME	Murder

Executioners
- 1811	William Taylor
1812 - 1833	Donald Ross

Both Ross and the post were dispensed with at a meeting of the Town Council on 19th December 1833.

Old Castle of Inverlochy

The Place of Execution
A ruined feudal stronghold on the left bank of the Lochy, a little above its influx to salt water Loch Linnhe, and two miles north east of Fort William, the spot was chosen as being in the heart of the country inhabited by McIliog's brethren.

The Execution
26th June 1752	DONALD McILOIG	Cattle Stealing

Executioner
As McIliog was condemned at Inverness, it may be presumed that the hangmen was brought from there.

Janet Innes's Cairn

The Place of Execution
Although the robbery for which Leal was hanged was committed between Three Mile House and Janet Innes's Cairn, on the Elgin to Fochabers road, the latter spot was chosen for his execution. Janet Innes, accused of witchcraft and burnt on the hillock, was the last witch to perish in the county.

The Execution
7th July 1773	KENNETH LEAL	Robbery

Executioner
As with the execution of Gillan at Spey in 1810, the hangman at Leal's execution probably came from Aberdeen.

Jedburgh

The Places of Execution
There are no records of the place of execution in Jedburgh prior to 1831, when Thomas Rogers was hanged in front of the 'Castle', which was built as the county jail in 1823.

Executions
22nd May 1753	MARGARET MINNA	Murder
5th June 1770	JOHN BROWN	Sheep Stealing
17th May 1785	ADAM HISLOP & WILLIAM WALLACE	Robbery
31st October 1786	JOHN CLARK	Horse Stealing
9th June 1789	WILLIAM MURRAY	Theft
10th October 1809	CHARLES STEWART MERCER	Rape
29th May 1822	WILLIAM ROBISON	Theft by Housebreaking

The Castle
19th October 1831	THOMAS ROGERS	Murder
25th October 1849	THOMAS WILSON	Murder

Executioners
There are no records of Jedburgh having an executioner in its employment.

Kinghorn

The Places of Execution
Westwater was the first and last criminal to be executed at Gallowhill Plantation, 2½ miles west of the town. Catherine Wallange was burned there as a witch in 1644. Regelsen was executed somewhere on the beach.

Executions
Gallowhill
21st June 1806	JOHN WESTWATER	Murder

The Sands
28th June 1811	HANS REGELSEN	Rape

Executioners
There are no records of a resident hangman in the town.

Kirkcudbright

The Place of Execution

The 1843 Statistical Account notes Greig's execution, saying it took place in the vicinity of the ancient Gallow-hill, on an eminence at the side of the public road.

The site, to the south east of the junction of Victoria Park and Millflats was later opened as a quarry. The minute book of the Squaremen Incorporation contains the following entry:

> 'Kirkcudbright, 25th June 1750.
> The Squaremen Incorporation being employed by the Magistrates and Toun Council to make and set up a new gibbet in the ordinary place of execution, and it is agreed by the Incorporation that every member shall attend the Deacon in the Milburn Yeards to cut down a tree for that purpose on Thursday next, by six o'clock in the morning, and then proceed to the said work, it is hereby enacted that any member not appearing in time and giving proper assistance, shall be fined six pounds Scots, and immediately distressed for the same.'

The Execution

9th July 1750	HENRY GREIG	Theft by Housebreaking

Executioner

Prior to Greig's execution, Newall, like his father before him, was employed as, 'Common Whipper of the Town and Stewartry'. The post was not filled again after his death.

1750 - 1765	John Newall

Leith

The Place of Execution

In 1822 as Heaman and Gautiez were brought down Constitution Street and on to the famous Leith Sands, the view, if they noticed, was the Fife coast - Imperial, Albert and Edinburgh Docks were then undreamt of.

The Execution

9th January 1822	PETER HEAMAN & FRANCOIS GAUTIEZ	Piracy

Executioners

There are no records of the town having employed an executioner.

Linlithgow

The Places of Execution

McDonald and Jamieson were executed at the village of Linlithgow Bridge, 3/4 of a mile west of the town, for a robbery committed there, whilst the remainder were hanged at a gallows in the market place.

The Executions
Linlithgow Bridge

21st September 1770	ALEXANDER McDONALD & CHARLES JAMIESON	Robbery

The Market Cross

27th August 1819	RALPH WOODNESS	Theft by Housebreaking
2nd February 1857	PETER McLEAN	Murder

Executioners
There are no records of the town having an executioner.

Montrose

The Tolbooth and Council House, Montrose, circa 1825

The Places of Execution
Dating from early times, the old Tolbooth jail in High Street, was demolished and replaced by a prison in 1832. It was little used, prisoners sentenced to more than 14 days being transferred to Dundee.
    For some reason Brown was hanged outside the police office in George Street.

The Executions
The Tolbooth

7th December 1821	MARGARET TYNDALL or SHUTTLEWORTH	Murder

George Street

31st January 1866	ANDREW BROWN	Murder

Executioners
There are no records of Montrose having employed an executioner.

Paisley

The Places of Execution
The following extract from the burgh records contains one of the earliest references to the Gallowsgreen in Paisley:

> '8th May 1595 - "Act anent the Gallowgrein" - It is statut and ordaint that na ky, stirks, nor any other beists, except hors, be pastured upon the Gallowgrein.'

To execute Potts, the gallows was erected outside the Tolbooth, built 1757, at the Cross.

The final three were carried out on ground adjacent to the Prison and Municipal Building built between 1818 and 1821 - and demolished in 1968.

The Executions
The Gallowgreen
27th December 1753	ROBERT LYLE	Theft
7th November1765	ALEXANDER PROVAN	Murder

The Cross
17th August 1797	THOMAS POTTS	Stouthrief

County Buildings
29th October 1829	JOHN CRAIG & JAMES BROWN	Robbery
18th October 1837	WILLIAM PERRIE	Murder
14th January 1858	JOHN THOMSON	Murder

Executioners
There are no records of Paisley having employed an executioner - relying upon the functionary from neighbouring Glasgow.

Perth

The Places of Execution
The original common place of execution in Perth, where a permanent gallows stood, was on the Burgh Muir, to the west of the town, on the north side of Old Gallows Road. The 1860 Ordnance Survey map shows a Hangman's Well on the opposite side of the road.

In the 11 year period between Fisher in 1776 and Hacket in 1787 the gallows came to town, and was set at the foot of High Street, outside the Sheriff Court.

Penny's book *Traditions of Perth* gives the following description of the new gallows:

> ' ... a scaffold, with a drop, was introduced; but in this instance, a new method was adopted. A scaffold was erected in front of the centre window of the Council room; over which a beam was fixed, on the side of the window, with the same length of beam within as without. To the end of the beam within, a rope was attached, and a hole was cut in the floor, through which a rope descended into the weigh-house, where a heavy weight was fastened about 3 feet from the ground. When the signal was given, this weight descended, and the beam rose on the outside, raising the body from the scaffold.'

From Chisholm in 1832 until Myszka in 1948 the County Prison was used. The scaffold for the final three public hangings being erected at the west end of the prison building.

The Executions
The Burgh Muir
15th June 1750	ALEXANDER McCOWAN	Murder

The Old Prison and Town House, Perth, circa 1834

12th July 1751	HUGH KNOX	Horse Stealing
	JAMES ROBERTSON	Robbery
22nd June 1753	ROBERT DAVIDSON &	Robbery
	GEORGE BRUCE	
21st July 1753	JOHN BRECK KENNEDY	Cattle Stealing
23rd November 1753	JOHN DUBH CAMERON	Murder
13th June 1755	WILLIAM DOIG	Murder
15th July 1757	HECTOR McLEAN	Murder
29th June 1759	JAMES RUSSEL	Murder
2nd July 1760	ROBERT KEITH	Murder
19th October 1764	JEAN CAMERON	Murder
19th June 1767	DUNCAN CAMPBELL &	Murder
	JOHN CHAPEL	
27th November 1772	ALEXANDER McDONALD	Cattle Stealing
11th June 1773	WILLIAM BROWN	Horse Stealing
17th June 1774	FRANCIS THORNILOE	Theft by Housebreaking

High Street

25th May 1787	JAMES HACKET	Theft
31st May 1793	JAMES DORMAND	Robbery
21st June 1793	ROBERT ROGERS	Robbery
13th November 1795	DONALD McCRAW	Murder
11th July 1806	DONALD McCRAW	Murder
28th February 1817	JOHN LARG &	Theft by Housebreaking
	JAMES MITCHELL	
31st October 1817	MALCOLM CLARK	Stouthrief

The County Prison

31st October 1832	JOHN CHISHOLM	Murder
29th May 1849	JOHN KELLOCHER	Murder
22nd May 1866	JOSEPH BELL	Murder
4th October 1870	GEORGE CHALMERS	Murder
19th August 1908	EDWARD JOHNSTONE	Murder
6th July 1909	ALEXANDER EDMINSTONE	Murder
6th February 1948	STANISLAW MYSZKA	Murder

Executioners

The undernoted were indentured executioners in Perth, but whether any carried through an execution is unknown.

13th May 1785	JAMES KIER
1st April 1789	WILLIAM ROBERTSON
25th October 1792	ROBERT AITKEN

Rannoch

The Place of Execution

By tradition, Cameron was hanged on a 'gallows tree', which flourishes still, opposite the entrance to Annat House, on the B846, by the north side of Loch Rannoch and about one mile west of the village of Kinloch Rannoch. The tree is featured on the 'Clans of Rannoch Trail'.

Execution

7th August 1753	DONALD BANE LEANE CAMERON	Theft

Executioner

No particulars of the executioner have survived.

Speyside

The Place of Execution

The press report of Gillan's execution describes the place merely as being on the moor near Fochabers, but an article in The *Elgin and Morayshire Courier* of 3rd January 1868 more fully describes it as:

> 'A spot on the north west corner of Stynie Moor, about midway between Kenny's Hillock and the Red Kirk ... '

Gibbeted, he was later buried at the foot of the gallows, but disturbed about 1830 during the burial of a suicide. Before long, relic hunters carried off most of his remains

The Execution

18th November 1810	ALEXANDER GILLAN	Murder

Executioner

William Taylor, Inverness.

Stirling

The Places of Execution

Little is known of early executions at Stirling except that they appear to have been carried out beyond the Barras Yett, the town's south gateway.

From 1811 they took place outside the Tolbooth in Broad Street.

Executions
The Barras Yett
19th November 1773	THOMAS McLATCHIE	Theft by Housebreaking
21st September 1777	MARION WHITE	Murder
29th October 1784	SARAH CAMERON	Murder
2nd June 1786	JAMES MOIR	Murder
28th March 1788	GEORGE McKERRACHER	Forgery
16th May 1788	JOHN SMART	Forgery

The Tolbooth
11th October 1811	ROBERT BROWN ANDERSON & JAMES MENZIES	Theft by Housebreaking
21st February 1812	ALEXANDER O'KAIN	Robbery
8th September 1820	ANDREW HARDIE & JOHN BAIRD	Treason
11th May 1821	JOHN FLEMING	Forgery
14th May 1824	JOHN CAMPBELL	Theft byHousebreaking
26th May 1826	JOHN McGRADDY	Theft by Housebreaking
28th July 1826	PETER MOFFAT	Murder
2nd October 1833	ROBERT TENNANT	Murder
8th April 1837	ALEXANDER MILLAR	Murder
4th October 1843	ALLAN MAIR	Murder

The Staffman's House, Stirling

Executioners
That Stirling had an executioner, or Staffman as they called him, over many years is apparent from the payment of his salary shown in the Treasurer's accounts, but the single line entries give no name:

> By Staffman.
> 1 year's wages to Martinmas 1788.
> £9.2.6.

For the execution of James Dun at Ayr in November 1781, the Magistrates hired the functionary from Stirling, and in their accounts name him as John Cuthill.

The Town Council Minutes for 21st April 1781, record the following unique request regarding the hangman, possibly again Cuthill:

> 'The Managers having considered a Petition from Carron Company praying that the Staffman may be allowed to go to Carron works to execute a sentence of the Justices of the Peace upon a person who stole goods from the Company, They grant the desire thereof, provided Mr Campbell the Companys agent grant a bond upon stamped paper to the Town Treasurer binding himself to pay the

Town five hundred merks Scots money unless the Staffman is returned safe and sound'.

The Council Minutes also record that John Rankine, Staffman, was dismissed on 2nd February 1771, but do not give his term of office.

Symington Toll

The Place of Execution
The exact place of execution is now difficult to pinpoint with accuracy. The contemporary *Ayr Advertiser*, says only that it was in the vicinity of Symington Toll. In his autobiography, *Retrospect of an Artist's Life*, John Kelso Hunter says Jeanfield Farm.

A contributor to the *Kilmarnock Standard*'s regular feature, 'Ayrshire Notes and Queries' of April 1877, goes further, saying it was, 'on the high ground on the left hand side of the road going from Kilmarnock to Ayr', which places it on the spur of ground to the south east of Jeanfield Farm - Helenton Hill.

Execution
17th February 1815   JOHN WORTHINGTON   Robbery

Executioner
The first execution of THOMAS YOUNG, Glasgow.

3

The Executions – 1750 to 1963

1750

January 26th;   **Charles GRANT**   Aberdeen

A native of Inveravon in Banffshire, condemned at the 1749 Aberdeen Autumn Circuit, on a plea of guilty to Wilful Fire Raising.

Brought to the Laigh Council House dressed in Grave-linnen, he declared himself a Roman Catholic and refused the prayers of the town's clergy.

Executioner; Unknown

June 15th;   **Alexander McCOWAN**   Perth

Hanged for murdering his pregnant, common law wife, Alison McCowan, with his dirk, and one of their children with a razor.

At the gallows, his right hand was severed with an axe, and afterwards nailed to the gibbet top. When the cart was driven from under his feet, the rope broke and it took a pulley to hoist him up.

The reported motive for the murder was; 'in order to carry on the filthy Intrigue more easily with another Woman whom he had debauched; and that he had gone through a long Tract of unclean Practices both at home and abroad'.

Executioner; Unknown

July 6th;   **Henry GREIG**   Kirkcudbright

Arrested with Margaret Stewart and Anne Gibson on charges of theft and robbery, Greig's execution was to warn ' the bands of depredators called gipsies or tinkers ... which harass the inhabitants by their insolence, their threats, and their robberies'.

Coming before the Stewart Depute [Sheriff] at Kirkcudbright on 31st May 1750, the offer to subject themselves to transportation was accepted from the women, but not Greig. He was condemned.

It could not be decided whether the execution was the responsibility of the Town Council or the Steward of the Stewartry, or who would carry the sentence through. There was John Newall, 'Common Whipper of the Town and Stewartry', but he refused, until incarcerated in the Tolbooth for a few days, after which, a fee of five guineas and elevation to the post of 'Executioner for the Stewartry' secured his attendance at Gallow-hill.

Executed on a newly built gallows, Greig was afterwards buried close to the northern wall of St Cuthbert's Churchyard.

Executioner; John Newall
Kirkcudbright

July 9th;   **Kenneth Dow KENNEDY**

Inverness

A notorious thief for 20 years Dow was condemned for cattle stealing.

From the ladder, he appealed to any McDonald or Campbell in the crowd who would see to his burial in the churchyard. The three or four who came forward fulfilling his request 'in a remote corner appointed for such Malefactors'.

Executioner; Unknown

December 19th;   **John YOUNG**   Edinburgh

A Sergeant-Major in the 4th Regiment of Foot (Colonel Rich's Regiment), Young was executed for forging and fabricating Bank Notes, whilst the soldiers who engraved the plates were cited as prosecution witnesses.

With his execution to take place between two and four o'clock, Young hoped to save himself by delay, and barricaded his cell. He was wrong. The Magistrates opened the floor above, and on the offer of a bounty, six of the city guard dropped on Young, and secured him.

At six o'clock that evening he was suspended in the Grassmarket.

Executioner; James Alexander
Edinburgh

1751

June 25th;   **Alexander GEDDES**   Aberdeen

A farmer from Kinnermony in Banffshire, Geddes was condemned for 'reiterated acts of the monstrous crime of bestiality with a mare, downward from the year 1736 to the time of his being taken up'.

At 5.00am he was strangled on the gibbet at Castlehill, but cut down alive and his body burnt to ashes.

He was the last culprit in Scotland to suffer for the crime, or to be burnt following execution.

Executioner; Unknown

July 12th;   **Hugh KNOX**   Perth
James ROBERTSON

Hugh and James Knox, a father and 18-year-old son, tried for Horse Stealing. Whilst the father was condemned, the son, on the jury's recommendation to mercy, was sentenced to transportation to the Plantations, never to return, under the usual, 'Pains of Whipping and Re-transportation'.

Knox was joined on the scaffold by Robertson, condemned for robbery.

Executioner; Unknown

October 25th;   **Ewan McPHERSON**   Inverness
Duncan KENNEDY

Executed for robbing John McDonald, a travelling chapman, between Garviemore and Fort Augustus.

Executioner; Unknown

December 6th;   **Hugh FRASER**   Inverness

Condemned at the Autumn Circuit and hanged for cattle stealing.

Executioner; Unknown

1752

January 8th;   **James WILSON**   Edinburgh
John McDONALD

Hanged at the Grassmarket for being Gypsies, Thieves and Sorners [beggars].

Executioner; James Alexander
Edinburgh

January 10th;   **Normand ROSS**   Edinburgh

On the night of Monday 9th August 1751, when noise of a struggle roused the servants at House of Linthill, near Eyemouth, they found their mistress, Mrs Margaret Home, widow of Ninian Home of Billy, lying in her blood-soaked bed.

She told of waking to find Ross, her manservant, taking a money drawer key from her pillow, and of him cutting and stabbing her in the panic of being discovered, before fleeing.

Next day, he was found in a nearby plantation and incarcerated in Greenlaw Prison, on a charge of assault - until Lady Billy died on the Saturday, when he was charged with murder.

His declaration gives his birth at Inverness on 16 April 1728, where, after an eight-year education, he served overseas in the army and as a Gentleman's Servant. He denied involvement in the '45 Rebellion, claiming he was out of the country between 1745 and 1749.

The High Court ordered his execution at the Gallowlee, '... there to have his Right Hand struck off, then to be hanged by the Neck till he was dead, and afterwards hung in chains, and the Right Hand fixed above him'.

The following rhyme may or may not be contemporary with the execution:

'The Lady's gane and Norman's ta'en,
Norman wi' the bloody hand,
Now he will have to pay the kain
For being at the De'il's command.
Norman Ross wi' pykit pow,
Three corbies at his e'en;
Girnin in the gallows tow,
Sic a sight was never seen!'

Executioner; James Alexander
Edinburgh

March 18th;   **Helen TORRANCE**   Edinburgh
Jean WALDIE

Hanged at the Grassmarket, 'for stealing and murdering 9-year-old John Dallas, a "living child", and soon after selling and delivering his body to some

The Stewart Monument, Ballachulish (*Author's Collection*)

surgeons & students of physic', Torrance and Waldie were the Burke and Hare of the 1750s.

When the surgeon's apprentice called to collect the Dallas body, and there had probably been many more, the women haggled over the price of 2s, and received an extra 10d - Torrance earning another 6d for carrying the body to their college in her apron.

The corpse was found four days later, in a solitary part of the town, 'bearing evident marks of having been in the surgeons' hands'.

Executioner; James Alexander
Edinburgh

June 26th;   **Donald McILOIG**
Old Castle of Inverlochy

A notorious cattle thief, McIloig alias Cameron, was captured by a party of General Pultney's Regiment and condemned at Inverness Spring Circuit.

The court ordered his execution to take place at Old Castle of Inverlochy, a mile distant from Inverness, 'being in the Centre of the Camerons his Relations, with a view to deter others there from the like Crimes so frequent in this Country, and where there are great Numbers of these Villains'.

Executioner; Unknown

November 8th;   **James STEWART**   Appin

With a jury said to have, 'approached the trial with a predetermined conviction of his guilt', Stewart was charged with the murder of 44-year-old Colin Campbell of Glenure, 'The Red Fox', late on the afternoon of 15th May 1752. Campbell had been Crown Factor on the forfeited estates of Ardsheal, Callert and a portion of Lochiel. He was a victim of the politics of post-1745 Scotland.

On a mission to evict farm tenants, Campbell and three others were going up through Lettermore Wood, on the south side of Loch Linnhe and a little west of Ballachulish, when the silence was broken by a single shot. Campbell slumped forward on his horse, two musket balls having passed through his body from back to front.

The trial opened at 6.00am on Friday 22nd September 1752 and finished at 8.00am on the Sunday

Plaque on the Stewart Monument (*Author's Collection*)

Near five o'clock his body was put up in chains, and 16 men from the command at Appin left to guard him through his first night. It would be 18 months before he was left unguarded.

In January 1755 when his remains were blown off the gibbet, the Lord Justice Clerk ordered it to be wired together and re-suspended. Piecemeal, it came down over the years.

Executioner; Unknown
Glasgow

November 24th; **Christian PHREN**   Aberdeen
William WAST

When discovered attempting to dispose of her newborn illegitimate child in a bonfire, Phren, a farm servant in the neighbourhood of Aberdeen, was brought to the city in a cart with the half consumed infant in her apron.

Her gallows companion, William Wast, a ship's captain from Auchmedden in the parish of Aberdour, had murdered his wife. He denied the murder of his wife to the last, but confessed to the murder of a boy at sea, some years before, by throwing him overboard.

On the scaffold, when the hangman complained he could not reach the rope, Wast calmly said he would pass it to him.

Both were gibbeted, although within a few days Phren's body was taken by the surgeons for dissection, leaving Wast 'till his bones were bleached by the winds of Heaven'.

Many years later, his remains were laid at the Methodist Meeting House in Queen Street, Aberdeen with a label tied to the breast:

'I, William Wast, at the point of
damnation,
Request the prayers of this
congregation.'
Executioner; Unknown

1753

May 22nd;   **Margaret MINNA**   Jedburgh
Condemned at Jedburgh Circuit court and hanged for child murder.

Executioner; Unknown

June 22nd;   **Robert DAVIDSON**   Perth
George BRUCE

Condemned on 11th May at Perth Spring Circuit, with Bruce's 17-year-old son David, for two robberies.

morning. The verdict of guilty was returned on the Monday morning.

Stewart would be transported from Inverary to Fort William on 5th October and thence to Appin where he would be, 'hanged nigh to the place where the murder was committed, where he is to remain hung in chains'.

An iron-plated gibbet was erected a few days before the execution.

On 7th November, escorted by three companies of soldiers, he was brought down from Fort William, reaching the Ballachullish Ferry in the evening. However a storm had laid up the ferry and it was midday on the 8th before they reached Appin on the south side of Loch Linnhe.

In a small tent, soon to be carried away in the storm, he had his last words with the ministers before mounting the ladder, and delivering his speech. In a wind so great that standing was difficult, he was pushed off.

When condemned, the boy cried most piteously, declaring in the greatest agony that he was forced to take part in the robberies by his father holding a pistol to his breast and threatening him with immediate death. He was reprieved.

Executioner; Unknown

July 21st;   **John Breck KENNEDY**   Perth

In his speech before being executed for cattle stealing, Kennedy, a notorious thief, acknowledged guilt of every crime - except murder and that for which he was about to suffer.

Executioner; Unknown

August 7th;   **Donald Bane Leane CAMERON**
Rannoch

When sentenced at Perth Autumn Circuit to be hanged at Kinloch Rannoch, 'on a Public Mercat Day', for two of the many charges of theft libelled against him, the verdict was translated into Gaelic.

> 'An innumerable crowd of his countrymen flocked from every glen to behold this unusual phenomenon in that country', where those who understood his language said he died protesting his innocence.

His execution appears to have been the last carried out on a tree, which, known as the 'Gibbet Tree', still stands.

A D Cunningham in his book, *A History of Rannoch*, writes that the commanding officer of the execution party watched Cameron hang, knowing a reprieve had been granted.

Executioner; Unknown

October 31st;   **Robert McILYMONT**   Dumfries

Condemned and hanged at Dumfries for horse stealing.

Executioner; Unknown

November 2nd; **Anne CAMPBELL**   Inveraray
                     Sarah GRAHAM

Condemned at Inveraray Autumn Circuit, Campbell was indicted, 'for stealing at 2 different times, Money to the extent of about £50 and concealing and hiding same in the thatch of a low house'.

Graham, about 80-years-of-age, had stolen 'out of the pocket of Alexander McLean, Merchant in Glasgow', a billbag containing promissory notes and Instructions of Debt to the value of £900, at the Whitsunday Fair at Kilmichael Glassary, a few miles

north of Lochgilphead. Her home is given as Kintrea, which may have been Kintra on Islay.

Executioner; Unknown

November 16th; **James MILLER**   Aberdeen

Within days of being whipped through the streets of Aberdeen and banished the county as a reputed thief, Miller was caught stealing from a house at Inverury, and condemned at the Autumn Court.

When his body was cut down, 'some friendly sailors saved it from the surgeons, by soon after taking it up, and carrying it out with them in a yawl, and sinking it in the sea'.

Executioner; Unknown

November 23rd; **John Dubh CAMERON**   Perth

Cameron alias McMartine alias Bottie, but commonly called 'Serjeant Mohr', was found guilty of murdering John Bruce of Inneredrie, sundry acts of theft and being a common thief.

When the Dempster came to pronounce the sentence, 'he struck him with his hands and feet, and would not allow him to come near'.

Reputedly a veteran of Charles Edward Stuart's army at Culloden, he survives in legend as a Highland Robin Hood, plundering Whigs and Sassenachs and giving to the poor.

Executioner; Unknown

December 27th; **Robert LYLE**   Paisley

From the parish of Kilbarchan in Renfrewshire, Lyle was condemned by a sheriff and jury at Paisley for theft, aggravated by being a habit and repute thief. He had stolen from James King's bleachfield at Causeyend of Stanely.

Tradition says his executioner was a fellow prisoner, whose punishment was remitted for undertaking the disagreeable office.

Executioner; Unknown

1754

February 27th;   **Richard MUIR**   Edinburgh

Condemned by the Lord Provost of Edinburgh, as High Sheriff, for several acts of theft by house-breaking, he was hanged in the Grassmarket.

Executioner; James Alexander
Edinburgh

May 1st;   **Hugh LUNDIE**   Edinburgh

Executed for five highway robberies committed in

and around Edinburgh during December 1753, from which he netted £1.15.10.

The night before his execution he was found unconscious with his coat and shirt tied about his neck, and was only revived when blooded by a surgeon.

From the gallows ladder in the Grassmarket, he related having lived a sober and innocent life - until his arrival in Edinburgh.

Executioner; James Alexander
Edinburgh

June 14th;   **Murdoch CURRY**   Dumbarton

A butler with Stonefield of Levenside, Curry was condemned by the sheriff at Dumbarton for theft of £5 from his master's house.

His case excited unusual commiserations - 'The very jailor at the time appears to have been afflicted with the prevailing sentiment.' His connivance in Curry's escape the week before execution, led to his dismissal by the magistrates, albeit Curry was captured within minutes.

His scaffold speech, published as a broadside, was titled:

> 'True and Genuine Account of MURDOCH CURRY, taken from his own Mouth, at the place of Execution, in Shorthand, being a Pious Exhortation to people of ranks to take Warning by his untimely end.'

The standard phrase, 'taken from his own Mouth', meant the taking of words, put in his mouth by the clergy, sandwiched between an account of the event.

> ' ... my petition is, that my body may get leave to be in the place appointed for the bones to rest, and that the good people in this place may take care of my grave, that it is not lifted.'

Throwing off his coat, he bid farewell to his sister and friends, and mounted the ladder. Removing his neckcloth, the executioner was ordered to feel his neck - it was not unknown to find concealed, leather or metal, collars around culprits necks. Then with the halter around his neck, he pulled down the cap - and went over.

Executioner; Unknown

September 18th; **Nicholas COCKBURN**
Edinburgh

Cockburn, who murdered both her husband and step-mother within a month was, by modern criteria, insane.

Her husband, James Kid, died at home in Kirknewton on 18th March 1754 and was buried without suspicion. She had stirred arsenic into his broth at dinner.

On 2nd April 1754 she went to Ormiston on the death (of natural causes) of her father, Alexander Cockburn, and next morning, with her father not yet buried, she added arsenic to her step-mother's pottage. As Susan Craig's agonising day ended in death at 5.00pm, Cockburn was arrested, and later tried and condemned.

Following her execution in the Grassmarket her body was given for anatomical dissection.

Executioner; James Alexander
Edinburgh

1755

April 23rd;   **Nicol BROWN**   Edinburgh

Brown, a flesher, condemned for the murder of his wife by burning was hanged and gibbeted at the Gallowlee.

On Sunday 8th June 1755 his body was found in a nearby quarry by a boy watering horses and put back on the gibbet - only to disappear again a fortnight later. It was never found.

Executioner; James Alexander
Edinburgh

June 13th;   **William DOIG**   Perth

Executed for the murder of 14-year-old Peter Maxton, a fellow chapman, Doig was more repentant for the bad life he had lived - especially for swearing, lying, sabbath breaking and disobedience to his parents - than the killing of Maxton.

His body was given for anatomical dissection.

Executioner; Unknown

1756

September 7th; **Agnes CROCKAT**   Edinburgh

Hanged in the Grassmarket for the murder of her seven-day-old bastard child.

Executioner; James Alexander
Edinburgh

1757

July 15th; **Hector McLEAN** Perth
Executed and hung in chains for the murder of Isabel McEuen, a fellow servant at Buchanty, a decayed hamlet on the south bank of the River Almond, ten miles from Crieff, McLean was about 18-years-old.

Learning that she was pregnant, he followed her on a walk, and when she refused to deny the child was his, murdered her, 'by knocking out her brains'.
Executioner; Unknown

October 22nd; **William STEWART** Inverness
Donald McILROY
Condemned at the Autumn Circuit - Stewart for the murder of Anne McRae, wife of John McLea - and McIlroy, a butcher at Kilbochy in Ross-shire, for murdering Kenneth Happy, gardener to Sir Lewis McKenzie of Scatwell.

Ironically, Stewart's body was given for dissection, whilst that of the butcher was hung in chains.
Executioner; Unknown

1758

June 30th; **David EDWARDS** Ayr
A sergeant with General Holmes's Regiment of Foot (later the 53rd Regiment of Foot), Edwards was condemned at Ayr Spring Circuit Court for murdering and robbing the regimental shoemaker, George Simson, whilst they were foraging potatoes at Stranraer in the January. The trial lasted from 6.00am on Saturday until 5.00am on the Sunday - with the jury delivering its verdict of guilty at 7.00am.

Executed on Ayr Common, his body remained on the gibbet until 1779. The following account was tendered to the Magistrates by the contractors:

'Ayr Julley the 3 day 1758.
An account of the town to William Parker and others for drain [drawing] to the Gibet.

to taken a stik for the Gibet	0. 1. 6
to 10 Draight of Stons from the mill	0. 3. 4
to 31 Draight of stons from the Shor	0.10. 4
to 3 Draight of timer from the Shor	0. 1. 0
to 14 Daills [planks] and barells out and fetched in to the tooun agin with Sume chairs	0. 4. 0
to 2 Kearts [carts] of lime attendens with ahors [a horse]	0. 0. 8

and keart [cart] to keree [carry]
the man to the Gibbet 0. 1. 0
£1. 1.10

This gibbet served Ayr for the remainder of the eighteenth century.
Executioner; Robert Jamieson
Ayr

1759

March 7th; **Ann MORRISON** Edinburgh
Hanged in the Grassmarket for the murder of her illegitimate child.
Executioner; James Alexander
Edinburgh

June 29th; **James RUSSEL** Perth
Like Edwards who suffered at Ayr the previous June, Russel was a soldier in General Holmes's Regiment.

Condemned for robbing Alexander Barland of 11s 6d, on the north inch of Perth the previous December, he was executed despite a recommendation to mercy from the jury.
Executioner; Unknown

1760

July 2nd; **Robert KEITH** Perth
A tinker from Star of Brunton, Markinch, Fife, Keith was hanged for murdering his step-daughter Margaret Graham on 22nd March 1760, and seriously assaulting his wife.

Leaving an alehouse near Balbirnie about 5 o'clock, all the worse for drink, the women were attacked within the hour. After stabbing his wife in the collarbone, he felled the girl with a staff then thrust the knife through her back.
Executioner; Unknown

1761

April 22nd; **Janet HEATLY** Edinburgh
A 22-year-old servant girl executed for the murder of her illegitimate child.
Executioner; James Alexander
Edinburgh

1762

January 13th; **William RIPLEY** Edinburgh

After conviction at Inverness of a rape on six-year-old Elizabeth Grinsal, Ripley, a soldier in Petitet's Regiment, was brought to Edinburgh, condemned and hanged in the Grassmarket.

Executioner; James Alexander
Edinburgh

1763

June 29th; **Thomas PRICE** Dumfries

A soldier in Leighton's Regiment, hanged for breaking into the premises of Messrs Wilson, merchants in Dumfries and carrying off watches and other goods.

Executioner; Unknown

1764

October 19th; **Jean CAMERON** Perth

Executed for child murder, Cameron had been servant to James Thomson, Officer of Excise at Dundee. She had become acquainted with Alexander McGregor, a soldier in Lord Sutherland's Highlanders, and got with child by him on a proposal of marriage. She concealed the birth for fear of being turned out of her service.

Of six women indicted for child murder at the Autumn Northern Circuit (Perth, Inverness and Aberdeen), only Cameron and Douglas at Inverness were hanged.

Executioner; Unknown

November 2nd; **Christian McKENZIE** Inverness
Margaret DOUGLAS

McKenzie was hanged for the murder of Mary Taylor, her husband's mother, and Kenneth McKenzie his 13-year-old brother - although his murder, 'had not proceeded from premeditated malice'.

A servant to Captain John McKenzie of Castle-Leod in Ross-shire, Margaret Douglas had been convicted of child murder.

After coming to Castle-Leod, Alexander McKenzie, the principal servant had watched his opportunity to debauch her - and had finally succeeded. She had also been before the Kirk Session for alleged guilt with another of the Captain's servants.

At the beginning of May 1764, hearing that some people were in the area from her native area of Assynt, she went to enquire of her mother and friends. About noon and two miles on the road her pains came, and about six o'clock the following morning she was delivered of a male child.

Whether it was alive or not she could not tell, but as she could not save both their lives, she wrapped its head in linen, and buried it under a thin stone and some earth.

On returning to her master's house it was obvious she had been delivered, but she continued in her denials until her breasts were examined and the minister and schoolmaster were brought.

In her dying speech she confessed to the murder of John McKenzie, son of a previous employer Murdoch McKenzie, by throwing him into a deep burn. She had taken a dislike to the boy, but was never suspected of murder, it presumed that his death had been accidental.

Executioner; Unknown

1765

June 28th; **John HUTCHEON** Aberdeen

A farmer from Cranabog of Carnousie, in the Banffshire parish of Forglen, Hutcheon was hanged for many crimes of dishonesty.

In December 1763 he broke into Mr Fullerton's house at Dudwick, and stole a gold watch, £50 in money and a bill of exchange due by himself. He had formerly worked Ardargue Farm at Dudwick.

Demolished in the last century no trace of the Dudwick Mansion remains.

Apprehended in October 1764 after stealing cattle from the parks of Waterton, he was taken to Aberdeen and tried at the Spring Circuit.

After execution, his body was taken by the surgeons.

Executioner; Unknown

July 10th; **Hugh BILSLAND** Glasgow

Responsible, with an accomplice, for a series of robberies through the previous winter, Bilsland was arrested after robbing a gentleman of £6 and a case of surgeon's instruments, at the west end of Argyle Street.

He was the first to be hanged at Howgatehead.

Executioner; Unknown

November 7th; **Alexander PROVAN** Paisley

A detestable ruffian, executed for the murder of his wife the previous July, Provan was employed at Smithhills Distillery, Paisley.

Before execution, his right hand was to be cut off and nailed to the head of the gallows but, according to tradition, the trepid hangman severed the hand through the palm, leaving Provan screaming, 'the tow, the tow, the tow!' - which was hurriedly placed about his neck and his suffering brought to a close.

A writer in 1829 reports the axe being long kept as a relic 'for those curious in these matters'.

Executioner; Unknown

November 13th; **Patrick OGILVIE** Edinburgh

In the cause célèbre of the 1760's, Lieutenant Patrick Ogilvie, 89th Regiment of Foot, and Katherine Nairne, his sister-in-law, were tried at Edinburgh for incest, and the murder of Thomas Ogilvie of Eastmiln in Forfar. Some reports stress that the incest was the graver charge.

Committed to Forfar prison on 14th June, they were taken to Edinburgh on the 21st and served with their indictments on 20th July 1765:

> '... THAT WHEREAS by the law of God, and the laws of this and all other well governed realms, the crime of INCEST, committed betwixt a man and the wife of his brother, especially when such crime is committed within the dwellinghouse of the injured husband, where the offenders were cherished and entertained by him with confidence and trust, is a heinous crime, and most severely punishable. '... AND ALSO, by the same holy law of God, ... all wilful HOMICIDE or MURDER, especially when perpetrated by poison, and above all, when such murder is committed under trust, or upon a person to whom fidelity and affection are due by the most sacred ties, is also a crime of the most heinous and atrocious nature.'

In January 1765, 19-year-old Nairne married Thomas Ogilvie, a 40-year-old with a sickly constitution, and settled at his family home of Eastmiln. Just prior to the wedding, however, Patrick Ogilvie, on recuperation leave from the East Indies, came to live at the house, and formed an incestuous relationship with Katherine.

The relationship soon led to a 'wicked design' to murder the husband, for which the lieutenant

Lord Dunsinnan, uncle to Katherine Nairne (*Kay's Edinburgh Portraits*)

obtained laudanum and arsenic. Thomas died from their effects during the night of 6th June 1765.

Knowing of the relationship, the servants realised the cause of Ogilvie's death - and the pair landed in Forfar Jail the following week.

Their trial was a formality - Ogilvie was sentenced to be hanged on 25th September, but Nairne's counsel presented a petition stating that she was pregnant. Five midwives later swore to the pregnancy being near six months. She had won a respite.

A great violin player, Ogilvie devoted his final weeks to the instrument.

After four respites, Ogilvie was brought to the Grassmarket gallows on 13th November, where a 'very moving incident happened ...'. When turned off, the noose of the rope slipped, and he fell to the ground.

> 'He was immediately taken up, and dragged up the ladder by the assistance of the city-servants, he making what resistance he could; and then the executioner, having again put the rope about his neck turned him

over for a second time, and he continued hanging till dead.'

Meanwhile, Katherine Nairne was lying in the Tolbooth, but not without hope. Her uncle Sir William Nairne, the future Lord of Justiciary, Lord Dunsinnan, now took a hand. With his connivance Katherine escaped the Tolbooth on the night of Saturday 15th March 1766, dressed as Mrs Shiells, one of the midwives.

At the foot of Horse Wynd, Sir William's clerk Mr James Bremner, the future Solicitor of Stamps, waited with a carriage. He accompanied Katherine as far as Dover, on her way to France.

Two rewards, each of £100, were offered for her apprehension, one by the Government and one by the city of Edinburgh, went unclaimed.

It was said she married a Dutchman, by whom she had a large family, before retiring to a convent. She died in England sometime in the nineteenth century.

Executioner; Isaac Gibbs
Edinburgh

1766

July 11th;   **James TAYLOR**   Inverness

Both on the journey from Pluscardine in Elginshire to Inverness for trial, and in court, Taylor displayed such bizarre behaviour that a jury was set to decide his sanity. They decided the madness feigned.

During his trial for robbery, he continued to sing, whistle, dance and talk incoherently to those around him, taking no notice of the proceedings. Finding him guilty, the jury did not add a recommendation to mercy.

Back in prison, he would not suffer the ministers; tore to pieces the grave cloaths which were brought to be tried on; and had to be tied strongly into the cart, from where he was handed up by the neck to the gallows.

Executioner; Unknown

1767

March 25th;   **Robert HAY**   Edinburgh

A 22-year-old soldier in the 44th Regiment of Foot, executed in the Grassmarket for street robbery.

Executioner; John Liddle
Edinburgh

June 19th;   **Duncan CAMPBELL**   Perth
John CHAPEL

Soldiers in the 6th Regiment of Foot, 20-year-old

Campbell, an Irishman, and 22-year-old Chapel, an Englishman, were executed and hung in chains for murdering and robbing James Imrie, tenant in Claytown, Dunbarny parish in south east Perthshire, the previous December.

Following Imrie from the market place, they attacked him on the South Inch, stabbing him through the heart with a bayonet. Leaving the weapon behind led to their arrest.

Executioner; Unknown

November 4th;   **Agnes DOUGAL**   Glasgow

Executed and dissected for murdering her 8-year-old daughter, James Cleland writes of 31-year-old Dougal in the 1817 edition of *The Annals of Glasgow*:

> 'This atrocious woman had lived a very lewd and wicked life, having had four children in adultery; a person with whom she then cohabited pretended he would marry her, provided Joanna Finlay, her daughter, was taken out of the way; from that moment Dougal determined to murder the child. Having concealed a table knife under her apron, she asked Joanna to take a walk with her by the River side, and when they passed the Anderston boundary she pressed her daughter into the root of a hedge and almost severed her head from her body.'

Executioner; Unknown

1768

February 24th;   **John RAYBOULD**   Edinburgh

Condemned and executed for forging and uttering notes of the Thistle Bank of Glasgow.

Executioner; Andrew Boyle
Edinburgh

1769

October 25th;   **Andrew MARSHALL**   Glasgow

The only culprit to be gibbeted in Glasgow, Marshall, a soldier with the 38th Regiment of Foot, was hanged for murdering and robbing Allan Robert at Slamannan the previous July.

The hangman omitted to bind his arms before pushing him off, allowing Marshall to catch the gallows arm. And unable to pull him down, the hangman resorted to beating his hands with a stick.

Stolen from the gibbet in the night, his body was never found. Tradition has it that gardeners in the vicinity, 'felt the prejudice against their vegetables was so strong ... that the cause was clandestinely removed'.

Executioner; Unknown

1770

April 25th;   **Andrew McGHIE**   Edinburgh

Hanged in the Grassmarket, aged 18 years and 3 months, for street robberies in the city.

Executioner; Edward Hay
Edinburgh

May 30th;   **William HARRIS**   Edinburgh

On 25th August 1768 Harris, a merchant in Ayr, was incarcerated in the town's Tolbooth:

'By virtue of a mittimus [warrant] from William Logan, Sheriff Substitute of the shire of Ayr, proceeding upon a petition presented to the said Sheriff by John Alexander, one of the tellers to James Maxwell, James Ritchie & Co. [Thistle] Bankers in Glasgow, as being in knowledge of and accessory to the forgery of a quantity of twenty shilling notes [to the value of £10,129] upon said Bank and as being not only the holder of some of said notes but was attempting to burn and otherwise destroy them, therein to remain till he shall be liberated in due course of law'.

In the October, dangerously ill, he was transferred to the debtors apartments till taken to Edinburgh on 3rd December 1768 for trial.

On 7th November 1769 he escaped from Edinburgh Tolbooth by cutting through the bars in his room, and a reward of 50 guineas was offered by the magistrates. He was recaptured by a Mr Blagdon, water baillie at Shields, (who claimed the reward) on 15th November 1769.

He was not tried until April 1770, when, 'coming into court his behaviour indicated some appearance of insanity'. This was put to a jury - which found him sane - and his case to a second jury - which found him guilty.

He was executed in the Grassmarket.

Executioner; Edward Hay
Edinburgh

June 5th;   **John BROWN**   Jedburgh

A labourer from Newcastle, hanged for the theft of 70 sheep from Soutrayhill Farm near Duns.

Executioner; Unknown

June 29th;   **Thomas STEWART**   Aberdeen

Whilst resisting apprehension at Stonehaven market in February 1770 on suspicion of theft, Stewart mortally stabbed the arresting constable, John Buchan, in the thigh.

Following execution his body was given to Doctor Livingstone at Aberdeen University for dissection.

Executioner; Unknown

September 21st; **Alexander McDONALD** &
                 Charles JAMIESON   Linlithgow

Tried at the High Court for robbery, they were held in Edinburgh Tolbooth until 20th September when they were taken to Linlithgow and executed on a gallows at the end of Linlithgow Bridge.

Neither confessed and McDonald declared that he suffered innocently.

Executioner; Unknown

1771

September 25th; **William PICKWITH**   Edinburgh

A 24-year-old soldier in the 22nd Regiment of Foot, Pickwith was hanged for several robberies in and around Edinburgh.

Executioner; Edward Hay
Edinburgh

1772

November 27th; **Alexander McDONALD**   Perth

Tried at the Autumn Circuit Court with George Buchanan, McDonald for stealing two horses and a watch, and both for stealing five head of cattle, and being habit and repute thieves. Buchanan was acquitted and McDonald condemned.

Executioner; Unknown

1773

June 11th;   **William BROWN**   Perth

A lacemaker from Dundee condemned at Perth for two acts of horse stealing.

Executioner; Unknown

July 2nd;   **Alexander McINTOSH**
Inverness

The 1773 Inverness Spring Circuit cause list carried the names Edward Shaw McIntosh of Borlum, Alexander McIntosh, his natural brother, John Forbes, miller at the Mill of Reatts, William Davidson in Beldow of Reatts, and Euan Dow McLauchlan and Donald Dow Robertson, both servants to Borlum - indicted for robbery - and entering into an association to murder and rob passengers on the highway. They had become the terror of the neighbourhood.

When on Thursday 13th May, the Advocate Depute learned that Edward McIntosh's wife and five 'gentlemen' had abducted his two principal witnesses, he obtained warrants, and despatched a messenger at arms and military escort to bring them to court.

Edward Shaw McIntosh and his two servants, and Forbes were outlawed for non-appearance and only Alexander McIntosh and William Davidson appeared for trial.

Both were found, 'Guilty, art and part, of the haill crimes, except stealing bear [barley] from Mr Blair', and Davidson of, 'robbing the house of James McPherson, weaver of Laggan of Killihuntly', and condemned.

Davidson was reprieved, but McIntosh, as the greater offender, was executed and hung in chains.

The remainder of the gang were never traced, despite a substantial reward.

Executioner; William Taylor
Inverness

July 7th;   **Kenneth LEAL**
Janet Innes's Cairn

A messenger at arms in Elgin, Leal was executed and hung in chains for robbing the North Mail postboy, 14-year-old John Smith, on the night of 23rd December 1772, between Three Mile House and Janet Innes's Cairn on the Elgin to Fochabers road. One letter contained £70 and another a bill of exchange for £200.

Condemned at Inverness, he was hanged before a crowd of 5000 at the Cairn raised to Janet Innes, the last witch burned in the district.

On the ladder he pleaded that his wife, Helen James, who was then in Elgin Tolbooth for 'theftuous practices', and his 9 children would be treated with humane compassion.

After receiving sentence he confessed his guilt, and 50 guineas were recovered from Helen's possession.

Buried at the gibbet's foot, Leal lay peacefully until 1829 when foresters employed by John Sellar, millwright at Longhill, were cutting wood on an adjacent knowe, and set about digging 'Kenny's Hillock'. Three feet under the surface they found his corpse in its gibbet irons.

From a report in the *Elgin and Morayshire Courier* of 3rd January 1868, we learn;

> "The chain was first got hold of, and on pulling it up all the hoops attached to it and encircling the body were brought to light.'

Their curiosity satisfied, the men re-interred the body and its iron suit, but retained the head-piece and chain, which they took back to Longhill. Their trophy dangled on a fence post by Longhill burn until swept away in a spate.

Executioner; William Taylor
Inverness

September 15th; **James WILSON**   Edinburgh
John BROWN

Executed for murdering Adam Thomson, and robbing his house on Carnwath Muir on the night of 27th January 1771.

Executioner; Edward Hay
Edinburgh

November 17th; **William MITCHELL**   Glasgow
Christopher JARDYNE

Hanged for four acts of robbery in Glasgow
Executioner; Unknown

November 19th; **Thomas McLATCHIE**   Stirling

Tried at Stirling Circuit with David Balfour and David Anderson, sailors in Leith, and James McLean of Gateside in East Lothian, for breaking into James Allan's house at Dunsmore Park, and stealing £34 4s in cash and bales of cotton cloth.

A carter from Portsburgh, McLatchie was the only one to pay the full penalty.

Executioner; Unknown

November 19th; **Alexander McNAUGHTON**
Perth

From Rotmell in Dowally, Perthshire, McNaughton was hanged for murdering Donald Keir, son of William Keir, the previous March. His diet for the Spring Court was deserted and not until 23rd September was he tried and condemned.

Executioner; Unknown

1774

March 2nd;   **Margaret ADAMS**   Edinburgh

On the evening of Friday 29th October 1773, Adams and her sister Agnes entered Janet McIntyre's huxtery shop in Glasgow's Argyle Street - bolting the door behind them.

They murdered McIntyre, but were disturbed plundering the shop. Neighbours, alarmed by the noise, broke in and found the sisters hiding under a bed.

Condemned at Edinburgh on 25th January 1774, Agnes was granted a reprieve on 25th February.

Executioner; Edward Hay
Edinburgh

June 17th;   **Francis THORNILOE**   Perth

A sergeant in the 67th Regiment of Foot, Thorniloe was tried and condemned for breaking into the house where Captain Croasdaile of the regiment was quartered and stealing 140 guineas from his bureau.

Executioner; Unknown

1776

September 11th; **Anne MACKIE or MATHER**
Edinburgh

Relict of David Mather, land surveyor in Tranent, hanged for murdering a bastard child of which she was delivered on 13th June.

Executioner; Donald Cameron
Edinburgh

November 1st; **Alexander MORISON** Aberdeen

The last culprit to be hanged at Gallowhill, and the final gibbeting in Aberdeen, Morison had murdered his wife, Agnes Yule, by fracturing her skull with an axe blow, in their house at the north end of the Guestrow.

Dressed in a red nightcap and red waistcoat, he came to the gallows in a cart with the rope already around his neck, where he managed to secure his feet so securely to the cart that the horse had to be driven with a whip.

Executioner; Robert Welsh
Aberdeen

1777

September 21st; **Marion WHITE**   Stirling

From Kinross, White was hanged, and dissected and anatomized, for child murder, following her conviction at the Circuit Court.

Executioner; Unknown

1779

June 25th;   **James McLAUCHLANE**   Ayr

Jean Anderson was travelling from Bo'ness to visit a brother at Irvine in Ayrshire on Sunday 28th February 1779, when McLauchlane joined the coach at Kilmarnock.

They alighted near Thornton, a few miles from Irvine, where next morning Jean was found dead and stripped of her cloak, stockings and silver buckled shoes.

The following week McLauchlane, a discharged soldier was arrested at Maybole and tried at Ayr Spring Court.

Executed on Ayr Common, his body was stolen from the gibbet 36 hours later. Tradition says the culprits had removed McLauchlane to protect their kailyards from the flies his body would attract.

Executioner; John Sutherland
Glasgow

1780

May 10th;   **David DALGLEISH** Edinburgh
                William DONALDSON

Dalgleish, for a robbery committed at Fountainbridge on 1st February 1780, and Donaldson, a soldier in the 31st Regiment of Foot, for theft by housebreaking, executed in the Grassmarket.

Executioner; John High
Edinburgh

September 11th; **David REID**   Edinburgh

Executed for forging and uttering notes of the Bank of Scotland.

Executioner; John High
Edinburgh

October 13th;   **Matthew HAY**   Ayr

As the last resting place of James McLaughlane, whose body was stolen from the gibbet, is a mystery, so too is that of Matthew Hay of Holms Farm, Dundonald, his successor on the gallows at Ayr.

A farmer, aspiring to be a gentleman farmer through the marriage of his daughter to Sir William Cunningham of Caprington, Hay's business interests included smuggling and counterfeit banknotes - and more than a passing interest in Lizzie Wilson, the daughter of his overseer, until Lizzie told him she was pregnant.

With his aspirations in question, he resorted to arsenic, but killed the overseer and left Lizzie unscathed.

Unlike his predecessor on Ayr's gallows, he would not be left on the gibbet - his body would be anatomically dissected by Dr George Charles of Ayr.

However, John Kelso Hunter in his autobiography, 'Retrospect of an Artist's Life', writes of being at the opening of Matthew's grave at Dundonald in 1812 when the coffin was found to contain a man's weight of sea sand. So what became of the body?

Did Dr Charles, boyhood friend of the poet Robert Burns and future Provost of Ayr, sell it to a medical school and dupe the family, or save it from an ignominious end and dupe the authorities?

Executioner; John Sutherland
Glasgow

November 1st;   **William JOHNSTON**   Dumfries

Innkeeper and deputy post master at Moffat, Johnston was hanged for stealing bank notes from letters. In his confession, he blamed his ruin on his love of drink.

Executioner; Roger Wilson
Dumfries

1781

June 6th;   **Robert HISLOP**   Glasgow

A weaver from Gorbals who had taken to theft by housebreaking, Hislop was the last to pay the penalty at the Howgatehead.

Executioner; John Sutherland
Glasgow

November 23rd; **Robert DUN**   Ayr

Condemned for robbing James Hutchison, banker and ex Provost of Ayr, of a considerable sum of money, Dun saw his brother-in-law accomplice John

Kay reprieved and handed over to the Navy Impress Service.

Before being pinioned at the gallows, the story goes, he took a roll of banknotes from the buckle of his back hair and handed them to a friend. It was Hutchison's money, but in forfeiting his life, it would go to his illegitimate child.

He was buried in St Quivox churchyard to the east of Ayr.

Executioner; John Cuthill
Stirling

1782

January 8th;   **John McAFFEE**   Edinburgh

When condemned at Inveraray for forging and uttering nine British Linen Company 20s notes, McAffee appealed, claiming that forgeries made in Dublin were outwith the jurisdiction of the Scottish Court.

The High Court did not agree and he was hanged in the Grassmarket

Executioner; John High
Edinburgh

1783

October 31st;   **William BURNETT**   Aberdeen

From Strachan, Aberdeenshire, Burnett was condemned at the Circuit Court and executed at the Market Place for theft of a mare and an ox. The morning after the theft, a farmer who recognised the beasts found him asleep at the roadside and apprehended him.

Confirming a local belief that it was unlucky to bring an offender to justice, the farmer was reduced to destitution, and was last known carrying coals in Aberdeen.

Executioner; Robert Welsh
Aberdeen

1784

February 4th;   **James ANDREW**   Edinburgh

A 21-year-old from County Down, Andrew was hanged for robbing John Dykes of his silver watch and money at Hope Park near Edinburgh.

Coming to Scotland a linen weaver, he married a Dalkeith woman who bore him two sons, but joined the South Fencible Regiment which, 'freed me from the clamours of a wife'.

'Perverted into the bewitching sins of drunkenness and whoring', he admitted from the scaffold being, 'a Sabbath breaker, a drunkard, rake and fool',

Executioner; John High
Edinburgh

July 7th;   **James JACK**   Glasgow

Accused of robbing William Barclay, schoolmaster at Calder Kirk, with an accomplice Archibald Jarvis, who absconded, Jack was the first to be hanged at the Castleyard.

After attempting to take his own life on the morning of his execution, he attempted to take the life of one of the town officers with the same knife. He was kept in fetters till hoisted from the cart by a pulley.

Executioner; John Sutherland
Glasgow

July 25th;   **Jean CRAIG**   Aberdeen

A daring and enterprising thief from Huntly, with three court appearances in two years, Craig was condemned for theft from a bleachfield in October 1783.

She should have been hanged on 11th June, but a respite saved her until the July.

Executioner; Robert Welsh
Aberdeen

October 29th;   **Sarah CAMERON**   Stirling

Hanged for murdering her six month old child by throwing it over Stirling Bridge, her body was conveyed to Glasgow for dissection.

Executioner; Unknown

November 3rd;   **James BRODIE**
William BRODIE
Jean SCOTT   Glasgow

Twenty four-year-old James Brodie, a soldier in the 96th Regiment of Foot, was condemned with his 20-year-old brother William, a sailor aboard HMS *Shrewsbury*, for theft by housebreaking.

Scott, the first woman in living memory to be hanged at Glasgow for theft, was paying the penalty for theft by housebreaking, receiving stolen property and being a habit and repute common thief. Twenty years of age, she was the daughter of Shavie Davie, a well known character about Glasgow.

Attended by five ministers, the trio came out to face an immense crowd and a new style scaffold. The

Glasgow Mercury reported;

'The Gibbet and Scaffold was constructed on the plan of the London Scaffold with springs, and it sunk down with ease so that the unhappy criminals were launched into eternity without any apparent struggle'.

Executioner; John Sutherland
Glasgow

1785

January 14th;   **Elspet REID**   Aberdeen

Condemned at the previous Spring Circuit for theft by housebreaking and being a habit and repute thief, Reid should have perished on the Market-place gallows with Jean Craig, but was respited due to pregnancy.

Executioner; Robert Welsh
Aberdeen

March 19th;   **Andrew LOW**   Forfar

Known about Forfar as a thief from the age of nine, Low, then 20, was condemned by Sheriff-Depute Patrick Chalmers on 28th January 1785 on multiple charges of theft by housebreaking.

Saturday being Forfar's market day, the town was thronged when the steeple bell commenced its death knell at midday and the cart drew up to the Tolbooth door.

Low, accompanied by the minister and the hangman, came out and mounted it, using the coffin as a seat, before the cart joined the procession of the town's officers with halberds, the provost and town officials, and a body of 150 baton armed special constables.

At the gallows, he was launched into eternity as the cart was driven off.

Alex Lowson's book, *Tales and Legends of Forfarshire*, mistakenly names the long dead John Chapman of Aberdeen as the hangman.

Executioner; Robert Welsh
Aberdeen

May 17th;   **Adam HISLOP**
William WALLACE   Jedburgh

Condemned for knocking down and robbing Captain Craes, a shipmaster from Eyemouth, in their home town of Kelso in February 1785.

When turned off, their halters broke and both sustained severe head injuries through striking the edge of the scaffold. Wallace remained sensible, but was 'much hurt by his fall'. They remained on the ground for the half hour it took to procure new ropes.

Later that night they were buried in Kelso Churchyard.

Executioner; Unknown

May 20th;   **William MOSSMAN**
            Bernard MEANS &
            John BARNS   Ayr

The Ayr Autumn Circuit brought together Mossman, a local man, condemned for repeated acts of theft, and Means and Barns, two Irishmen for breaking into a shop at Stranraer and stealing £20.

Their execution brought a difficult and embarrassing day for Ayr's Magistrates. With their irons struck off the previous night, the trio barricaded their cell and were got out with great difficulty.

As at Jedburgh earlier in the week - all three ropes broke and the trio were seated at the gallowsfoot until fresh rope was brought from town.

Executioner; Peter Grant
Ayr

June 1st;   **Neil McLEAN**   Glasgow

An armourer by trade, McLean was hanged at Castleyard for forging and uttering notes of the Glasgow Arms Bank.

Executioner; John Sutherland
Glasgow

June 8th;   **David STEVEN**   Glasgow

Hanged for murdering his one time partner in crime, Thomas Morton, a stocking maker, by shooting him through the workshop window of John Black, stocking manufacturer, in Gallowgate, Glasgow.

In November 1783 Steven, his father William Steven, portioner of Flender, and Morton were detected circulating forged notes of the Aberdeen Banking Company in Paisley, but Morton turned King's evidence.

David and William Steven were indicted to appear at Glasgow Spring Court of 1784, but as Morton was in Ireland, probably for his own safety, the diet was temporarily deserted.

Steven and his family excited great terror in Ayrshire, where they lived.

His body was given to Professor Hamilton of Glasgow University for anatomical dissection.

Executioner; John Sutherland
Glasgow

September 21st; **William MILLS**   Edinburgh

When hanged at the west end of the Tolbooth for theft by housebreaking:

"The place of execution was improved by the addition of a scaffold for the Magistrates and Clergy etc. which undoubtedly gives a greater degree of solemnity to the scene'

Executioner; John High
Edinburgh

November 4th; **John McDONALD**   Aberdeen

A vagrant, and by modern standards an imbecile and hence unfit to plead, McDonald was tried at Aberdeen on two charges of wilful fire raising, by which the stacks and yards, of two farmhouses were burnt out.

Shortly before one of the fires, he was seen with a burning peat, which he pretended was to light a tobacco-pipe.

When the courthouse candles were lit, about the time he received sentence, he fancied he was to be hanged immediately, and cried out - 'Och, ye'll surely no hang me here wi can'le licht!'

Executioner; Robert Welsh
Aberdeen

November 9th; **Thomas VERNON**   Glasgow

A 20-year-old soldier in the 28th Regiment of Foot, Vernon was hanged for robbing James Maxwell of £8 2s, with an accomplice Richard Davies, who was reprieved.

Executioner; John Sutherland
Glasgow

1786

March 22nd; **John HAUGH**   Edinburgh

Sons of William Haugh, of Daldarroch Farm, Glencairn, Dumfriesshire, John and William Haugh were condemned for breaking into William Smith's shop at Kirkland of Glencairn and stealing hats, silk handkerchiefs and several dozen silver plated buttons.

Both were condemned at Edinburgh, although William won a reprieve 'during his Majesty's pleasure'. By July 1787 that pleasure was exhausted and he too paid with his life.

Executioner; John High
Edinburgh

April 19th; **Walter ROSS**   Edinburgh

A flax dresser from Edinburgh, Ross was hanged at the Luckenbooths for three acts of theft, which included picking a wallet containing £25 from the pocket of the Lord Provost of Glasgow.

Executioner; John High
Edinburgh

June 2nd;   **James MOIR**   Stirling

Awaiting execution for murdering his wife, Margaret Keydon, by arsenic poisoning, Moir, from St Ninian's, also confessed to poisoning his father-in-law with arsenic - and previously smothering his two children, aged one month and 12 days.

His body was given for anatomical dissection.

Executioner; Unknown

June 7th;   **James SPENCE**   Glasgow

Condemned at Glasgow Spring Circuit for breaking into the house of Provost Campbell of Glasgow, a verdict of not proven was returned against his sister Ann.

The Old Parochial Register shows him to have been a 21-year-old weaver who 'died of asthma'.

Executioner; John Sutherland
Glasgow

October 25th;   **Elizabeth PAUL**   Glasgow

Widow of John Ritchie of Greenock, and a habit and repute thief, 58-year-old Paul had previously been dealt with by a Circuit Court - 'banished Scotland for life - and whipt through the streets when she returned'.

Now she was paying the penalty for stealing 4 pieces of cloth valued at £6 6s. from a bleachfield near Paisley.

Executioner; John Sutherland
Glasgow

October 31st;   **John CLARK**   Jedburgh

Thomas Martin, portioner at Gallowside, commonly called Craigieknowe, was whipped through the streets and banished Scotland for resetting horses he bought from Clark, knowing them to have been stolen. Nothing further is known of Clark.

Executioner; Unknown

1787

January 17th;   **Daniel DAVOREN**   Edinburgh

A soldier in the 56th Regiment of Foot, 22-year-old Davoren was held in Edinburgh Castle until executed at the west end of the Luckenbooths for Robbery.

Executioner; John High
Edinburgh

January 29th;   **Charles JAMIESON**   Edinburgh
               James JAMIESON

About midnight on Wednesday 13th September 1786, the Jamiesons, and their mother Eupham Graham, a tinker family, entered the stable yard of Kinross post office, and stole mail bags from the Aberdeen to Edinburgh coach.

With associates as illiterate as themselves, they were unable to separate the valuable bills of exchange from ordinary letters, and when arrested at Falkirk on 26th September, had made no profit from the theft.

The jury at Edinburgh found the brothers guilty, but saved their mother with a not proven verdict.

Executioner; John High
Edinburgh

March 21st;   **John REID**   Edinburgh

Whilst servant to James Stuart of North Platt Farm, Reid murdered his 8-month-old natural son by drowning him near Ratho Byres.

Executed at the Luckenbooths, his body given for dissection.

Executioner; John High
Edinburgh

May 23rd;   **Thomas GENTLES**   Glasgow
            John McAULAY
            Thomas VEITCH

Condemned at the Spring Court - Gentles for stealing cloth from Kirklee bleachfield, and McAulay and Veitch for knocking down and robbing Charles Wilson, surgeon in Glasgow.

It took an hour for the procession to make the half mile journey up High Street from the Tolbooth to the Castle Yard and near the Bell of the Brae, Gentles and Veitch had to be revived with wine and 19-year-old McAulay with water.

Executioner; John Sutherland
Glasgow

May 25th;   **James HACKET**   Perth

Son of Thomas Hacket, a wright in Kirriemuir, James was executed for theft of goods and money.

'A very ignorant man, who could neither read nor write', he appeared, 'very undaunted and unconcerned', on the scaffold outside Perth Prison.

Executioner; Unknown

June 1st;   **William WEBSTER**   Aberdeen

Returning from the army, Webster had operated a 'wheel of fortune' at the weekly market until banished as a swindler by the magistrates - when he turned his hand to theft by housebreaking.

The case against him was clinched by a young girl identifying a stolen gown from a small blood stain left when she pricked her finger whilst sewing it.

In the condemned cell, he attempted both prison breaking, using a saw brought by his wife, and suicide with a razor and laudanum.

His execution was marked by an unusual number of pickpockets in the crowd

Executioner; Robert Welsh
Aberdeen

June 30th;   **William RICHARDSON**
Dumfries

Executed for murdering 19-year-old Elizabeth Hughan who was seven months with child by him, his body was given to the surgeons.

Executioner; Roger Wilson
Dumfries

4th July;   **William HAUGH**   Edinburgh

Condemned with his brother John in February 1786 for breaking into a shop at Kirkland of Glencairn in Dumfriesshire, William was later reprieved.

However on 18th June 1787, he was back in court when a letter from the Home Secretary was read;

'signifying his Majesty's pleasure, that the respite granted to William Haugh, prisoner in the Tolbooth of Edinburgh of sentence of 7th February 1786, should cease on account of his atrocious behaviour'.

His attempt to break jail on the Sunday before John's execution, and again in May 1787, rendered him no longer worthy of the Royal Clemency.

Executioner; John High
Edinburgh

October 19th;   **James McNAB**   Ayr

Whilst awaiting trial at Ayr for horse stealing, the young Irishman escaped Ayr Tolbooth and was outlawed by the Spring Circuit Court.

The following week he was captured at Maybole, with another stolen horse, and condemned at the Autumn Court.

Executioner; James Grant
Ayr

1788

March 28th;   **George McKERRACHER**
Stirling

A tenant at Ward of Goodie in Perthshire, McKerracher was condemned at Edinburgh on 18th February 1788 for forging and uttering bills of exchange for £48 and £49, the previous April and May.

Executioner; Unknown

May 16th;   **John SMART**   Stirling

A reputable shopkeeper from Falkirk, 49-year-old Smart forged 18 bills of exchange to the value of £1400 over a three month period.

Executioner; Unknown

June 27th;   **James GRANT**   Aberdeen

Condemned for theft by housebreaking, the contemporary Aberdeen Journal reports:

'He was executed in the way now used in England; a scaffold being erected in front of the prison, over which the gibbet projected; the place on which the criminal stood was made to fall down, and leave him suspended.'

Executioner; Robert Welsh
Aberdeen

July 2nd;   **Peter YOUNG**   Edinburgh

A vagrant and thief, Young broke Perth Jail in 1786, but was captured, with his wife Jean Wilson, after breaking into a shop at Portsoy, and lodged at Aberdeen.

Both were condemned to be executed on 16th November 1787, but Wilson, on account of her being pregnant, had her execution postponed till 9th August 1788.

On the night of 24th October 1787, they broke Aberdeen Jail, releasing all the other prisoners. The Reward Notice which offered a bounty of 20 Gns described Young as:

'a stout young man, pockpitted, aged about twenty two, with a remarkably sharp eye; about five feet ten inches high, thin made, has an arch sneering look; is a native of Deeside in the county of Aberdeen, the language of which county he speaks. His dress is described as being; a tartan short jacket with large squares or lozens, trowsers of the same stuff, and a bonnet, so that he is rather a remarkable figure'.

Although not mentioned in the description, his remarkably small hands allowed him to slip from handcuffs.

Arrested at Montrose in December 1787, he was taken to the High Court at Edinburgh, where, when asked if there was reason why execution of his former sentence of death should not be carried out, he replied, 'I am not the man'.

After great deliberation, the bench of six judges adjourned the court until the following day, when the macer and clerk from the Aberdeen Circuit were called - and identified him as Peter Young.

Sentenced to be executed at Edinburgh on 2nd April a respite was granted until the July date.

Executioner; John High
Edinburgh

October 1st; **William BRODIE** Edinburgh
George SMITH

Brodie and Smith – 'The First Interview in 1786'. (*Kay's Edinburgh Portraits*)

'Mr Brodie' in the Condemned Cell (*Kay's Edinburgh Portraits*)

That Deacon Brodie's name lives on, may have more to do with the man and his place in Edinburgh society than his crimes, for in press reports of his trial and execution he is consistently referred to as, 'Mr Brodie'.

His father, Convener Francis Brodie, had been a successful wright and cabinet maker in the Lawnmarket, and a Town Council member. On his death in 1780, William succeeded to the business, and in 1781 was chosen a councillor of the City, as Deacon of the Incorporation of Wrights and Masons. He was also an inveterate gambler.

Smith on the other hand was quite different - and treated as such. A hawker from Berkshire, he and his wife had arrived in Edinburgh in mid 1786, when ill health forced him to part firstly with his goods and then his horse, in order to support himself and his wife.

Taking residence at Michael Henderson's, 'a house much frequented by the lower order of traveller', he

Brodie and Smith on the Scaffold   (*Edinburgh City Library*)

met Brodie, and later Andrew Ainslie and John Brown - the main prosecution witnesses at their trial.

At the latter end of 1787, a series of thefts were committed in and around Edinburgh - shops were opened and goods seemed to disappear, as if by magic. The theft at the Excise Office in Chessel's Court, Canongate on the night of 5th March 1788, dispelled the magic.

Whilst Brodie and Ainslie kept watch, Smith and Brown entered the office by a false key procured by Brodie, but missing a cache of £600 in a concealed drawer, they came away with £16.

Disappointed at the small return, and with an English sentence of transportation on his head, Brown resolved to barter a pardon with information on the Edinburgh crimes. He was successful - he and Ainslie became 'King's evidence'.

As Brown, Ainslie and the Smiths were arrested, Brodie fled. From London he reached Amsterdam but was arrested before he could embark for America.

When their trial opened on 27th August 1788, with Brown and Ainslie the principal prosecution witnesses, the only unknown was the date of their execution.

At eleven o'clock, with their irons knocked off,

Brodie was visited by a few select friends, during which time he wrote to the Lord Provost, requesting that certain named gentlemen be permitted to take charge of his body - 'and do the last offices to it with decency'.

'The last offices', he hoped, would include reanimation, to which end the body was to be placed in a cart, and driven at a furious rate round the back of the Castle, on route to a surgeon. What had worked for 'half-hangit Maggie Dickson', 60 years earlier, might work again.

They were ready at two o'clock, Brodie dressed in a full suit of black with his hair dressed and powdered, and Smith in white linen trimmed with black.

Coming from their cell, they passed the room holding Bruce and Falconer. As His Majesty had granted them a six week respite, Brodie told them, a pardon would soon follow. On first hearing of the respite, Brodie had expressed satisfaction, and to Smith's observation that six weeks was but a short period, Brodie had cried, 'George, What would you and I give for six weeks longer? - Six weeks would be an age to us!'

Coming onto the platform, preceded by two white-robed magistrates with white staves, and the three ministers. Brodie bowed politely to both the magistrates and the crowd.

After prayers, the white nightcaps were put on, and Brodie, clasping Smith by the shoulder and pointing to the steps to the drop said, 'George Smith, you're first in hand'. Slowly Smith ascended, followed by Brodie, 'with briskness and agility'.

Brodie examined the scaffold, and his halter, and deciding it was too short, stepped down whilst it was adjusted. When this was repeated he began to show impatience. That Brodie had the audacity, and the magistrates the patience to suffer such behaviour, illustrates the influence he had held in Edinburgh. Throughout these theatricals, Smith had remained placidly on the drop.

Finally satisfied, he untied his neckcloth, buttoned up his waistcoat and coat, and helped the executioner fix the rope. With the nightcap over his face he, 'placed himself in an attitude expressive of firmness and resolution', and Smith dropped the signal.

When cut down, his body was taken on the furious cart ride, but neither it nor the bleeding carried out in his Lawnmarket workshop, restored animation.

Executioner; John High
Edinburgh

October 17th; **William CORMACK** Inverness

Whilst the Inverness Autumn Circuit sent Cormack to the gallows for theft by housebreaking, it accepted a petition from Margaret Smith for banishment from Scotland for life for the murder of her child.

Executioner; Unknown

October 22nd; **William McINTOSH** Glasgow

Condemned for robbing John Hamilton, a day labourer at Scotstoun, of one pound, 19-year-old McIntosh was the first to suffer at Glasgow Cross.

From a raised platform in front of the jail he was suspended from a rope attached to a beam projecting from a second storey window.

Executioner; John Sutherland
Glasgow

December 3rd; **William SCOTT** Glasgow

William and his brother John, from Old Monkland, could not have guessed when they appeared before William Honeyman, Sheriff Depute in the County of Lanark at Glasgow on three charges of theft by housebreaking that he would condemn them. It was unusual enough to be unique.

Hearing the sentence, William cried out, 'O, I am a gone man, I am a guilty man, my brother is not so guilty as me'. He was proved correct, John was reprieved.

Executioner; John Sutherland
Glasgow

December 24th; **James FALCONER** Edinburgh
Peter BRUCE

During the night of 16th February 1788, Falconer and Bruce, merchants in Dundee, broke into the offices of the Dundee Banking Company, through the ceiling, and stole £422.2.6.

Tried at the High Court in Edinburgh in August, they were twice respited. Despite Deacon William Brodie's hopes, they were executed.

The chief prosecution witnesses, Alexander McDonald and Alexander Menzies, were later convicted of another crime and transported - but hanged at the yard arm for mutiny on their passage to Botany Bay.

Executioner; John High
Edinburgh

1789

May 27th; **John CARMICHAEL** Dumfries

A journeyman shoemaker, 22-year-old Carmichael had been condemned with Robert Leggat (later reprieved) of theft by housebreaking.

Executioner; Joseph Tait
Dumfries

June 9th; **William MURRAY** Jedburgh

Found guilty at Jedburgh of stealing a large quantity of books from a carrier's cart in Greenlaw, Murray was condemned whilst James Agnew, his co-accused and fellow chimney sweep, was transported for 14 years.

Murray's return from banishment had aggravated his case.

Executioner; Unknown

July 3rd; **John MONRO** Aberdeen

Monro, a notorious thief, was in Aberdeen Jail awaiting trial for theft by housebreaking, when he escaped with Peter Young in October 1787.

Recaptured, he was tried at the Spring Circuit, found guilty, whipped through the streets in June 1788 and banished the County. However, using the assumed name John Stewart he returned to his old haunts. It was to prove a mistake.

On 16th November 1788, he was committed to Banff Jail accused of theft by housebreaking at Cairnbulg three nights before. He now used the additional aliases of John Brown and John Young. At the May Circuit of 1789, with the help of a little perjury, he was found guilty and condemned.

Despite warnings from his spiritual guide that denial would only assure him a place in Hell, his last breath denied his guilt.

It later transpired that perjury had been committed to save the real John Stewart, and that Monro had merely participated in the non-capital crime of reset.

Executioner; Robert Welsh
Aberdeen

1790

February 8th;   **Bartholomew COLLINS**
Edinburgh

Thirty three-year-old Collins, a brewer's servant in Edinburgh, was executed for murdering Marjory Cowan, his wife of 5 weeks, a few days after the birth of their child. They had lived together for three years.

After condemnation he confessed to killing her in a fit of drink induced jealousy.

Hanged in his shirt, having neither coat nor waistcoat, his body was given to Dr Alexander Monro at Edinburgh University for anatomical dissection.

Executioner; John High
Edinburgh

June 9th;   **John BROWN**   Glasgow

When condemned for issuing forged notes of the Paisley Banking Company, 32-year-old Brown, a farmer from Dreghorn in Ayrshire, told the judge, 'he would have esteemed it a favour if his execution could have been fixed for 9th May'.

> 'The feeling and humane judge re-
> plied that most people had a desire to
> live as long as they could, and hoped
> he would be convinced of the pro-
> priety of enjoying life, and improve the
> time allowed him in preparation for
> eternity'.
>
> The *Glasgow Mercury*.

The prospect of living under the shadow of a death sentence might have altered his Lordship's opinions.

Executioner; John Sutherland
Glasgow

June 9th;   **Patrick FITZPATRICK**   Dumfries

Condemned with James Muldroch at Dumfries Circuit Court in April for theft by housebreaking, 25-year-old Fitzpatrick was hanged, whilst Muldroch was reprieved.

Executioner; Joseph Tait
Dumfries

October 20th;   **James DAY**   Glasgow

Unable to support her 5-year-old natural son, the mother gave him to Day, a gardener to Mr Fulton of Park near Inchinnan in Dunbartonshire. He in turn placed him with a baby farmer - £6 for the initial year and £5 per annum thereafter - but being unable to pay, the child was sent back.

In November 1789 the couple left Inchinnan, ostensibly to seek work in the Highlands, taking the child along. After dining at Old Kilpatrick, Day drowned the now 6-year-old boy in the Clyde, before setting for the north.

On the scaffold, when Day reeled backwards in a convulsive fit, Sutherland immediately let the drop fall.

Executioner; John Sutherland
Glasgow

October 29th;   **James HENDERSON**   Aberdeen

Hanged for the murder of Alexander Gillespie, a slater in Touch, whom he claimed broke into his house at Bainshole, parish of Forgue, early one July morning.

The prosecution proved Henderson the aggressor - having murdered Gillespie with an axe when he called peaceably at the house for drink.

His body was given for dissection.

Executioner; Robert Welsh
Aberdeen

1791

February 23rd;   **William GADESBY**   Edinburgh

A 7th Regiment soldier, thrice tried for capital crimes, Gadesby was finally convicted for robbery and condemned to be executed on 2nd February 1791.

In the condemned cell he confessed to the Dundee Bank housebreaking for which Falconer and Bruce had forfeited lives in December 1788, and won a respite of two weeks.

The confession was fantasy - but with 2nd February now passed he submitted he could no longer be competently hanged. The High Court refused to consider the question, and he was duly executed.

Executioner; John High
Edinburgh

July 27th;   **John PAUL**   Edinburgh
             James STEWART

Paul, a 24-year-old weaver from Paisley, and Stewart, a 23-year-old soldier, executed for robbing a gentleman of his watch, hat and 14s in Nicholson's Square, Edinburgh.

> 'In the execution broadside, Paul expressed the hope that, ' ... no person will be so cruel as to mention my untimely death to my aged parents'.

Executioner; John High
Edinburgh

October 12th;   **William SMITH**   Edinburgh

Thirty two-year-old Smith, alias John Gun, executed at the west end of the Luckenbooths for theft by housebreaking at Long Newton, where he stole clothing from the house of a George Gibson.

Executioner; John High
Edinburgh

1792

January 11th;   **James PLUNKET**   Glasgow

Condemned to be executed at Glasgow on 26th October 1791 for robbing Robert Wilson, a silversmith, in New Vennal of his watch, money and shoe buckles, Plunket escaped from the Tolbooth on 11th October.

The reward notice circulated to magistrates throughout the country led to his apprehension at Aberbrothie in Angus, but not knowing him, the escort from Glasgow took him before the High Court at Edinburgh. There he admitted his identify, and was ordered to be executed on the new date.

At his trial, two jurymen who failed to appear were each fined 100 merks and an order made to place their names first at every ensuing Circuit till they did appear.

Executioner; John Sutherland
Glasgow

May 16th;   **James DICK**   Glasgow

A shoemaker, 32-year-old Dick ended the last of many disputes with his wife Isobel Russell, by

A REWARD OF

One Hundred and Fifty
GUINEAS,

By the Honourable LORD PROVOST *and* MAGI-
STRATES *of* GLASGOW.

WHEREAS GEORGE DAVIDSON and JAMES PLUNKET, late prisoners in the Tolbooth of Glasgow, under sentence of death by a judgment of the last Circuit Court of Justiciary held here, effected their escape, between ten and eleven o'clock in the evening of Tuesday the eleventh day of October current, in company with JOHN RUSSEL, weaver in Calton of Glasgow, who aided them in their escape:

A reward of FIFTY GUINEAS for each of the above-named persons, is hereby offered, to any person or persons who will apprehend and secure, in any safe prison, the said George Davidson, James Plunket, and John Russel, besides the necessary charges of apprehending and securing them.

GEORGE DAVIDSON, is a native of Caithness, between 17 and 18 years of age, about 5 feet 7 inches high, smooth faced, of a fair complexion, wears his own darkish brown hair, tied behind; is slender and well made, a little in kneed; wore, when he escaped, a round hat, a close-bodied green coat, with metal buttons, thickset breeches, a light coloured striped waistcoat, and dark ribbed worsted stockings.

JAMES PLUNKET, a native of Ireland, is about 22 years of age, 5 feet 8 inches high; smooth faced, of a fair complexion, wears his own hair, of a sandy colour, tied behind, and the locks curled; wore, when he escaped, a round hat, a dark brown close bodied coat, with yellow metal buttons, a light coloured waistcoat, corduroy breeches, and plain white worsted stockings; he was lately discharged from the 35th Regiment of foot, on account of a scorbutic complaint in his right leg, which retains marks of a late sore.

The above John Russel is a native of Glasgow, about thirty years of age, about 5 feet 4 inches high, stout made, wears his own dark brown hair, powdered, and tied behind, and large frizzled locks; wore, when he went out of prison, a round hat, green stript close-bodied coat, with yellow metal buttons, a light coloured waistcoat, and corduroy breeches.

All Magistrates, and other Officers of the Law, are requested to use their utmost exertions to discover and secure these three persons. Officers of the Customs, at the sea-ports, are likewise requested to employ their utmost vigilance for the same purpose; and it is expected that Masters of Vessels, to whom any of these three persons may offer themselves for passage, will apprehend and secure them as above.

Council-Chamber, Glasgow, *12th Oct.* 1791.

Wanted Notice for James Plunket   (*Ayr Carnegie Library*)

murdering her in their home in Glasgow's Bridgegate. His body was given for dissection.

Executioner; John Sutherland
Glasgow

November 7th;   **Mortimer COLLINS**   Glasgow

Coming along Goosedub Street [then off Stockwell Street] on the night of 25th July 1792, 22-year-old

Collins, and Peter Owens, both of the 37th Regiment, had knocked down everyone they met.

Both very drunk, they next came upon John Panton, keeper of the city's Bridewell, who paid with his life for upbraiding them. Chasing him into Jaffray's Close, Collins murdered him with his bayonet.

Executioner; John Sutherland
Glasgow

1793

May 22nd; **Agnes WHITE** Glasgow
James McKENZIE

Encouraged by the hope that should the crime be discovered, she would only be banished, White murdered her five month old child at Paisley on 5th January 1793 by giving it oil of vitriol in milk.

Her scaffold companion, McKenzie, a carter in Glasgow, was hanged for robbery. A charge of being a habit and repute thief was found not proven.

Executioner; John High
Glasgow

May 31st; **James DORMAND** Perth

Condemned at the Circuit Court for four robberies committed near Dundee on 30th November 1792, whilst acting with Robert Rogers, 19-year-old Dormand was hanged on the appointed day, whilst Rodgers was respited until 21st June.

Executioner; Unknown

June 21st; **Robert ROGERS** Perth

See James Dormand - 31st May 1793

Executioner; Unknown

1794

October 15th; **Robert WATT** Edinburgh

Of the many in Scotland caught up in the revolutionary fervour then fomenting in France, Watt alone paid with his life.

Tried in Edinburgh before a Court of Oyer and Terminer under the Lord President and seven judges, including two from England, and a jury of twelve, Watt and David Downie (condemned and later reprieved) were charged with being members of the Friends of the People Society, and forming, 'a distinct and deliberate plan to overturn the existing Government of the country'.

David Downie, co-conspirator with Robert Watt
(*Kay's Edinburgh Portraits*)

The Society's plan was this:

'A fire was to be raised near the Excise Office (Edinburgh), which would require the attendance of the soldiers in the Castle, who were to be met there by a body of the Friends of the People, another party of whom were to issue from the West Bow to confine the soldiers between two fires, and cut off their retreat; the Castle was next to be attempted; the Judges (particularly the Lord Justice Clerk) were to be seized; and all the public banks were to be secured. A proclamation would then be issued, ordering all farmers to bring in their grain to market as usual; and enjoining all country gentlemen to keep within their houses, or three miles from them, under penalty of death. An address would be sent to his Majesty [George lll] commanding him to put an end to the war [with France], change his ministers or take the consequences.'

The court commenced at 8.00am on Wednesday 3rd September and rose a little before 6.00am the following morning. The verdict came as no surprise.

During his confinement, Watt was held in Edinburgh Castle, and it was from there he was brought for execution to the west end of the Luckenbooths.

About half past one o'clock, the two junior Magistrates walked from the council chamber to the Castlehill, preceded by the city constables and town officers, in a hollow square formed by the city guard.

At the Waterhouse (the limits of the burgh) they were met by the procession from the Castle, consisting of two Chief Constables of the shire of Edinburgh, dressed in black, with batons, and the Sheriff-depute and Sheriff-substitute. They too were in black, with white gloves and white rods.

Next came the black painted hurdle (drawn by a white horse) in which sat the Executioner (in black) from Perth, with the axe in his hand - and Watt, with his back to the horse, and tied to his seat.

As escort, there were six constables on each side of the hurdle, and twelve on the outside of them, with a further twenty in the rear. To keep off the mob, 200 of the Argyleshire Fencibles followed, walking the dead march.

With the culprit in the hands of the Magistrates, the soldiers retired to the Castle, and the procession made its way to the Tolbooth.

By a quarter to three, Watt was on the scaffold, where after prayers and farewells, he dropped the signal on the hour.

When the body was cut down after thirty two minutes and laid on a table, the executioner stepped forward and severed the head with two strokes - "This is the head of a traitor", he pronounced, holding it up to the crowd.

On Monday 13th October, the Executioner of Perth was brought to Edinburgh at the request of the Sheriff depute, but whether this man, whose name is unknown, or Edinburgh's John High performed the whole duty, is unknown.

Executioner; John High
Edinburgh

James McKean at the Bar, Edinburgh (see overleaf) (*Kay's Edinburgh Portraits*)

1795

November 13th; **Donald McCRAW**   Perth

A weaver to trade, McCraw was hanged for murdering his pregnant wife, Anne Adams. She had purchased an ounce of tea on credit, and unknown to McCraw, who when asked by the shopkeeper to settle flew into a rage.

His body was given for dissection.

Executioner; Unknown

1797

January 25th;   **James McKEAN**   Glasgow

On Friday evening, 7th October 1796, James Buchanan, the carrier between Glasgow and Lanark, called at McKean's house in Glasgow's High Street, apparently on business, and was taken into the room where McKean worked as a shoemaker. The room had, 'neither fire nor candle'.

A few minutes later, when McKean called for a towel, as Buchanan had, 'wet the floor on making his water', his wife saw blood on the floor, and shrieked, 'Murder! - Murder!' Picking up his hat McKean made off.

He hoped to escape to Ireland, but was captured in Lamlash Bay when his Irish bound ship from Irvine in Ayrshire was held by contrary winds. Returned to Glasgow, he was tried, condemned and executed.

Senex Reid, in *Glasgow, Past and Present*, writes of the case. When the body of 44-year-old McKean was given to Doctor Jeffray for dissection:

> 'Some gentlemen in Glasgow anxious to preserve part of the remains of this notorious murderer, asked the Doctor to give them the skin of McKean's back, with which request he very obligingly complied. These gentlemen then sent it to a tan-pit to be tanned, and what was very curious, the king's duty was demanded and paid for thus tanning McKean's hide, When the tanning operations were finished, the skin had much the appearance of a common piece of ben-leather. I had a small piece of it in my possession, about the size of a crown piece, and much about the same in thickness.'

Executioner; John Sutherland
Glasgow

By Order of the She-riff of Renfrew.

WHEREAS upon the night of Sunday the nineteenth current, the house of John Barr, Farmer, at Gryfe castle, in the parish of Houstoun, and Shire of Renfrew, was, betwixt the hours of Eleven and Twelve, broke into by eight or nine Men, armed with Cutlasses or Sticks, who, after committing great outrages in the house, and threatening the said John Barr, his Wife, and three Servants with instant Death if they did not make a discovery of all the money in the house, (with which the said John Barr and his wife were forced to comply,) carried off a Pocket Book of sewed worsted of various colours, chiefly green, containing Four Guinea Notes of the Royal Bank of Scotland, Six Guinea Notes, partly of the Paisley Bank, and partly of the Union Bank, and one Guinea Note of the Greenock Bank, with several Bills and Papers, the property of the said John Barr, together with about forty Shillings in Silver, and a pair of Silver Sugar Tongs, and two Silver Tea Spoons, the Tongs and Spoons having the letters I. B. engraved on each of them.

AND WHEREAS, amongst others, there is the greatest reason to suspect William Oak, Weaver, at Bridge of Johnston (better known by the name of Billy Oak) George Aitcheson and William Pealing or Pullens, weavers in Irvine, all Irishmen, who have since absconded, of having been concerned in the above House-breaking and Robbery, A REWARD OF TEN GUINEAS is hereby offered to any person, or persons, who shall apprehend and secure them, or either of them, to be paid by Edward Jamieson, Procurator Fiscal of the County, upon Conviction.

OAK is a man about sixty years of age, straight and well made, fully six feet high, has grey coloured eyes, broad lips, large nose, his face a little pitted with the Small Pox, and retains the Irish accent; he wears a brown tied Wig, pretty far back on his head, in speech and articulation he is full and formal, in address and conversation, smooth and insinuating, he resided several years in Kilmarnock, came to Paisley about thirteen years ago, and has for these last three years lived in Johnston, and in all these places maintained a very suspicious character. He is by trade a Weaver, but has for these some years past occasionally travelled the country with an Ass or Poney vending Stone Ware. Oak's wife has absconded with him and there is a probability of their travelling together.

George Aitchison is of a fair complexion, thin and pale-faced, has short hair, is about five feet six inches high, and generally wore a white drab-coat, He made his escape from Irvine on Thursday last about eight o'Clock at night, after being taken into custody, leaving his hat behind him.

William Pealling or Pullens, is of a black complexion, round-faced pitted with the small pox, stout made, about 5 feet 9 inches high, has black tied hair, and generally wore a blue coat. He is supposed to have left Irvine the same day.

If the Tongs and Spoons are offered for sale, it is entreated they may be detained, and information given as above.

Sheriff Clerk's Office,
Paisley, 25. March, 1797.

Reward Notice for the Stouthrief at Gryffecastle Farm
(*Paisley Library*)

August 17th;   **Thomas POTTS**   Paisley

A weaver from Williamsburgh, 35-year-old Potts was condemned at Edinburgh for stouthrief committed at Gryffecastle Farm, Houston, on the night of 19th March 1797, and hanged by the Tolbooth.

Ironically, when the initial reward notice was published; Potts was unknown.

Executioner; John Sutherland
Glasgow

1798

May 16th; **John McMILLAN** Glasgow

On the evening of Tuesday 13th September 1791, McMillan, a 55-year-old Chelsea Pensioner, got into an argument with Alex Moodie, a gardener in Glasgow, over a trifling sum of money.

Lifting a dirk, McMillan plunged it into the gardener's breast and fled, leaving the others in the room to tend the dying Moodie.

An advertisement, offering twenty guineas for his arrest, described him as:

'5 foot 5 inches, stout, face pitted with smallpox, greyish eyes, short curly bushy hair mixed with grey, and wearing a round hat, dark blue coat and waistcoat, brown corduroy trousers and blue ribbed worsted stockings. He has an English/Gaelic accent, and was in the 21st Regiment.'

He was next heard of in a newspaper report of 16th March 1798:

'Monday morning, Mr Williamson, messenger, arrived in Edinburgh from London having in custody John McMillan, late change keeper here, accused of murder of Alex Mudie, some time ago.'

Fleeing to London and re-enlisting, he was posted overseas. In early 1798 he returned to Savoy Barracks in London where, boasting of the killing of Moodie, he was identified and arrested.

Now a 62-year-old, he was tried at Glasgow Spring Circuit in proceedings that lasted less than two hours.

He frequently said he would meet death with courage and boldness - and he kept his word.

Executioner; John Sutherland
Glasgow

1799

March 6th; **James STEWART** Edinburgh

A letter carrier with the General Post Office in Edinburgh, Stewart was executed at the west end of the Tolbooth for abstracting five £20 notes from a letter whilst at Grangemouth the previous December.

The day after the theft he exchanged two of the notes in Edinburgh - one in a haberdasher's and one in a grocer's.

Several trial witnesses were Quakers who refused to be put on oath, giving declarations instead, but despite losing the benefit of their evidence, the Crown still won a conviction.

Executioner; John High
Edinburgh

1800

March 12th; **Griffith WILLIAMS** Edinburgh

A native of Caernarfon, 24-year-old Williams came to Leith as a sailor aboard the *Susannah* of Charlestown, South Carolina, in November 1799.

Condemned at the High Court for murdering Ann Wilson or Bruce, who stole money from him in her house at Smeiton's Close, Leith, on 10th December, he declared his resolution had been to, 'beat her so as just to leave life in her'.

Executed at the west end of the Tolbooth his body was given for dissection.

Executioner; John High
Edinburgh

June 11th; **Peter GRAY** Glasgow

Convicted at Glasgow Spring Circuit Court of hamesucken committed at Lieutenant Colonel Colquhoun's house of Ross Hall in Dunbartonshire the previous December. He was 45 years old.

Executioner; John Sutherland
Glasgow

September 3rd; **Samuel BELL** Edinburgh

Executed for fraudulently issuing notes of the Bankers, Carrick, Brown & Co. of Glasgow.

Executioner; John High
Edinburgh

1801

February 11th; **Richard BROXUP** Edinburgh

Condemned and executed for the following thefts committed in July and August 1800:

1) Picking open a chest of drawers in the house of Nicol Watson, change keeper, near Green Tree, Leith and stealing £30.
2) Breaking open a chest belonging to John Fairgrieve, change keeper, Leith Walk, Edinburgh and stealing clothing.
3) Opening a chest of drawers in the house of William Wilson at Stockbridge and stealing £26, and

4) Stealing clothing from George Binnie, change keeper, Coltbridge.

Executioner; John High
Edinburgh

June 12th;   **John WATT**   Dundee

In Dundee's first execution in over a century, Watt was hanged for theft by housebreaking following his condemnation at Perth. He gave his occupation as weaver.

The *Edinburgh Advertiser* of 12th-16th June 1801 reports:

'We understand it is the intention of the Lords of Justiciary, that in future all criminals sentenced to die, shall be executed in the places where they committed the crimes. This is certainly a wise and salutary measure.'

Circuit towns fought a long battle with successive governments over this question - which was not resolved with the decision in Watt's case. They would continue to bear the costs for crime committed elsewhere.

Executioner; Unknown

December 11th; **John YOUNG**   Aberdeen

A brother of Peter Young, hanged at Edinburgh in July 1788 for theft by housebreaking, John had roamed Aberdeenshire with a group of tinkers until arrested for the murder of Hugh Graham, a fellow gypsy.

Graham had attacked Young, near Chapel of Garioch, and in defence, Young had stabbed him. Despite Graham having initiated the attack, Young was condemned. With his family background, there was no hope of mercy.

From a contemporary report we learn of the Aberdeen custom for the hangman, in this case Robert Welsh, to dress the condemned in their grave clothes, but that Young objected. He did not, 'like to hae that creature Robbie Welsh's hands about him'.

His body was publicly dissected by the Lecturer on Anatomy at Marischal College.

Executioner; Robert Welsh
Aberdeen

1802

April 7th;   **George LINDSAY**   Edinburgh

Hanged at the head of Libberton's Wynd, 60-year-old Lindsay had murdered John Allan, a Dragoon

with the 23rd Regiment, in the January. His body was given for dissection.

Executioner; John High
Edinburgh

1803

June 8th;   **William CUNNINGHAM**
Glasgow

A tall, stout made man of 45 years Cunningham was hanged for theft and reset of theft.

Executioner; Archey McArthur
Glasgow

1804

January 20th;   **John COWIE**   Edinburgh

Arrested on 21st May 1803 for murdering his wife, Isobel Scott, by knocking her head on the hearthstone of their lodgings in Borthwick's Close, High Street, Edinburgh.

The press said their home was; 'a house of bad fame, and indeed there is hardly a house of any other description in the close'.

His road to the scaffold was protracted. His trial date was set for 11th July 1803 but put off till 26th August, and finally 30th November. To be executed on 4th January 1804, he was reprieved until the 20th.

Executioner; John High
Edinburgh

1805

June 5th;   **David SCOTT**   Glasgow
       Hugh ADAMSON

When the penny post brought anonymous information to the Jailor at Glasgow Tolbooth that Scott and Adamson were attempting to escape, they had already sawn through the bar securing their irons - but needed one more night to cut the window stanchel.

Elizabeth Allanton, a servant in the jail, was later convicted by the Magistrates of having brought them six spring saws in a water stoup, and sentenced to six-months imprisonment with hard labour.

They had been condemned for forging and uttering banknotes of Carrick, Brown and Company, Glasgow.

Executioner; Archey McArthur
Glasgow

1806

June 21st;   **John WESTWATER**   Kinghorn

Condemned at the Spring Circuit Court which opened at Perth on 9th May, Westwater was hanged in his home town for the murder of a fellow flax dresser, John Orr, by stabbing him with a knife.

Westwater was one of three culprits condemned at this court and executed. The others being Donald McCraw hanged at Perth, and Margaret Cunningham who was hanged at Edinburgh.

Executioner; Unknown

July 11th;   **Donald McCRAW**   Perth

A former Serjeant in the 42nd Regiment of Foot, McCraw was a 70-year-old merchant in Perth, with a premises in Kirkgate, when condemned for murdering 9-year-old Euphan Couper, daughter of John Couper, baker in Perth.

The circumstances of the case were, 'so repugnant to common decency that strangers were excluded from the court'.

Ironically, as a former serjeant in the town guard, he attended many previous executions in Perth

Executioner; Unknown

1807

January 7th;   **Margaret CUNNINGHAM**

Edinburgh

Convicted at the 1806 Perth Spring Circuit of murdering her husband John Mason, with arsenic, in their home at Path-head in Fife, whilst her accomplice, John Skinner, absconded. It was their second attempt.

Being pregnant, she was referred to the High Court for sentencing, and held in Edinburgh Tolbooth where the child was born in the December.

Executioner; John High
Edinburgh

January 21st;   **Thomas SMITH**   Edinburgh
George STEPHENSON

When condemned for stealing two horses from the farm of the Rev. James Maitland Robertson, Minister of Livingston; and one from William Glendenning at Livingston Mill, Smith and Stephenson fell on their knees and beseeched their Lordships and the jury to recommend them to his Majesty's Mercy.

Both from Newcastle, Smith was described as a little man, pretty far advanced in life; and Stephenson genteel and not exceeding 30 years.

Executioner; John High
Edinburgh

June 10th;   **Adam COX**   Glasgow

A native of Dungannon in County Tyrone, 46-year-old Cox drowned his infant son in a clay hole near his Tradeston home, following the death of his wife.

He went to the scaffold leaving three other children in the care of the magistrates.

His body was given to the University for dissection.

Executioner; Archey McArthur
Glasgow

October 21st;   **Maitland SMITH**   Dumfries

A stocking maker in Dumfries, Smith was condemned for murdering and robbing Alexander Williamson, a drover at Dalwhat in April 1807.

The indictment stated that:

> '... the said Maitland Smith did wickedly and feloniously discharge a pistol, loaded with ball, at the said Alex Williamson, whereby he was wounded on the left side of the body, about one inch from the spine, the ball having broken the first false rib, gone through the heart, ... in consequence of which he died.'

When apprehended, Smith was in possession of a silver watch, a purse and padlock, 17s in silver, a pocket book containing a bill of exchange for £800 and a bad shilling.

Executioner; Joseph Tait
Dumfries

November 28th; **Peter McDOUGALL**   Inveraray

A native of Perth, McDougall was condemned at Inveraray Autumn Circuit for murdering his wife, Mary Stewart, by throwing her into the River Etive, on a stormy December night the previous year, near King's House Inn. They had been crossing the Black Mount accompanied by his mother and step-father.

After a 14-day respite, he was hanged at the Crags, on the outskirts of Inveraray, and given to John Anderson, surgeon at Inveraray, for anatomical dissection.

Executioner; Archey McArthur
Glasgow

1808

February 10th; **Barbara MALCOLM**   Edinburgh
Condemned for murdering her 18-month-old daughter, Margaret Sutherland, on 8th December 1807, by pouring oil of vitriol over her throat, in the pretence of it being raw sugar.

After execution her body was given for anatomical dissection.

Executioner; John High
Edinburgh

July 20th;   **James GILCHRIST**   Glasgow
After strangling his wife Margaret Brock, Gilchrist, a Slateford stockingmaker, tried to allay suspicion by placing her chair by the fire and setting her clothing alight. He denied the charge to the last.

'I go as a sheep to the slaughter', he told the Lord Provost at the pre-execution service.

His body was given to Glasgow University for anatomical dissection.

Executioner; Archey McArthur
Glasgow

1809

February 22nd; **Robert STEWART**   Edinburgh
A journeyman bookbinder, Stewart was executed for breaking into the workshop of Peter More, calico glazer in Edinburgh on the night of 1st November 1808, and stealing webs of cloth.

Executioner; John High
Edinburgh

May 26th;   **William DORNAN**
                Robert SMITH   Ayr
Executed for breaking into Miss McMurray's drapery shop in Ayr's High Street the previous September. Her shelves were empty and her counter, except for a flint left by the thieves, cleared. The theft and a full description of the stolen property was reported in the local press.

The following week, Smith's wife was at the harvest on a farm near Ayr, where some of Miss McMurray's goods were recognised in a bundle she carried.

Condemned at the Spring Court, Dornan and Smith were the first to suffer outside the Tolbooth.

The new gallows and two coffins cost £20 - and the executioner was paid a five guineas fee

Executioner; Archey McArthur
Glasgow

October 10th;   **Charles Stewart MERCER**
Jedburgh
A weaver in Traquair, Mercer was condemned at the Autumn Court on 1st September for the rape of Isobel Nicol, a girl of 10 years and 6 months.

Executioner; Unknown

November 8th;   **John Gordon McINTOSH**
                George STEWART   Glasgow
Whilst McIntosh and Stewart were condemned for theft by housebreaking at a Glasgow calico dealer's warehouse, the case against their accomplice, John Armstrong, was found not proven. Arrested and taken to Edinburgh - his meeting with a hangman would come the following January.

On the scaffold they were attended by the Rev Dr William Taylor jun., the Rev Dr John Lockhart, the Rev John Love, the Rev William Routledge - and the hangman.

Executioner; Archey McArthur
Glasgow

1810

January 17th;   **John ARMSTRONG**   Edinburgh
Leaving McIntosh and Stewart to their fate, Armstrong had stepped from the Glasgow dock with his not proven verdict, and into the arms of officers from Edinburgh - with an apprehension warrant for another theft by housebreaking.

On 15th October 1809 he had broken into a Mr Robertson's shop at Dalkeith and stolen cloth and silver watches. The Edinburgh jury found him guilty.

Executioner; John High
Edinburgh

May 25th;   **John McMILLAN**   Ayr
From Kirkinner in Wigton, McMillan was tried at Ayr for the murder of his paramour, Barbara McKinnel, by supplying her with muriate of mercury as an abortifacient.

With medical experts unable to say positively that corrosive sublimate had occasioned McKinnel's death, McMillan's counsel made four strong points in his defence:

1) No person saw the powder given.

2) By the time the girl named McMillan as the person responsible, her mind was weakened by disease.

3) She had expressed no animosity towards him, and,

4) Admitting the possibility that he had given her the poison or medicine, he had done so in the belief that it would be harmless to her.

Despite the doubtful medical evidence the jury found him guilty, and he was condemned.

His body was given to Professor James Jeffray of Glasgow University for dissection.

Executioner; John High
Edinburgh

June 15th; **Andrew HOSACK** Aberdeen

A quarrier from Rubislaw, 56-year-old Hosack was pursued across fields after disturbing a dog whose master's house he robbed by way of the chimney in August 1809.

After execution at Castle Street, he was buried in a shallow grave on Gallowhill, but later removed and sold to the surgeons.

Executioner; John Milne
Aberdeen

November 18th; **Alexander GILLAN** Speyside

Condemned at Inverness for the murder and rape of 11-year-old Elspet Lamb, after her elder sister had rejected his attentions, Gillan was hanged and gibbeted on the moor near Fochabers.

Escorted from Elgin Jail by a detachment of the 78th Regiment of Foot from Fort George, he attempted, unsuccessfully, to address the crowd, before ascending the ladder:

'There he was detained in awful suspense by the unskilfulness of the hangman, but at last when the drop gave way, yielded his spirit without a struggle'.

After hanging an hour he was cut down, put in irons and suspended on the gibbet.

Taylor, the hangman, would later pay for his incompetence with his life.

William Taylor
Inverness

1811

March 27th; **Adam LYALL** Edinburgh

At the High Court in January, Adam and his brother John were tried for robbing Matthew Boyd, cattle dealer, on Sheriffmuir the previous October.

Meeting Boyd on the road, they robbed him at pistol point of a large sum of money, and made off. They hired a chaise from Newhall's Inn at Queensferry, and made for Edinburgh where they spent the night at a Princes Street hotel.

Their luggage was following them, they explained, and in response to comment of it being unusual to come from Glasgow by Queensferry, they said they had been visiting respectable family connections in Stirlingshire.

After they left the hotel next morning, Matthew Boyd arrived. He described them - and yes, the gentlemen had slept the night in the hotel. At this moment the Lyalls passed the door - now dressed in elegant clothes, with new boots and spurs, and whips in their hands. With the help of a soldier, Boyd arrested them.

At the trial, John feigned insanity and got away with his life, leaving Adam to the scaffold.

Tried on the same evidence in June 1812, despite again feigning madness, John was convicted and transported beyond the seas for life.

Executioner; John High
Edinburgh

June 7th; **George WATSON** Ayr

The Spring Court at Ayr dealt with two cases of horse stealing.

In the first, William Gillespie, a 70-year-old Irishman was sentenced to twelve months imprisonment for stealing a horse to carry off blankets he had already stolen. His appearance, 'indicated extreme wretchedness. With his meagre and squalid countenance, long beard and projecting teeth, he excited in the spectators, a degree of horror tempered with compassion'. His fatuous appearance saved him from the gallows.

In the second case, a 55-year-old itinerant stoneware dealer, George Watson, and his 25-year-old son, were charged with the theft of two horses at New Cumnock. A broken shoe on one of them had made pursuit into Argyllshire relatively easy.

The son was sentenced to banishment beyond the seas for 7 years and the father condemned.

The full report of the execution in the local paper ran:

'On Friday last, George Watson senior was executed here pursuant to his sentence, for the crime of horse stealing - During the period of his imprisonment, he displayed extreme ignorance, but expressed a sense of his guilt, and when the awful crisis arrived, he behaved with a degree of Stoical indifference, which in a better cause might have been mistaken for magnanimity.'

Executioner; John High
Edinburgh

June 28th; **Hans REGELSEN** Kinghorn

Regelsen, a young Danish seaman, hanged on the sands at Kinghorn for a rape on the body of a girl, Margaret Budge, the previous March. Condemned at Perth his sentence was respited one week.

Executioner; Unknown

October 11th; **Robert Brown ANDERSON**
James MENZIES Stirling

Executed for breaking into the shop of James Russell, merchant in Grahamston, near Falkirk, and stealing a quantity of goods.

Executioner; Unknown

December 26th; **Thomas McNAIR** Falkirk

On the night of Friday 5th April 1811, McNair, a 22-year-old slater, and Andrew Easton were on a spree in Falkirk, when Luden Tantzen, a German seaman asked directions to Grangemouth. The young men obliged, and Tantze set off.

In court, Easton, as a prosecution witness, related McNair's suggestion of robbing the seaman - and their getting 15 Falkirk Bank guinea notes, several shillings and two pamphlets from the German's pockets.

The jury's recommendation to mercy, fuelled strong local feeling against the sentence, and fears of an attempted rescue at the gallows grew.

The execution passed without incident, but even when cut down after forty five minutes, the friends who carried the body to his father's house, were escorted by dragoons, and patrols were maintained in the town throughout the night.

Executioner; Unknown

1812

February 21st; **Alexander O'KAIN** Stirling

Condemned at Edinburgh for robbing Archibald Stewart, a drover and cattle dealer, near Stirling.

Stewart was returning to Glenlyon from Falkirk Tryst on the evening of 11th October 1811 (the day Anderson and Menzies expiated their crime at Stirling) when O'Kain and at least one accomplice waylaid and robbed him of £1,010, chiefly in twenty pound notes of the Falkirk Bank.

As a result of a countrywide search for the robbers, O'Kain was traced to a Dumfries public house 11 days later.

Taking £49 from his pocket, he said it was all the money he had - until a further £120 was found about his person. After much difficulty and long search, a further £340 was found concealed in the chimney of his room.

Returned to Stirling from Edinburgh on 20th January for execution, he appeared on the scaffold, before a crowd of 4,000, dressed in white and attended by the magistrates bearing their ceremonial white rods.

Executioner; Unknown

April 22nd; **Hugh McDONALD** Edinburgh
Neil SUTHERLAND
Hugh McINTOSH

The festivities in the ember hours of the year 1811 were marred in Edinburgh by 'a band of idle apprentice boys', some of whom were responsible for breaking 70 public lamps, at least 10 robberies and one murder.

The murder had occurred at the head of the Stamp Office Close in High Street, where police watchman Dugald Campbell was attacked with sticks and bludgeons. He later died in the Royal Infirmary.

In seven of the ten robberies, the complainers reported losing 'a man's round hat', besides watches, watch keys, seals, penknives and a small amount of money.

Six men aged between 16 and 19 years were apprehended and committed for trial at the High Court in March. Of these, one absconded, two were sentenced to 14 years transportation, and McDonald, Sutherland and McIntosh condemned.

They would be executed on High Street opposite the Stamp Office Close, and McIntosh, found guilty of the murder, would have his body given for dissection.

Four hundred men from the Perth and Renfrewshire Militias were charged with keeping order of the largest crowd ever seen in Edinburgh. Every place which could command a view of the procession and the gallows was taken up - to the very rooftops.

Executioner; John High
Edinburgh

June 5th; **Moses McDONALD**   Greenock

Tried at Glasgow with an accomplice, John Gray, for theft by housebreaking in Greenock, both were found guilty, whilst another, Alexander Gibson, was outlawed for non-appearance.

Gray was sentenced to 7 years transportation, whilst McDonald, a 35-year-old docker, was condemned.

When thrown off, the rope broke and he was sat at the gallowsfoot till another was brought.

Executioner; Unknown

November 13th; **Robert FERGUSON**   Inverness

Condemned for murdering Captain Munro of the 42nd Regiment of Foot, he addressed the gallows crowd in Gaelic, denying implication in any other murder, and confirming that his wife had no hand in Munro's killing.

His body was given for anatomical dissection.

Executioner; Donald Ross
Inverness

1813

May 26th; **James FERGUSON**   Glasgow

Escaping Glasgow Tolbooth shortly after his arrest for street robbery in September 1812, 19-year-old Ferguson made for Perth, but was captured a fortnight before the opening of the Glasgow Circuit Court.

The manner of his execution was a disgrace. After giving the signal, he was kept standing an inordinate time before the drop fell. The rope then slipped several inches at the top, allowing his feet to rest on the staging before being pushed off.

Executioner; Archey McArthur
Glasgow

June 11th; **James MERRY**   Ayr

The evidence against Merry for presenting forged bills of exchange to the Bank of Scotland in Ayr's Sandgate was strong enough for the Judge to say, 'The charges are serious and it behoves the jury to weigh the matter, but in my opinion there is not a shadow of doubt with respect to the case'. The jury agreed.

A reaper and thatcher from Ochiltree in Ayrshire, Merry had the following letter published by the *Ayr Advertiser* the day before his execution;

'When I call to mind the many crimes I committed in my past life against my fellow creatures they wound my very heart. I beg all ... to forgive me, and my poor unfortunate family ... as they are perfectly innocent'.

The expense of bringing John High from Edinburgh, and the bill for the Magistrates levee after the execution, brought the cost to £49.10.10.

Executioner; John High
Edinburgh

July 14th; **John McDONALD**   Edinburgh
James Williamson BLACK

Ordering their execution on the Corstorphine Road, where they had robbed and murdered William Muirhead, a blacksmith from Calton, two months before, the Lord Justice Clerk told 19-year-old McDonald and 18-year-old Black that out of respect for the inhabitants in the neighbourhood he would not appoint their bones, 'to wither in the winds of Heaven'. They would instead be given for dissection.

Their contemptuous behaviour throughout the trial had shocked the court. And when the judge concluded the condemnation with the wish that the Almighty would have mercy on their souls, McDonald called out, 'He will have none on yours!'

At half past eleven on the day, a cart from the College arrived at the Tolbooth escorted by the City Guard. The Lawnmarket and the environs of the jail were guarded by 900 men of the 7th Dragoon Guards from the Castle, under a field officer.

At 12.30pm the procession was ready to move - it consisted of: The High Constable; the Magistrates; Mr Wilson, the Sheriff Substitute; Mr Brown, the Superintendent of Police; The Revd. Professor David Ritchie, Minister of St Andrews Church, The Revd. Mr Porteous, Chaplain to the Tolbooth; The Revd. Mr Badenoch; a Catholic priest; The cart with McDonald and Black, drawn with their backs to the horse, and the Executioner in front of them; and a large force of city constables.

By way of the Lawnmarket, the Mound and Princes Street, they made their way out to the west, where Mr Muirhead was found lying, a little more than a quarter mile from Coltbridge, and 30 yards west of the road to Ravelston.

They mounted the scaffold at 2.40pm in heavy rain, where a psalm was sung and suitable prayers offered by the Messrs Ritchie and Porteous, before Black dropped the signal and they were launched into eternity.

After hanging for one hour, their bodies were placed in the cart, without being put in shells, and taken to the College for dissection.

Executioner; John High
Edinburgh

November 18th; **William MUIR**
William MOODIE Glasgow

Condemned on three counts of robbery committed whilst acting together in the vicinity of Glasgow.

On the gallows, and before the caps could be placed on their heads, Muir dropped the signal leaving Moodie supported by the rope in a faint. When he was restored, their faces were covered, and on another signal being given the drop fell.

Thirty four-year-old Muir, a native of Dalry in Ayrshire, was a deserter from the Berwickshire Militia and the Royals. Imprisoned at Glasgow for robbery in 1808, he escaped - as he had from jails at Ayr, Irvine, Paisley, Linlithgow and Berwick. He left a wife and five children.

An Irishman, Moodie had also deserted from the Royals. Now 28 years old, he had married at 13 years of age and left a widow, who was pregnant, and three children.

A public subscription was opened for the support of their families.

Executioner; John High
Edinburgh

December 29th; **Christian SINCLAIR** Edinburgh

60-year-old Orcadian tried at Edinburgh for poisoning her 8-month-old niece with arsenic in the parish of St Ola, she was brought from Kirkwall to Leith on the Excise Cutter, Prince of Wales.

Carried to the scaffold on a chair, her 'poor and mean looking' body was afterwards given for dissection.

Executioner; John High
Edinburgh

1814

May 12th; **John GIBSON** Hawick

Condemned at Jedburgh, Gibson, a 40-year-old nailer, was hanged on a scaffold opposite the home where he murdered his wife, Janet Renwick or Gibson, the previous 19th November.

His body was given for dissection to Drs Monro, Senior and Junior, at Edinburgh University.

Executioner; John High
Edinburgh

May 27th; **John McMANUS**
Robert GIBSON Ayr

In March 1814, 21-year-old McManus from Magheraboy in County Sligo, was with a detachment of the 27th Regiment of Foot assisting the Revenue Service at Irvine in its war against the smugglers.

On the evening of Monday 7th March, he was returning to his billet - a little drunk - when he had an exchanged of words with a group of locals, including a weaver named Alan Hutton who punched him to the ground. When knocked down again he ran for his lodgings to the cheers of the crowd. They were next aware of a flash - a report - and Hutton falling with a musket ball through his heart.

The next place in the dock at Ayr Spring Court was taken by Robert Gibson, a collier from Riccarton, accused of assaulting the footpost between Kilmarnock and Tarbolton and robbing him of his bag. Letters in the bag had contained some £30.

The evidence of his accomplice, James McCormack, assured his place on the drop with McManus.

High returned to Edinburgh the next day, but the following week the City Chamberlain had to write to Ayr requesting settlement of his fee to, 'rid this office of his importunities'.

Executioner; John High
Edinburgh

August 10th; **James McDOUGALL** Edinburgh

A 60-year-old cattle dealer from Edinburgh, McDougall was hanged for uttering forged Bank of Scotland notes.

Crown Office proceeded on only two of the five charges against him: receiving change for a forged £5 note at Belhaven Toll; and passing 3 forged guinea notes to John Dove, a tailor in St Mary's Wynd, Edinburgh, for a great coat and vest.

Executioner; John High
Edinburgh

October 19th; **William HIGGINS** Glasgow
Thomas HAROLD

The first to be hanged in front of the new prison, Irishmen Higgins and Harold had been condemned for highway robbery.

'The Hanging Stanes', Braid Road, Edinburgh (*Author's Collection*)

The fatal apparatus was of a new design, which the broadside on their execution describes as being, 'much better adapted for the melancholy purpose than the old one'.

Executioner; John High
Edinburgh

1815

January 25th; **Thomas KELLY** Edinburgh
Henry O'NEIL

With a view of checking, by a severe example, the deprivations which have prevailed to so alarming an extent for some time past', Kelly and O'Neil were executed at the spot where the last of their three robberies, that of David Loch, a carter from Biggar, was committed on 23rd November 1814. They had been arrested two days later.

The spot, then described as being, 'between the Briggs of Braid and Braid's Burn, on the high road leading to Dumfries', is today at the junction of Braid Road and Comiston Terrace, Edinburgh - where the two gallows stones can still be seen set in the roadway.

Both aged about 50 years, Kelly was tall, stout and fair complexioned, whilst O'Neil was lower, and very black.

The Hanging Stanes' plaque (*Author's Collection*)

Reward Notice for John Worthington, 2nd November 1814, Ayr Advertiser
(*Ayr Carnegie Library*)

Immediately after the execution their bodies were placed in coffins and taken for burial to Greyfriars church yard.

In 1993, a plaque, erroneously claiming the pair to be, 'the last two highwaymen in Scotland to be executed ...' was erected at the spot.

Executioner; John High
Edinburgh

February 17th;   John WORTHINGTON
Symington Toll

As 48-year-old Worthington and his three tinker accomplices set out on the Kilmarnock road from the hostelry in Monkton, the publican, suspicious of the strangers' conspiratorial behaviour over their mutchkins [a Scots liquid measure], expressed his fear for the safety of villagers returning from the Kilmarnock Dudd's Day Fair.

By the time news of the three robberies reached the village and a hue and cry had been organised, the robbers were in Fenwick, north of Kilmarnock, dividing the meagre spoils.

The others were never traced but within the week Worthington was in Ayr Tolbooth, and the authorities had the evidence to satisfy an Edinburgh jury at his trial the following January.

He was kept in Edinburgh until the day before, when, passing from sheriff to sheriff, with an overnight stay in Glasgow, he was brought across the country and finally to Helenton Hill - 'at or near to the place where the crimes had been committed'.

The immense crowd had been entertained throughout the morning by Tam Young as he practised with the 'vile trigger' of the scaffold. This was Tam's first execution, and the cheer which went up from the crowd with each 'practice' drop did nothing to steady him. By the time he was leading Worthington to drop he was more nervous than the condemned man.

Worthington dropped the signal almost immediately, barely giving Young time to reach the trigger, and the drop fell at twenty minutes to three.

The following account of the burial in the Low Churchyard at Kilmarnock comes from John Kelso Hunter's *Retrospect of an Artist's Life*:

'A few friends performed the solemn service of making the body of non-avail for dissection. They had surmised, owing to the shallowness of the grave, that it was meant for less trouble to those who contemplated a robbery.

One friend had a bottle of vitriol and another a bucket of quicklime. The coffin lid, which was slenderly nailed down, was lifted by the edge of a spade being inserted and lever power applied ... The vitriol was applied from the face down to the toe of one leg then up the other. This done, the lime was applied and the lid hurried on, and in this shallow grave was left the now decomposing body.'

Executioner; Thomas Young
Glasgow

March 29th; **John MURDOCH**　Edinburgh
Hanged at the west end of the Tolbooth for murdering and robbing James Murdoch, a shopkeeper at Langrig, near Whitburn on 25th January 1815.

'Having had the benefit of a religious education from his parents (who are still alive) he pointed out several passages of scripture applicable to his condition'.

Executioner; John High
Edinburgh

November 1st; **John SHERRY**　Glasgow
In August 1814 Sherry was lodged in Glasgow Prison on a charge of breaking out of Carlisle Jail, whilst awaiting trial on a charge of burglary. On the return to Carlisle he leapt from the top of the coach and made his way back to Glasgow. One of his co-accused was hanged at Carlisle.

Returning to crime, he was arrested in May 1815 on a charge of highway robbery on the Paisley road.

Thirty years of age and a native of Monaghan in Ireland, he left a widow and five children.

Reporting Thomas Young's first execution in Glasgow, the *Glasgow Chronicle* wrote, 'He appears to be master of his business'.

Executioner; Thomas Young
Glasgow

1816

March 13th;　**David THOMSON**　Edinburgh
A carter from Broughton near Edinburgh, Thomson, 'a decent looking young man', was executed at the west end of the Tolbooth for five counts of theft by housebreaking.

Executioner; John High
Edinburgh

May 31st;　**William EVANS**　Ayr
An overseer with the Duke of Portland's estate at Troon, Evans was condemned at Ayr Spring Circuit for the forgery of bills of exchange. On the drop, and with the signal handkerchief in his hand, his last utterance, 'I take it upon myself to say that I am a murdered man, by the liberty of God my Saviour', caused a minor sensation. Some believed him to have been wrongly condemned.

John Kelso Hunter speaks in his autobiography of being at Symington Toll as a boy in February 1815 for the execution of John Worthington, when Evans passed through. The old tollkeeper asked Mr Evans if he would not wait and see the man hanged. 'I attend no such gatherings, Sir', came the haughty reply.

Executioner; James Aird
Ayr

December 11th; **John BLACK**　Edinburgh
In the early hours of Thursday 4th July 1816 John Allan, a farmer at Pentland, was attacked at Libberton and robbed - the thief getting away with his gold watch, a twenty pound note of the East Lothian Banking Company and several one pound notes.

The bloodied Allan raised the alarm and Black was arrested, tried and condemned.

With John Simpson as their newly appointed Executioner, Edinburgh's magistrates hired Young of Glasgow to initiate him in the craft - it was money ill-spent - his next would lead to his dismissal.

Black's trial had a sequel. The following February, the High Court dealt with Black's cousin, John Morris, a defence witness for Black, on a charge of perjury. Pleading guilty, he was sentence to nine months imprisonment - and to stand one hour on the pillory. It too had a sequel.

The Scotsman newspaper reported:

'We are sorry to learn, that when John Morris was suffering punishment of the pillory at the Cross, Edinburgh, on Wednesday last, the executioner [John Simpson], who was necessarily present, was first pelted by the mob with stones and mud, and afterwards knocked down, kicked, and subjected to the most cruel and barbarous treatment, till he was rescued by some of the spectators.'

Executioner; Thomas Young
Glasgow

1817

February 28th;   **John LARG**   Perth
James MITCHELL

Tried and condemned at the High Court for stouthrief, having forcibly entered the toll-house at Friarton, on the Perth to Kinross road on the night of 12th November 1816, and robbed the tacksman, William McRitchie.

An accomplice, Alexander Steel was outlawed for not appearing at court.

Executioner; Unknown

May 28th;   **William McKAY**   Glasgow

Accused of forging and passing guinea notes of the Bank of Greenock in Belfast, Ayr, Renfrew and Lanark in the years 1811, 1816 and 1817, and particularly on 14th March 1817 vending notes in the house of George Ferguson, Grocer, near Barrowfield Toll, Glasgow.

The jury found these not proven, but a verdict of guilty on having passed a note at the Pointhouse, Govan Ferry brought a capital conviction. The case against a co-accused, James McNeill, was found not proven.

A stocking maker from Carrickfergus in Ireland, McKay was duly hanged.

Executioner; Thomas Young
Glasgow

October 10th;   **Bernard McILVOGUE**   Greenock
Hugh McILVOGUE
Patrick McCRYSTAL

Convicted at Edinburgh for theft by housebreaking, robbery and rape committed at Everton Farm, near Greenock on the morning of 23rd March 1817.

Breaking into the farmhouse, they assaulted and robbed Robert Morris of money, then raped his sister in law, Janet Crawford, and his servant Mary Black. They received their sentence, 'with much unconcern'.

Watched by a crowd of 10,000, they were executed in front of the New Church in the Square and buried next morning in the new burying ground.

The execution incurred the following expenses:

Alex Leith - Chaise for 3 days	6.10.0
Fee to Thos. Young	15.15.0
Fee to Angus McKie	3. 3.0
Expenses at Bishopton	4.0
	£25.12.0

Executioner; Thomas Young
Glasgow

October 17th;   **Margaret CROSSAN**   Ayr
Willaim ROBERTSON &
Joseph CAIRNS

Ayr's only triple execution of the nineteenth century - with the three culprits coming from Galloway.

Thirty-year-old Crossan, who would leave an infant child to the parish, had set fire to a byre at Carsegowan Farm in Wigtonshire, in which twelve cows, a bull and three calves had perished - the farmer having threatened to evict her from her cottage.

Robertson and Cairns had been capitally convicted of robberies committed at New Luce and Mochrum.

As they came out of the Tolbooth door to the scaffold:

> 'In Robertson's eye there stood a tear, and his countenance wholly indicated a mind affected by the deepest grief; Cairns was unmoved, but sedate; but in the countenance of the woman nothing could be discovered save a smile, but not of levity'.

Robertson was so weak that he was supported by the rope even before he was suspended. Cairns stepped onto the platform with a slow steady pace, whilst Crossan, dressed in a white robe and a cap knotted with black ribbons followed with a hasty but firm step.

As Cairns was to give the signal, he enquired if the others were ready. Robertson waved his hand and Crossan answered cooly in the affirmative. When the drop fell Robertson died quickly and without a struggle, leaving Cairns and Crossan to convulse for some time.

All three were buried in the Auld Kirk Yard, where the register shows Robertson to have died of an unknown cause, and Cairns and Crossan to have succumbed to consumption.

Executioner; James Aird
Ayr

The Byre at Carsegowan Farm (*Author's Collection*)

October 29th; **Freebairn WHITEHILL** Glasgow
William McKECHNIE
James McCORMICK

A 20-year-old Glaswegian, Whitehill was condemned for robbing Thomas Barre, the Glasgow to Slamannan carrier, of a purse containing £3 6s in Glasgow's Havannah Street in May 1817.

McKechnie and McCormick were indicted for breaking into William Cublick's haberdashery shop in Greenock's Cathcart Street and stealing cloth, threads and ribbons to the value of £396. Both were found guilty, 30-year-old McKechnie on his own confession, and condemned.

'During confinement, McCormick conducted himself in a manner becoming his dreadful situation, but McKechnie and Whitehill, who too confidently expected the Royal mercy, were not so attentive to religious matters, and, when no hope of pardon was left became melancholy and dejected ...'

Born in Antrim and a tailor to trade, McKechnie was a deserter from the Royals when arrested. Thirty years of age he left a wife and four children.

Although born in Caithness, McCormick was bred in Stirling and latterly worked as a gentleman's servant near Greenock. He left a wife and six children.

Executioner; Thomas Young
Glasgow

October 31st; **Malcolm CLARK** Perth

Accused of stouthrief with a George McMillan, who failed to appear for trial, Clark pleaded guilty to the charge at the Perth Autumn Circuit, and was condemned.

Although the jury recommended him to mercy,

the judge warned him that due to the aggravated nature of the crime which had become too prevalent in the country, he should cast delusive thoughts from his mind.

He is described as a good looking young man not quite twenty.

Executioner; Unknown

1818

June 3rd;   **William BAIRD**   Glasgow
              Walter BLAIR

The day before their execution for acts of highway robbery on the Cumbernauld road near Haghill, Baird and Blair made a desperate attempt to escape the Tolbooth.

About two o'clock, when the turnkey, accompanied by two soldiers, took a boy to shave them, Blair produced a pistol and demanded his keys. The soldiers ran for assistance, pulling the door behind them and the turnkey threw the keys from the window.

When overpowered, another pistol was found, and both discovered to be loaded with powder and pieces of pewter spoon.

Near midnight some ten days before, former army companions had got the pistols to them by throwing a ball of twine into their cell from the street below, and tying the pistols to its end.

Next day they appeared peaceably on the scaffold, dressed in black with white gloves and weepers.

Executioner; Thomas Young
Glasgow

June 5th;   **John RITCHIE**   Aberdeen

Apprehended in January 1818 for stealing 30 sheep from the parks of Gordon Castle, Ritchie celebrated his 17th birthday whilst awaiting trial.

Such was the contemporary incidence of sheep stealing, that the trial jury's recommendation to mercy was ignored. On the scaffold, his youthful and comely appearance was so striking that many spectators left - unable to bear the sight.

Ritchie however, stepped onto the drop with great firmness and composure, after bowing to those around him on the platform. He died with very little struggle.

Executioner; John Milne
Aberdeen

November 4th;   **Matthew CLYDESDALE**
                  Simon ROSS   Glasgow

Little could 19-year-old Simon Ross have realised that his gallows companion that November afternoon would become a latter day Glasgow legend - far less Clydesdale himself.

Ross had been condemned for a theft by housebreaking at Rutherglen with three accomplices - the youngest of them aged 14 - and Clydesdale for the motiveless murder of an old man near Clarkston.

When cut down from the scaffold, Ross's body was given to his relatives, but as a murderer, Clydesdale's was taken up High Street to the College in a trundle, where Professors James Jeffray and Andrew Ure were waiting to carry out the anatomical dissection.

With the contemporary medical interest in Galvanism, Clydesdale's body would be subjected to a series of experiments to study and demonstrate the effects of electricity on the body.

In the lecture theatre, Professor Andrew Ure produced a range of dramatic effects; smiles and grimaces; 'violin player like' movements of the

Professor James Jeffray

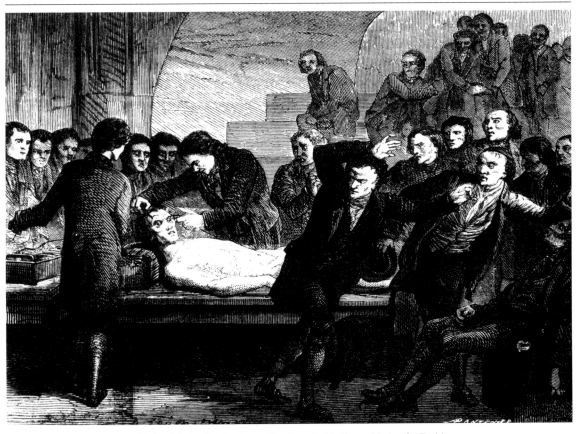

Clydesdale in the Anatomy Theatre (*Bibliotheque Nationale, Paris*)

Dr Andrew Ure

fingers; and the restoration of the mechanics of breathing, though not, as Ure was later to report with regret, the restoration of life.

In the 1850s Clydesdale rose again as a myth, when Peter Mackenzie published his *Reminiscences of Glasgow and the West of Scotland*.

In a chapter entitled, 'The Case of Matthew Clydesdale the Murderer - Extraordinary Scene in the College of Glasgow', Mackenzie wrote of Clydesdale returning to life - rising from the chair where he had been seated and looking around him in amazement.

According to Mackenzie, Professor Jeffray:

> '... pulled out his unerring lancet and plunged it into the jugular vein of the culprit, who instantly fell down like a slaughtered ox.'

McKenzie's fantasy has been recounted so often over the years that it has become accepted as a true account.

Executioner; Thomas Young
Glasgow

November 6th; **John BARNET** Aberdeen

Arrested in the Autumn of 1817 for theft by housebreaking, Barnet, from Kirktown of Peterhead, broke prison and was not dealt with until the Autumn of 1818.

A stout man of five foot nine or ten inches, with brown hair and red whiskers, the reward notice published after his escape recorded his, 'downcast and thoughtful look'.

His body was buried at sea, but within a few days came ashore at the mouth of the River Don and fell to the surgeons.

Executioner; John Milne
Aberdeen

December 30th; **Robert JOHNSTON** Edinburgh

The execution of 22-year-old Johnston for the robbery of a candlemaker the previous October was dubbed by the press a 'Shameful Outrage'. It was also a grave embarrassment to Edinburgh.

Johnston, no stranger in the petty courts and the Tolbooth, appeared unbowed on coming from the lock-up house and mounting the platform.

After praying and shaking hands with the clergymen, he mounted the scaffold and looked boldly round him, before helping the executioner adjust the rope, and giving the signal.

The drop fell - but the excessively short length of rope enabled him to stand on the platform. As the Magistrates ordered carpenters to cut a wider opening, the first cries of 'Murder' came from the crowd.

The cries were followed by a shower of stones, which sent the Magistrates and the carpenters to the shelter of the Tolbooth Church doorway, through which they passed into the police office.

Almost every window glass in the church suffered from the stones, as did Johnston who had been abandoned on the platform.

'Cut him down - he's alive!', rang out, as the crowd took possession of the scaffold. Johnston, despite hanging many minutes, was alive, and after taking the rope from his neck and arms and the cap from his head, he was carried off towards High Street. The scaffold structure proved too robust, but Johnston's waiting coffin was broken up and thrown through the church windows.

With more police and military on the streets, Johnston was taken from the crowd at the head of Advocate's Close, and carried to the police office. After being bled in the arms and temple by a surgeon, he was fit to be taken back to the scaffold.

The platform had been retaken by troops from the Castle, and carried by six men, Johnston was placed on the drop. Again the executioner made a bungle of it. The rope was now too long and Johnston had to be lifted while the rope was shortened by winding it round the hook.

Again shouts of 'Murder!' and 'Shame!, Shame!' rang out, and only the military presence prevented another riot. Johnston struggled for many minutes before passing into eternity.

Next morning the Magistrates dismissed both their master of works and the executioner. The fifty guinea purse offered for the discovery of Johnston's rescuers was unclaimed.

Executioner; John Simpson
Edinburgh

1819

April 7th; **Alexander ROBERTSON**

Glasgow

A genteel-looking 24-year-old from Falkirk, hanged for breaking into the City Auction Mart in Candleriggs the previous October.

Executioner; Thomas Young
Glasgow

April 14th; **George WARDEN** Edinburgh

A clerk in Aberdeen Post Office for 2 years, earning £40 per annum plus benefits of £60, twenty one-year-

Robert Johnston on the scaffold

"	"	John McDowall Grave Digger for interring the body of John McNeill alias Boag, a Criminal executed here yesterday	" 3 "	
"	"	William Fergusson Coals for the Town Guard from 29 April to 29 May inclusive, and for the Executioner	" 8 "	
June	3	" Thomas Dunn for entertainment to the Lockman while in confinement for some days previous to the execution	" 16 "	

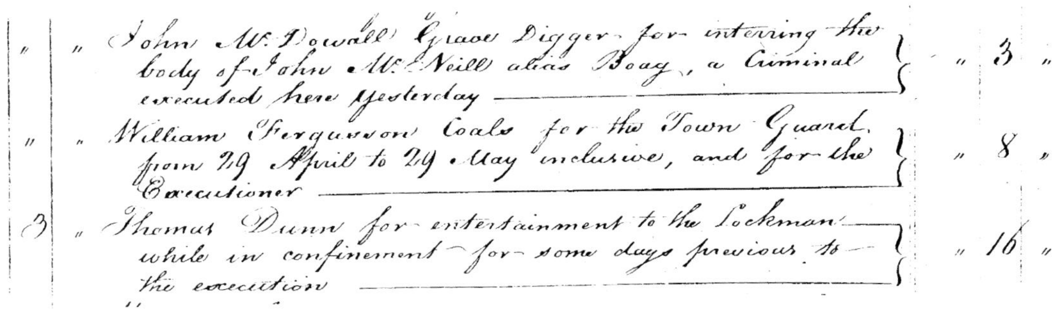

Execution Expenses — John McNeil — Ayr Burgh Treasurer's Account (*Ayr Carnegie Library*)

old Warden was condemned for abstracting money from letters.

On the drop, he fainted before Young, the executioner, could get to the lever, evoking cries of, 'Let down the drop!,' from these near the platform. Others at a greater distance, alarmed by the shout ran with violence from the scene.

He left a widowed mother and two younger sisters to lament his fate.

Executioner; Thomas Young
Glasgow

May 28th; **John McNEIL** Ayr

Condemned at Ayr Spring Circuit with his 18-year-old brother Joseph, on four charges of theft by housebreaking committed in North Ayrshire, 22-year-old John was left to pay the full penalty, when Joseph was reprieved.

Executioner; James Aird
Ayr

August 27th; **Ralph WOODNESS** Linlithgow

Described as hardened offenders, 20-year-old Woodness and 17-year-old Richard Smith were tried at Edinburgh for theft by housebreaking; from a haberdasher's shop in Linlithgow they stole woollen cloth, sarcenet and burial crepe to the value of £350.

The charge against Woodness, who called one of the witnesses, 'a damned liar', was found proven, whilst that against Smith was found not proven. Smith's day would come the following August.

Executioner; Unknown

November 3rd; **Robert McKINLAY & William BUCHANAN Robert GUTHRIE & Alexander FORBES** Glasgow

Glasgow's first quadruple execution brought together two sets of housebreakers.

Twenty three-year-old McKinlay and 18-year-old Buchanan, cotton-spinners from Glasgow, had broken into Bothwell Castle and stolen a variety of gold and silver articles. Although McKinlay was said to gain his livelihood by fraud and theft it was Buchanan's first offence.

Arrested for theft by housebreaking at Kilmarnock, 25-year-old Guthrie, a weaver from Paisley and 18-year-old Forbes, a cloth lapper, 'given to idleness and thieving' were old offenders. Guthrie had appeared before the Spring Circuit at Glasgow the previous year when a charge of stealing 15 cheeses from a shop in Paisley was found not proven.

They appeared on the platform as decently dressed and good looking young men.

Executioner; Thomas Young
Glasgow

November 17th; **John BUCHANAN** Glasgow

Executed for the murder of his paramour, Jean McKenzie alias Duff, in October 1818 by stabbing her with a fork, Buchanan denied his guilt till the last.

Indicted to appear before the High Court at Edinburgh, he was released on £60 bail due to the absence of witnesses, and re-indicted for the Glasgow Autumn Circuit.

So confident was he of the outcome of his trial that against his counsel's advice he appeared in court

- sitting through the trial previous to his own. He was to be disappointed

Twenty three years of age, he was described as short but stout with a ruddy complexion. A flesher to trade, he had a small army pension as the result of wounds received whilst serving with the 91st Regiment of Foot.

Standing on the drop, he addressed Executioner Young, "Thomas, let me know when you are ready", and when told that it was, threw the signal napkin behind him, and was launched into eternity.

T M Tod in his book *The Scots Black Kalendar* writes:

> "He had been twitted by a companion ... that he would yet die 'with his face to the Monument'. This was the equivalent to saying he would be hanged in front of the centre piazzas at the Jail, which faces the Nelson monument on the Green. Buchanan swore that would never happen, and he kept his word, for he astonished the hangman by turning round with his face to the side".

This story is not borne out by contemporary reports.

His body was given to the Professor of Anatomy for dissection.

Executioner; Thomas Young
Glasgow

1820

January 5th;   **Brine JUDD**   Edinburgh
Thomas CLAPPERTON

Condemned for hamesucken at the house of James Bryden, Roadmains, Borthwick the previous September, Judd and Clappperton's appearance as decent looking young men impressed the gathering at their trial. They were both under 24 years.

After forcing a locked and barred door they had rendered Bryden and his wife insensible and robbed them of £41 in bank notes and a banker's deposit receipt for £268.

Leaving the courtroom, Judd saw Bryden and his wife, and 'his eyes swimming in tears', shook hands with them.

The crowd for their execution, owing to the wetness of the morning, was small but uncommonly quiet and sympathetic.

Executioner; Thomas Williams
Edinburgh

March 10th;   **William McGHEER**
Charles BRITTAN   Ayr

Condemned at Edinburgh for a stouthrief committed in the early hours of Sunday 19th December 1819 at Borland Farm near Dalrymple in Ayrshire, occupied by William Drennan. With McGheer's father, brother and another man, they were in custody at Ayr before the week was out.

All were well-known to the authorities, especially McGheer's father John, who kept a public house in Newton upon Ayr. Lying on the north side of the River Ayr, Newton was the poor relation to Ayr proper, to the south of the river.

In his book *Circuit Journeys*, Lord Cockburn wrote of the town:

> 'The great deduction from the comfort and respectability of Ayr proper is this horrid Newton, and the squalid lines of wretched overcrowded hovels, stared out of by unfed and half-naked swarms of coal black and seemingly defying inhabitants, that form its eastern approaches. They have a very Hibernian air.'

They appeared on the scaffold dressed uniformly in black coat, white vest and white trousers trimmed with black lace. Whilst 27-year-old McGheer looked pale and emaciated, his 22-year-old companion appeared composed and well, despite the involuntary quiver on his lip.

In his farewell speech, McGheer warned that he had come to this end by ignoring his religion and his father, well knowing that his father should have been on the drop with him.

Handed the signal handkerchief, he immediately dropped it, scarcely giving one of the clergymen time to clear the platform, which fell as the Tolbooth clock struck the hour of three.

When the bodies were cut down at five minutes to four, the families hurried them away, for the purpose, it was later learned, of attempting to reanimate them.

Executioner; James Aird
Ayr

May 21st;   **Richard SMITH**   Glasgow

An old offender, with four appearances before Glasgow's Magistrates for theft, Smith had narrowly escaped the gallows with a not proven verdict the previous year at Edinburgh, when his co-accused Ralph Woodness was condemned for theft by housebreaking.

Being aged only 15 may have saved him at

320

300 Pounds REWARD.

WHEREAS, certain Wicked, Evil-disposed, and Traitorous Persons, during the night of the 1st, or on the morning of the 2d of April instant, did, *feloniously, traitorously,* and *daringly,* in furtherance of a *Conspiracy* to compass or imagine the Death of Our Lord the King, or to *levy war against Our Lord the King* within his Realm, or to commit other Treasons, *publish* and *affix,* on the walls and public places in many parts of the City and Suburbs of Glasgow, and other parts of the County of Lanark, a most *Wicked, Revolutionary* and *Treasonable Address* to the Inhabitants of Great Britain and Ireland, dated at Glasgow, April 1, 1820, and bearing to be issued " by order of the Committee of Organi-" zation for forming a Provisional Government," directly and openly *proclaiming* Rebellion *against our Lord the King and the Laws and Constitution of this Realm,* inciting and stimulating the Subjects of our Lord the King to take up Arms for the overthrow of the Government and Constitution, as by Law established, and *to levy war against our Lord the King,*—and further endeavouring to seduce the Soldiers of our Lord the King to desert their duty and to join in a threatened Insurrection, and to intimidate and overawe all loyal and peaceable Subjects by threats of violence and devastation,—The LORD PROVOST and MAGISTRATES of the City of Glasgow, SHERIFF of the County of Lanark, and JUSTICES of the PEACE for the Lower Ward of Lanarkshire, hereby offer a

Reward of £300

to any Person or Persons who shall, within Fourteen Days from this date, DISCOVER AND APPREHEND, or cause to be DISCOVERED AND APPREHENDED, those guilty of this OVERT ACT of HIGH TREASON, by printing, publishing, and issuing the said Revolutionary and Treasonable Address, under the said Treasonable designation of the Committee of Organization for forming a Provisional Government.

Glasgow, 4th April, 1820.

Printed in the Herald Office, Glasgow.

Reward Notice for the 'Radical Rebels' (see Wilson, Hardie and Baird overleaf) (*Mitchell Library, Glasgow*)

Work commenced on the scaffold in Broad Street about 10.30pm the previous night:

> 'Two coffins, containing sawdust, one bearing the inscription, "Andrew Hardie, aged 27", the other, "John Baird, aged 37", were placed upon it; a board, covering about a third of the coffin, was placed to support the breast of the body; a square tub in which was a considerable quantity of saw dust, was placed at the head of each coffin; to that side of the tub nearest the coffin was affixed a block.'

At one o'clock they mounted a hurdle at the Castle gate and sat with their backs to the horse. Their travelling companion, the headsman, with axe in hand, was already on the cart. He was a young man of about 20 years.

Forty minutes later they were in Broad Street, circled by a crowd of 6000 spectators, and mounting the scaffold, which Hardie addressed, 'Hail! harbinger of eternal rest'. Many stayed away at the prospect of the beheadings.

Their request to address the crowd was acceded to - with the warning that nothing political would be allowed.

Baird came forward:

> 'Friends and Countrymen! - I dare say you will expect me to say something to you of the case which has brought me here - but on that I do not mean to say much ... the matter ... was for the cause of Truth and Justice ... '.

Hardie then stood where Baird had spoken:

> 'Countrymen! ... I declare before my God I believe I die a martyr in the cause of Truth an' Justice ... '

But for Sheriff McDonald that was too much, 'Hardie, remember Sir, your solemn promise, I cannot permit you to proceed in this manner; if you attempt it I must call the executioner to perform his duty'. Satisfied at having had his say, Hardie then spoke of the Bible.

At eleven minutes to three the executioner adjusted the ropes, pulled the caps over their faces, as Hardie seized Baird's hand and dropped the signal. The bible in Baird's left hand dropped as the trap gave way.

After half an hour the bodies were cut down and placed in the coffins, with the face downwards. With the necks resting on the blocks and the heads hanging into the tubs, the headsman came to perform his duty.

Delicately made and good looking, he wore black crepe over his face, a black serge gown and a boy's hairy cap. His initial agitation was heightened by the crowd crying, 'Murder! Murder!' at his appearance.

He severed Hardie's head at the third stroke, before holding it up in both hands and proclaiming, 'This is the head of a Traitor'. Baird was decapitated at two strokes.

The duty over, he retired hastily and was heard to say through his tremblings, 'I wish to God I had not had it to do'.

At 9.00pm that same night they were interred at the High Church.

In the romanticism of the Reform Movement it is easy to forget that lives were lost. In its report of the Bonnymuir Skirmish, the *Glasgow Chronicle* published the following:

> 'List of Killed and wounded on the evening of Saturday, the 8th instant, as collected from several Medical Practitioners in the Town, the 14th April 1820.

Names	Age	Wounds
A Clephane	48	Under the groin Dead
A Drummond	20	Shot thro' chest Dead
James Kerr	17	Through the belly Dead
J McWhinnie	65	Thro' shoulder & Chest Dead
H Paterson	14	Through the leg Leg amputd
J Patrick	80	Through the thigh Doing well
D McBride	14	Through cheek & jaw Doing well
A McKinnon	17	Through chest and arm Doubtfull
C Turner	65	Through the leg Leg amputd The above in Infirmary
Jno Boyce	33	Through the belly Dead
G Tillery	25	Through the thigh Doing well
R Spence	11	Slightly in the foot Slightly
W Lindsay	15	Shot dead on the spot Dead
Jas McGilp	8	Ball in the right thigh

ERECTED BY
PUBLIC SUBSCRIPTION JULY, 1847,
TO THE MEMORY OF
JOHN BAIRD,
AGED 32,
AND
ANDREW HARDIE,
AGED 28,
WHO FOR THE CAUSE OF
FREEDOM,
SUFFERED DEATH, AT STIRLING,
8TH SEP, 1820.

Detail from Baird and Hardie Monument   (*Author's Collection*)

G McArthur	18	Through the left thigh Flesh wound
J Turner	22	Through calf of the leg Flesh wound
P Cameron	14	Through the right leg Flesh wound
J Gunn	24	Through calf of left leg

Executioner; Unknown

Postscript

In 1847 the Hardie and Baird and Martyr's Stone Committee erected a memorial in Glasgow's Sighthill Cemetery. On 20th July, with the permission of the Home Secretary, the bodies were exhumed at Stirling, carried to Glasgow, and buried.

October 8th;   **Edward McRORY**   Dumfries

Thirty one-year-old McRory (or McLory or M'Grory), from Ballybreck in Ireland, condemned at Dumfries Autumn Circuit for assaulting Hugh Gallagher at Carse of Slaiks, between Gatehouse and Creetown, in the June, and robbing him of £5 of money.

Maintaining his innocence to the last, he twice lifted the cap to address the crowd, before pulling it down and giving the signal.

He revealed, whilst in prison, that his father and brother had been hanged in Ireland.

Executioner; Thomas Williams
Edinburgh

November 8th;   **Daniel GRANT**   Glasgow
Peter CROSBIE
John CONNOR
Thomas McCOLGAN

Tried at Glasgow for breaking into the house of Mrs Watt, near Crossmyloof, on the night of 19th December 1819, when (being armed) they approached her bed, and demanded her keys.

Two hours later they left with a gold watch chain, two pairs of silver plated candlesticks, two pairs of silver plated snuffers and stands, 12 silver table spoons, 12 silver desert spoons, a silver divider, knives and forks, three gold rings, 60 coins in gold, silver and copper and 4 suits of men's black clothing

- they were each found guilty and condemned.

Whilst the condemnation was being read, Connor called out, 'Thank you, my lord. I still have a month to live before I kick the bucket'. McColgan damned his Lordship for an old b_____ , crying out that, 'he would be in hell before them'.

In contrast, their behaviour on the scaffold was described as 'extremely decent and becoming'.

Executioner; Thomas Young
Glasgow

1821

January 14th; John DEMPSEY Glasgow

Dempsey and five fellow soldiers of the 13th Regiment of Foot, having drank away the night of Saturday 30th July 1830 at their billet in Greenock's Shaw Street, were long past conviviality on coming onto the street about midnight.

The group of sailors they met took umbrage at being called 'blue jackets', and a scuffle broke out. Forced back to the house the soldiers loaded their muskets and commenced firing over the heads of a gathering crowd.

Hearing the firing, Robert Simpson, a watchman on the quay came up and asked the soldiers to desist. They shot him dead. This drew another watchman, Henry Pearson, but his remonstrations ended with the same tragic result.

Pleas to desist whilst the wounded were attended to, drew more shots, and a sailor lad named Archibald Morrison was also killed.

The town guard commanded by magistrates and regimental officers finally forced entry to the house and arrested the soldiers.

Following an 18 hour trial at the High Court in Edinburgh on charges of maliciously discharging loaded firearms and murder only Dempsey and Robert Surrage (later reprieved and transported) were found guilty.

Dempsey dropped the signal protesting his innocence.

Executioner; Thomas Young
Glasgow

January 17th; Samuel MAXWELL Edinburgh

Maxwell and three accomplices, Robert Muir, James Donnelly and Alex. Hamilton, tried at the High Court for robbery, having broken into James Arniel's house at West or High Capley near Neilston on the night of 12th November 1819, armed with firearms, and

stealing wearing apparel, a gold watch, 9 one pound banknotes and other articles. They pled not guilty.

The jury returned a *viva voce* verdict, finding Maxwell and Hamilton guilty, and the libel not proven as to Muir and Donnelly, but unanimously recommended Hamilton to the mercy of the Crown.

Whilst sentence was being passed, Hamilton burst into tears, and at its conclusion broke out into loud and bitter cries. The jury's recommendation was heeded.

An immense multitude turned out to see 24-year-old Maxwell, a stout good looking young man, ascend the scaffold a few minutes after 8 o'clock. They were to see him struggle very hard and die in great pain.

Executioner; Thomas Williams
Edinburgh

May 11th; John FLEMING Stirling

Two nights before his execution for issuing a forged £5 note of the Paisley Banking Company, Fleming was so fevered that it was supposed the sentence of the law would have been anticipated.

He survived until the Friday morning, but appeared very careworn, and lost no time in dropping the signal.

Executioner; Unknown

May 16th; William Leonard SWAN
Glasgow

Convicted for passing forged £5 notes of the Paisley Banking Company to Agnes Mitchell, change keeper in Airdrie and John Smellie, change keeper at Clarkston.

Now 35 years old, Swan had appeared before the Circuit Court six years earlier charged with tendering a £100 bill of exchange he had abstracted from a letter box in Glasgow, when he was found not guilty.

He appeared on the scaffold genteelly dressed in black with weepers on his coat.

Executioner; Thomas Young
Glasgow

June 6th; James GORDON Dumfries

Executed for the murder of a simple-minded pedlar boy, John Elliot, the previous November near Upper Cassock Farm in the wilds of Eskdalemuir.

He came out to the scaffold on Buccleuch Street by a door struck through the prison wall - and into torrential rain.

The press report runs:

'What added unspeakable interest to the awful crisis, and gave it, indeed, the character of wild and appalling sublimity, was the remarkable circumstance, that the moment in which the prisoner took his place on the drop was indicated by a vivid flash of lightning and a tremendous burst of thunder!'

He did not make his expected speech, merely asking if anyone wished to speak to him - and on receiving no answer said, 'Fare you all well', and dropped the signal. A second peal of thunder announced his departure.

> Executioner; Thomas Williams
> Edinburgh

July 18th;   **David HAGGART**   Edinburgh

A 19-year-old native of Edinburgh, hanged for murdering Thomas Morrin, turnkey at Dumfries Jail, in October 1820, whilst effecting his escape.

> Executioner; Thomas Williams
> Edinburgh

October 25th;   **Michael McINTYRE**   Glasgow
William PATERSON
Wardrop DYER

At the Autumn Court, 28-year-old McIntyre and 17-year-old Paterson (or Kidston) were condemned for breaking into the house of John Niven, Tanner, Crawford's Dyke, Greenock, and stealing three women's shifts, a half sheet, a black coat, three waistcoats, a pair of black breeches, a pair of blue pantaloons, a bombazet gown, three printed cotton gowns, two shawls, two women's caps, three child's caps, two frocks - and being habit and repute thieves.

On hearing the sentence, McIntyre said, 'he didn't care a damn' - but he was no stranger to courts. Since leaving the army, where his repeated stealing and desertion had earned him 2000 lashes, he had been imprisoned five times.

Despite his previous experience, and convictions, Paterson burst into tears. The Spring Court of 1819 had sentenced him to 12 months imprisonment for theft.

Following them on the cause list, Dyer would guess his fate. He too was charged with theft by housebreaking - having stolen a silver teapot and stand, a silver sugar basin and ten silver table spoons from Mrs Barbara Urquhart's house in Russell Street, Glasgow. He was not disappointed.

> Executioner; Thomas Young
> Glasgow

November 16th; **George THOM**   Aberdeen

Some years after the death of his first wife, Thom married Jean Mitchell who, with two brothers and two sisters, resided at Burnside Farm in Keig Parish. He was sixty one years of age.

Shortly before the marriage, the Mitchells gained an inheritance through the death of another brother, and overcome with avarice, Thom planned to poison the family.

During a stay at Burnside, Thom's choice of sleeping in the kitchen afforded him the opportunity of adding arsenic to their salt. Next morning, saying he had to call at a neighbouring farm, he left the family to their milk pottage - and adulterated salt.

All suffered the effects of arsenical poisoning, but only William, who had eaten more heartily than the others, died.

The Thoms were arrested, although Jean was soon after released, leaving her husband to face trial.

In the courthouse, en route to the scaffold, he had to be supported whilst his shroud was put on, and on the gallows given a chair for the final service. He died without a struggle.

His body was taken to the College, where it was subjected to a series of galvanic experiments.

> Executioner; Unknown

December 7th;   **Margaret TYNDALL or**
SHUTTLEWORTH   Montrose

Condemned at Perth for murdering her husband, Henry Shuttleworth, in their public house in Castle Street, Montrose, on the night of Friday 28th April 1821. They were both addicted to drink.

Thirty-six-year-old Margaret had been drunk when put to bed by their servant girl, who left to attend a night wake. Next morning Henry was found battered to death and a blood stained poker found in Margaret's bedroom. She was arrested later the same day.

Doubts regarding the purely circumstantial evidence in the case won her a four week respite. These included: lack of motive; her state of intoxication at the time of the crime; and her guiltless behaviour in first raising the alarm.

The review came to nothing, but it was unclear whether the respite had been for a calendar or lunar month. The question was taken to a bench of twelve English judges, who decided that a further extension of five days should be granted.

Coming to the scaffold from the Tolbooth she ascended the steps in a steady manner, oblivious to the four thousand strong crowd, the funeral toll of the steeple bell and the weather. The wind was blowing a perfect hurricane with torrents of rain.

The Shuttleworth's shop in Castle Street, Montrose

An eyewitness wrote:

'A woman about thirty-six years of age, small, neat, and good looking, a face inclined to be, but not absolutely pale, with a slight obliquity of vision. The best idea of her appearance may be conceived by imagining a woman, in the middle rank of life, expecting a visitor to breakfast; her cap was a morning one with a handkerchief tied round her head, cleanly dressed in black clothes, a frill round her neck, blacking stockings, new boots, and black gloves, the lower part of her dress was confined by a white handkerchief'.

After shaking hands with those around her, Milne put the noose about her neck, but then had difficulty in getting the white cap over her head, it having shrunk in the rain.

'Lord have mercy on me; Christ have mercy on me; I die an innocent woman; I am innocent of and ignorant of the death of Henry Shuttleworth; I loved my husband as I loved my life. Drinking and threatening words have brought me to my ruin; Christ receive my soul'.

The signal was dropped, and Milne cut the cord supporting the beam with an axe.

Next morning her body was taken to Edinburgh

University for Dr Monro's anatomy class.

Local opinion, as shown from the entry in the parochial register, was of her innocence:

1821

December 7 MARGT. TINDAL was executed in front of the jail, for the supposed murder of her husband HENRY SHUTTLEWORTH, having been condemned on presumptive evidence.

Although he is believed to have left the post in 1818-19, *Tales and Legends of Forfarshire*, gives Milne as the executioner.

Executioner; John Milne
Aberdeen

1822

January 9th;   **Peter HEAMAN**   Leith
Francois GAUTIEZ

In the only capital conviction for a crime beyond Scottish shores, Heaman and Gautiez were condemned for piracy by the High Court of Admiralty at Edinburgh in November 1821.

Heaman, a 36-year-old from Karlskrona in Sweden, and Gautiez a 24-year-old Frenchman were charged with:

' ... piratically seizing the brig 'Jane of Gibraltar' on her voyage from Gibraltar to Brazil, freighted with 38180 Spanish dollars ... murdering Thomas Johnson, the master, and James Paterson, a seaman ... confining Peter Smith and Robert Strachan, seamen, in the forecastle, where, by attempting to suffocating them by smoke, they were terrified into com-plicity in seizing the vessel, which was afterwards sunk off the coast of Ross-shire having landed the money on the Isle of Lewis, where they were apprehended'.

The Maltese cabin boy, Andrew Camelier, told the Court that in the early hours of 19th June 1821 he was awakened by a shot, and coming on deck saw Heaman strike James Paterson with a musket. Gautiez then hit Captain Thomas Johnson [or Johnston(e)] , with another musket.

Two recalcitrant Scots seamen, Peter Smith and Robert Strachan, were confined in the hold and the hatch nailed down, before Johnson and Paterson, weighted with an anchor and stones, were thrown overboard. Captain Johnson, Camelier claimed, was only unconscious at the time.

Released after three days, 'when they appeared downhearted', Smith and Strachan vowed, under duress, not to divulge what had taken place.

The eight barrels of dollars were broken open and bagged, as Heaman steered for the Scottish coast. Calling at Barra they purchased a large boat and made for Lewis, where the *Jane* was sunk and the dollars taken ashore.

Using a pint pot as a measure, the coins were divided equally between Heaman, Gautiez, Smith, Strachan, the cabin boy Camelier and an Italian seaman named Johanna Dhura.

Their activities attracted the attention of the island's Excise Officers, who arrested them and seized the money.

Found guilty of piracy and murder, they would be hanged between nine o'clock and midday within the flood mark on the Sands of Leith, and their bodies given for dissection to Dr Monro of Edinburgh University.

Their final drive from Calton Jail to Leith was sitting in a black cart with their backs to the horse. As the procession wound through immense crowds, chiefly females and children, Heaman bowed incessantly - whilst Gautiez took no notice.

Arriving on the sands at the foot of Constitution Street, a portion of the 51st Psalm was sung, before they shook hands and stepped onto the drop. The cords were put about their necks, and Heaman threw the signal over his shoulder.

Gautiez left a widow in Spain, to whom he wrote that he was confined in hospital by illness.

The High Court of Admiralty was abolished in 1830 and its powers absorbed by the High Court of Justiciary.

Executioner Thomas Williams
Edinburgh

May 29th;   **William ROBISON**   Jedburgh
Hanged at the County Hall for theft by housebreaking at Moat House, near Selkirk, the previous October, when he stole a £5 note of the British Linen Bank, a £5 note of the Leith Bank and two bills of exchange worth £92

Executioner; Thomas Williams
Edinburgh

May 29th;   **William CAMPBELL**   Glasgow
Decently dressed in black with weepers, 19-year-old Campbell was hanged for theft by housebreaking.

On 3rd January, along with James Kerr and William Welch, he broke into William White's dye house, by the north side of the jail, and stole wearing apparel. They were also charged with being habit and repute thieves.

Welch was found not guilty and the case against Kerr not proven - leaving Campbell to face his fate alone.

Executioner; Thomas Young
Glasgow

May 31st; **Robert McKINTOSH**
William GORDON   Aberdeen

Aberdeen's first double execution since Phren and Wast in 1752, was again for two murderers.

MacIntosh, a 21-year-old farm servant from Crathie near Balmoral, had murdered his forty-year-old fiance, Elizabeth Anderson who was pregnant by him, after another had taken his eye. He had cut her throat from ear to ear.

His gallows companion, 45-year-old William Gordon, a fishing tackle maker in Aberdeen, had mortally stabbed his wife through the femoral artery with a sharpened poker.

Death by hanging was a disgrace, but such was the contemporary horror of anatomical dissection that MacIntosh's father made a fruitless trip to London seeking a remission from that part of the sentence.

Their appearance on the scaffold wearing black, broke the Aberdeen tradition of dressing the condemned in a shroud.

Gordon died without a struggle, but MacIntosh, owing to the rope having been improperly placed about his neck, cried out and struggled for some minutes. The crowd exceeded anything ever witnessed in Aberdeen.

The bodies were given to Drs Skene and Ewing at the Medical School for dissection, where McIntosh's skeleton was preserved for some years.

Executioner; Unknown

June 5th; **Thomas DONACHY**   Glasgow

Brought to the Circuit Court with three accomplices on a charge of breaking into a cellar in Oxford Street, Gorbals, and stealing wine and rum, Donachy alone pleaded not guilty.

Whilst his associates were sentenced to fourteen years transportation, Donachy was condemned. His previous bad character and apparent position as leader of the gang coupled with his resistance to arrest told against him.

'Owing', the papers reported, 'to the lamentable frequency of executions in this City, the number of spectators was less than that assembled on any former occasion in the memory of the oldest

inhabitants'.

Executioner; Thomas Young
Glasgow

December 20th; **James BURTNAY**   Ayr

Arrested in September 1821 for the rape of eight-year-old Janet Anderson at Prestwick Toll, 22-year-old Burtnay was the first to 'end up facing Arran' on the scaffold by the west wall of the new prison.

Executioner; James Aird
Ayr

1823

February 26th; **William McINTYRE**   Edinburgh

A native of Paisley, who had come to seek work in Edinburgh, the 17-year-old tailor had broken into Miss Ann Butler's house in Lothian Road.

His claim to have been asleep on a park bench, and only awakened by the cries of 'Stop thief!' was dismissed.

The *Glasgow Courier* of 23rd January 1823 concluded its report of his trial with the following paragraph:

> 'There are no fewer than 6 wretched beings at present under sentence of death in Scotland viz. G Mclaren, T Grierson, James McEwen and W McIntyre, all young boys lying in the jail of Edinburgh, and James Robertson and Robert Simpson, for robbing the porter of the Caledonian Coach at Inverness, in the jail of which place they are now confined.'

All except McIntyre were subsequently reprieved

Executioner; Thomas Williams
Edinburgh

April 16th; **Mary McKINNON**   Edinburgh

Condemned for murdering a solicitor's clerk in a brothel she kept in the South Bridge, 32-year-old McKinnon refused religious instruction in belief of a reprieve.

Neatly dressed in mourning she was seated on the drop, waving farewell to the crowd, estimated as the largest since Brodie and Smith in 1788, before giving the signal.

Her body was given to Dr Alexander Monro of Edinburgh University for public dissection.

In his book *Circuit Journeys*, Lord Cockburn, who defended her, wrote of her case:

'Her family had been respectable. It was sworn, by a person who had served with him, that her deceased father was a captain in the army. But by misfortune after misfortune, or more probably by successive acts of misconduct, she was at last, when not much, if at all, above thirty, reduced to the condition of being the mistress of a disorderly house in Edinburgh.

'So she died publicly, but gracefully and bravely; and her last moment was marked by a proceeding so singular, that it is on its account that I mention her case. She had an early attachment to an English Jew, who looked like a gentleman, on the outside at least; and this passion had never been extinguished. She asked him to come and see her before her fatal day. He did so; and on parting, finally, on her last evening, she cut an orange in two, and giving him one half, and keeping the other herself, directed him to go to some window opposite the scaffold, at which she could see him, and to apply his half to his lips when she applied her half to hers. All this was done! she saw her only earthly friend, and making the sign, died, cheered by this affection.'

But things were not all they seemed with Mary McKinnon. Her name was not McKinnon but M'Innes - and despite testimony at her trial, her father had not been an army captain, but a private in the 91st Regiment of Foot.

Executioner; Thomas Williams
Edinburgh

May 14th;   **John McKANA**   Dumfries
              Joseph RICHARDSON

Found guilty of uttering banknotes of the Ship Bank of Glasgow, they were convicted with Richardson's brother William, who was later reprieved.

Thirty-two-year-old Richardson from Gilmourbank near Lochmaben, had led an irreproachable life (the press report him as the son of a respectable farmer and kirk elder) until falling into McKana's company. A 39-year-old Irish emigrant, he had married a Lockerbie woman, and worked as a roadman.

Executioner; Unknown

May 23rd;   **Thomas DONALDSON &**
              William BUCHANAN
              William MacLEOD   Aberdeen

All three executed for stouthrief - Donaldson and Buchanan having violently assaulted and robbed John Couper, a 70 year farmer at Newton of Greens, whilst MacLeod had forced his way into the home of an elderly woman at Greenhill of Auchiries and robbed her of £4 16s.

Executioner; Unknown

June 4th;   **John McDONALD &**   Glasgow
              James WILSON

A seaman, belonging to Glasgow's Bridgegate, 32-year-old McDonald was convicted of breaking into Moss Moseley's jewellery shop in Candlerigg Street, and stealing 18 silver watches.

Eighteen months later the jeweller was in the news again:

'Between Friday night and Saturday morning the shop of Mr Moss Mosely, Jeweller in Glasgow, was broken into, and pillaged with great deliberation. The thieves entered an unoccupied cellar, forced their way through a brick wall, with an iron crow, into the jeweller's cellar, and got into his premises by the hatch which had been left open. The window, glass cases and drawers were swept of everything valuable. Fourteen silver watches, 50 gold seals, 20 or 30 gold keys, about 100 silver thimbles, 40 gold broaches, 50 gold pins, and a number of other articles were carried off. Mr Moseley has lost above a thousand pounds by housebreaking, since he came to Scotland. His first shop was broken in Edinburgh. It was also broken into while in the Candleriggs, and one McDonald was executed for the robbery, and now it is broken into a third time in King Street'.

Although only 21-years-old, Wilson was an old offender, having been previously imprisoned - and whipped through the streets by the Executioner. On this occasion he had broken into a house in York Street, Glasgow and stolen clothing. He came from Lochwinnoch in Ayrshire.

On the drop they saluted friends, and Wilson saluted the hangman, as he shook hands with him.

McDonald, due to his slight build asked Young to give him plenty of rope.

Executioner; Thomas Young
Glasgow

October 23rd;   **Robert SCOTT**   Fans Farm

A vindictive and passionate man, 36-year-old Scott was condemned at Jedburgh Autumn Circuit for murdering two men near to Fans Farm on the Earlston to Greenlaw road, on 30th June. Returning home from Earlston Fair the trio, all the worse of drink, had quarrelled.

The Indictment stated, that Scott did:

> 'wickedly, maliciously and feloniously attack and assault the deceased James Aitcheson, cooper in Greenlaw, and the deceased Robert Simm, horse dealer in Greenlaw, and did with a sheep-stake or bludgeon or stone ... cruelly and barbarously inflict various severe blows and wounds ... whereby the head and left leg of Robert Simm were fractured and broken, and the head of James Aitcheson was severely wounded; and did with a knife ... in a cruel and barbarous manner, cut and slit the noses of the said James Aitcheson and Robert Simm; in consequence of all which they were both and each or one or other of them bereaved of life'

The jury took eight minutes to reach their unanimous verdict of guilty - Scott would be hanged at a convenient place near where the murders had been committed.

From Jedburgh Castle the Sheriff of Roxburghshire would take him to the county boundary at Leader Bridge and pass him to the Sheriff of Berwickshire.

The procession left the Castle in the following order:

Two Carbineers.
Twelve Yeomanry, commanded by Adjutant Carruthers.
The Sheriff's Carriage.
Two Non-Commissioned Officers.
Detachment with the Colours, commanded by Lieutenant Walker.
The Chaise with the prisoner, guarded at each side by two Yeoman.
The remainder of the Yeomanry under Captain Ainslie, closed up the rear.

At Leader Bridge the Yeomanry changed and at Earlston, Scott was put in a cart with a rearwards facing seat for the final journey.

On the drop his voice rang out over the crowd - asking the Almighty to protect his wife, five children and his mother. To the crowd he gave warning of the dangers of drinking and violent passion.

This said he prepared to meet his fate with the utmost fortitude. Untying his neckcloth and placing it in his hat, he threw them over the side of the scaffold, before dropping the signal.

His body was given to Doctor Monro at Edinburgh University for dissection.

On 15th December 1823, an account for £243.2.7 was rendered to the Berwickshire Barons of Exchequer, including £150 for the construction of the gallows, which was afterwards kept at Blandfield Cottage at an annual rent of £6.0.0.

Executioner; Thomas Williams
Edinburgh

October 29th;   **Francis CAIN**   Glasgow
                  George LAIDLAW

Condemned at the previous Circuit Court; Cain for robbery of a Mr Maxwell on the King's Highway and Laidlaw for theft by housebreaking at the premises of Solomon and Hadkins, 1 Nelson Street, Glasgow, from where he stole £600 worth of jewellery.

Executioner; Thomas Young
Glasgow

November 12th; **David WYLIE**   Glasgow

Arrested and tried with William Johnstone, who was reprieved, for theft of £400 worth of property from the house of Mr Rodger in Gordon Street, Glasgow. A native of Paisley he was between 17 and 18 years.

Executioner; Thomas Young
Glasgow

December 12th; **James ANDERSON**   Ayr
                David GLEN

Condemned at the High Court in Edinburgh for the murder of John McClure, a 58-year-old weaver in Ayr, whom they had assaulted whilst on a drunken spree.

With the day of their execution 'one of the stormiest in a tempestuous season', the crowd was smaller than expected as the executioner led them onto the platform.

Their harrowing time was evident. Glen, who bowed to the spectators, was wasted and pale, whilst Anderson seemed to have lost all muscular power. The weather hurried things on, and after shaking hands Glen dropped the signal and the drop fell.

Next morning their bodies were on the road for Edinburgh and the anatomy theatre of the University.

Executioner; James Thomson
Ayr

1824

April 7th; **Charles McEWEN** Edinburgh

Condemned on circumstantial evidence for murdering his 30-year-old common law wife, Elizabeth Money, on the lonely road at Firmouth, Aboyne, Aberdeenshire, the previous October. Elizabeth travelled the country with him, selling tea canisters.

A fortnight after the murder, the body was disinterred and head wounds compared with a small anvil McEwen carried in his trade as a coppersmith. Although medical experts could not entirely agree to it being the murder weapon - their evidence was accepted. Thirty six-year-old McEwen's memory was hazy through drink.

After sentence had been passed he addressed the bench. "Thank you my Lord - I die innocent - there has not been a Doctor here this day but has perjured himself."

Executioner; Thomas Williams
Edinburgh

May 14th; **John CAMPBELL** Stirling

An inveterate thief, Campbell escaped Stirling Jail whilst awaiting trial at the Circuit court for theft by housebreaking, and was only captured in time to face trial.

When the jury returned to court, he became dreadfully agitated; 'Oh, mercy!, mercy!' - 'Oh, Gentlemen of the Jury, will you have mercy!' - 'Oh, Your Lordship, favour show on me'. As the clerk was recording the verdict, he started up again. 'Oh, restrict my libel! - Oh, let me suffer anything, but do not bring me to an ultimate end!'

Although the drop was considerable, he struggled a good deal. When cut down after 35 minutes, his body was hurried away in a cart by his father and a brother .

Days before the execution they found a St Ninians doctor agreeable to attempt a reanimation, but despite bleeding both temples and the jugular vein, Campbell was gone. He was 19 years of age.

Had he got Campbell to galvanic battery 10

minutes earlier, the doctor was confident he would have been successful.

Executioner; Thomas Williams
Edinburgh

May 19th; **William McTEAGUE** Glasgow

Whilst running a small shop in Hutchesontown, Glasgow, McTeague and his daughter Margaret were trading in forged notes of the Royal Bank of Scotland and Sir William Forbes & Co.'s Bank in Ireland.

She was sentenced to 14 years transportation, and he was hanged.

Executioner; Thomas Young
Glasgow

June 2nd; **John McCREEVIE** Glasgow

Executed for breaking into Mr Shepherd's house at Springvale, where he struck him, whilst in bed, with a crow bar and robbing the house, he was led to the scaffold shouting, 'I am innocent! - I am innocent!'

Executioner; Thomas Young
Glasgow

July 21st; **William DEVAN** Glasgow

Hanged for murdering his wife, Mary Jamieson, in their home in Paisley Loan, Gorbals by cutting her throat with a razor, 50-year-old Devan's execution attracted a larger than usual crowd.

Being Fair Week, the front of the jail had to be cleared of showmen's booths before the scaffold could be erected and the area fenced off. The ground was manned by police and town officers, and a small military presence.

The body was taken to the College, but disappointingly the galvanic experiments were not nearly so spectacular as those produced on Clydesdale five years earlier.

Executioner; Thomas Young
Glasgow

August 27th; **Alexander MARTIN** Aberdeen

In 1823, 31-year-old Martin, 'a reckless and hardened criminal' from Durris, appeared on indictment before the High Court of Justiciary for a rape committed in 1816, but as the girl could not positively identify him he was acquitted.

In July 1824 he came again to the court on charges of theft by housebreaking and a stouthrief committed at Kemnay in the April.

Lord Meadowbank's reference to, 'the awful example which had been witnessed lately in

Aberdeen' (the execution of Donaldson, Buchanan and MacLeod for stouthrief) dispelled any hopes of a reprieve.

Executioner; Unknown

1825

June 1st; **James STEVENSON** Glasgow

Condemned for highway robbery, by knocking down and robbing John Brown of £25 on the Cathcart Road the previous winter, Stevenson was also suspected of stealing watches, rings and gold seals from Mosely the jeweller in King Street, Glasgow.

Executioner; Thomas Young
Glasgow

1826

February 10th; **William ALLAN** Aberdeen

Whilst on the road from Coupar Angus to his home at Montquhitter in September 1825, 20-year-old Allan met Alexander Mackay, a cattle drover, making his way home to Sutherland from a sale in the south.

The drover's suspicions of Allan, who urged taking by-roads, were realised near to Fyvie, when he was struck down and robbed of the 34s from the cattle sale.

Despite a fractured skull, the drover crawled half a mile to the inn at Lewes of Fyvie and raised the alarm.

From a description, Allan was found the next day feeding cattle on a nearby moss, and brought to the inn where he was identified. The drover died there a fortnight later.

Condemned at Edinburgh and taken to Aberdeen for execution, he showed little repentance or emotion until his final night when the sound of the workmen erecting the scaffold seemed to shake his very soul.

His body was given to Marischal College for dissection.

Executioner; Unknown

May 26th; **John McGRADDY** Stirling

Hanged in front of the town's jail for a daring theft by housebreaking at Muiravonside Manse he was identified by the Rev William McCall and two female servants.

A co-accused, John Curran, was found not guilty, and a prosecution witness, Edward Quin, was claimed by 22-year-old McGraddy to have been a fellow perpetrator. Two petitions seeking clemency

failed to save him.

'The person who officiated as executioner wore a crape upon his face and appeared not to have been the ordinary executioner'.

Executioner; Unknown

June 2nd; **David BALFOUR** Dundee

At the first execution in Dundee in over a century, Balfour was hanged on a gallows erected outside the Guild Hall, facing High Street, for the murder of his wife, Margaret Clark, on 21st December 1825.

Executioner; Unknown

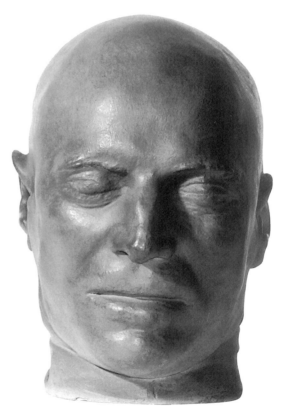

Lead cast of David Balfour's head (*Dundee City Council*)

June 7th; **James DOLLAN** Glasgow

A native of Gerock Bridge in Tyrone, 26-year-old Dollon was ostensibly a tailor, but in reality responsible for a minor Glasgow crime wave.

On a February night, he and an accomplice not only robbed Andrew Jack of 10s on the Old Bridge (now Victoria Bridge) in Glasgow, but attempted to throw him over the parapet.

He left a wife but no children.

Executioner; Thomas Young
Glasgow

July 28th; **Peter MOFFAT** Stirling

A weaver in Kilsyth, Moffat was condemned for murdering his father, also named Peter, in April 1822.

On the scaffold, after addressing the crowd on the dangers of drunkenness and Sabbath breaking, Young placed the rope about his neck - but found it too short.

Cries of, 'Shame! - Shame! - The rope's too short! - Hang the fellow himself!', (and similar expressions) sprang from the crowd. Moffat frantically pulled off the cap and leapt back.

When order was restored, and Moffat had regained his composure, the procedure started again. With the proper drop Moffat entered eternity.

Executioner; Thomas Young
Glasgow

October 18th; **James McMANUS** Dumfries

Condemned for assaulting and robbing Andrew Smail, farmer in Beckton, Dryfesdale, on the Dumfries to Lockerbie road on the night of 15th August. The case against two accomplices was found not proven. The press described him as 'quite a youth'.

Executioner; Unknown

November 1st; **Andrew STEWART** Glasgow
Edward KELLY

A broadside published for this execution closes with the paragraph:

'It is calculated that there are nearly 5000 people in the city [Glasgow] and suburbs, who, were they called upon to give an account how they gain a livelihood, could give no satisfactory answer.'

A weaver to trade, twenty four-year-old Stewart had violently assaulted (with others) Filippo Testti, a looking glass manufacturer, and robbed him of a gold watch, chain and three gold seals.

Kelly, a 21-year-old carter from Bridgegate, had robbed James Fleming of £108 16s.

Executioner; Thomas Young
Glasgow

1827

March 1st; **William THOMSON** Dalkeith

Condemned at Edinburgh for robbing a farmer at Cousland, whilst returning from Dalkeith Market the previous November. His brother John and John Fram, were later reprieved.

Held in Calton Jail until the last morning, immense crowds greeted his return.

After execution, his body was handed over to friends for burial.

Executioner; Thomas Williams
Edinburgh

June 6th; **John KERR** Greenock

At Greenock's first execution since 1817, Kerr paid the penalty for the murder of his wife the previous October.

From a scaffold erected in front of the New Church, the immense crowd extended from the foot of William Street on the north, to the Cross in Shore Street and Manse Lane on the east and west. Whilst many townspeople left to avoid the spectacle, floods of the curious came in from the country.

Fifty-four-year-old Kerr had settled in Greenock some 20 years earlier using his Royal Navy experience to set up a ship rigging business. Many of the Clyde's finest ships carried his ropes and sails.

His body was given to Dr Jeffray at Glasgow College.

Executioner; Thomas Young
Glasgow

Margaret Wishart's house in Orchard Street, Arbroath

June 16th; **Margaret WISHART** Forfar

Condemned for the murder of her blind sister, Jane, at Arbroath the previous October by giving her arsenic in porridge or gruel, Wishart was hanged on a gallows erected in front of the Town Hall.

For twenty five minutes she stood on the drop, fervently engaged in prayer, repeatedly shifting the signal handkerchief from hand to hand. When told it was time, she requested, 'Two minutes yet', before giving the signal.

Her body was given to Dr Monro at Edinburgh University for dissection.

Executioner; Thomas Williams
Edinburgh

Malcolm Gillespie

November 16th; **Malcolm GILLESPIE**   Aberdeen

As an exciseman in the north east, Gillespie was notoriously efficient at hunting down smugglers and illicit stills.

Behind this persona was a man of extravagant habits who attempted to relieve his debts through passing forged bills of exchange. When arrested in April 1827, there were 27 charges against him.

At the conclusion of his 15-hour trial, the judges, Lords Pitmilly and Alloway made reference to his changed circumstances. He had been a frequent witness in their courts.

He walked to the scaffold with great composure, and having taken leave of those around him, dropped the signal. He was buried at Skene.

Executioner; Unknown

December 12th; **James GLEN**   Glasgow

Whilst awaiting trial, 22-year-old Glen, a carter from New Kilpatrick, escaped from Glasgow Jail on the morning of Sunday 3rd June 1827 with ten others, but the following morning, gave himself up at the Jail door. Finding himself hunted from place to place, he could get neither peace nor rest, and thought it best to deliver himself into the hands of justice.

Justice had its way at the Autumn Court when he was condemned for the 'terrible, cruel and barbarous' murder of his 17-month-old illegitimate son, James, whom he had throttled and thrown into the Forth and Clyde Canal the previous May.

Suspended for 35 minutes, he was afterwards taken to the College for dissection by Dr. Jeffray.

Executioner; Thomas Young
Glasgow

1828

May 8th;   **Francis COCKBURN**   Falkirk

The orphaned son of an Edinburgh gold beater, Cockburn had been given as apprentice by the parish authorities to William Burt, nailer at Camelon, a woebegone place to the north west of Falkirk. Burt was a harsh master.

Entering Peter Black's change house on the evening of Saturday 1st September 1827, an intoxicated Cockburn found Burt drinking with a group. An exchange of abuse ended with Cockburn stabbing his master in the eye. He died in three days and the 18-year-old was incarcerated in Stirling Jail to await the Spring Court. His condemnation evoked much sympathy as did his execution.

He, however, expressed a cool and deliberate readiness to meet his fate, saying he would go, 'just the same as if he were going to his work!'

His body was given to Dr Monro at Edinburgh for anatomical dissection.

Within days of the execution Falkirk was flooded with copies of the doggerel poem:

A LAMENTATION
FOR
FRANCIS COCKBURN
You people all of Camelon town
Give ear to what I have penn'd down,
The fate of a young lad of fame,
Francis Cockburn, it is his name.

He's come of decent parentage,
And is scarce eighteen years of age
He ne'er was known in his lifetime
Till now to do a wicked crime.

In Camelon a comrade he had
Who was a nailer to his trade
Its one he thought he'd never hurt
His loving comrade William Burt

This love to hatred it did turn
And anger in each breast did burn
Their anger unto such height rose
It caused words and sometime blows

September last on the first day
Cockburn unto a friend did say
To Peter Black's I will repair
I hear that Willie Burt is there

He came to Black's without delay
It being on a Saturday
It's William Burt he there did spy
And thrust a large knife in his eye

I'm a gone man he did exclaim
He's pierced me to the very brain
So there in agony he lay
And did expire on the next day

Cockburn he was a prisoner made
And off to Stirling was conveyed
So there for seven months he lay
Filled with horror and dismay

Upon the twelfth of April last
His awful sentence it was past
The summons he had to obey
At Falkirk on the 8th of May

When the scaffold he did ascend
He told to each comrade and friend
I did commit that horrid crime
Which cuts me off now in my prime

Long in my breast I harboured spite
Which does my trembling soul afright
For killing of my comrade dear
In shame I'm doom'd to suffer here

Take warning now you young men all
By Francis Cockburn's sad downfall
He's cut off from this earthly stage
Tho' scarcely eighteen years of age

As a footnote, William Burt and his father Andrew, also a nailer at Camelon, are worthy of mention.

Andrew appeared at Stirling Circuit Court in 1804 charged with murdering an apprentice boy, David

Callender, and was whipped through the streets before being transported for 14 years.

Executioner; Unknown

October 22nd; **Thomas CONNOR** Glasgow
Isabella McMENEMY

The pair, both aged 22, had a well oiled scheme. McMenemy enticing men into quiet places and Connor robbing them.

In May 1828, Alex McKinnon, a boatman, in Glasgow to sell eggs, became their last victim when he was decoyed to a lonely spot on the Paisley Canal at Port Eglinton, knocked insensible, and robbed of 40s.

Connor, 'Urged on by his depraved mother ... who gave unbounded scope to his wicked designs', had never worked.

The first woman to mount a Glasgow scaffold since Agnes White in 1793, McMenemy, who had only thrice before had a bible in her hands, appeared on the platform in a black bombazeen gown, white shoulder napkin and white head cap. Though short in stature, a fair complexion and red hair set off her good looks.

Executioner; Thomas Young
Glasgow

1829

January 28th; **William BURKE** Edinburgh

William Burke (*Edinburgh City Libraries*)

WILLIAM HARE.
KING'S EVIDENCE

William Hare   (*Edinburgh City Libraries*)

Dr Robert Knox   (*Edinburgh City Libraries*)

For a man to have his name entered in standard English Dictionaries; be instrumental in the formulation of an act of parliament; and be the subject of innumerable ballads, songs and plays, says something about the good or evil in his life. In the case of William Burke, it was evil.

Between December 1827 and October 1828, he was responsible, with William Hare, for the murder of Daft Jamie and fifteen others, whose bodies they sold to Dr Knox at Surgeons' Hall at £8 or £10 each.

Unsure of securing a conviction against both men and their women, the Crown served indictments on Burke and his paramour Helen McDougall, and cited Hare and his wife as witnesses. McDougall had refused to give evidence against Burke.

The trial opened on Christmas Eve 1828 and ran for two days. The outcome was unsurprising - Burke was found guilty of the three charges the Crown had proceeded on, whilst the case against MacDougal was

found not proven. He would be hanged at the head of Libberton Wynd between 8 and 10 o'clock on the morning of Wednesday 28th January 1829.

When passing sentence, the Lord Justice Clerk assured him that he had no chance of a pardon.

In his last week in Calton Jail, he spoke of a dream. He was in the Grassmarket and saw the gallows erected and all the crowd assembled; 'but it was only a dream', he added, 'for, I doubt, they will not allow me to go that length'. Burke knew the temperament of an Edinburgh mob.

At 4 o'clock on Tuesday morning he was taken to the lock-up house behind Parliament Square, and in the afternoon with the street fenced off, a crowd watched the work start on the scaffold. At midnight, in heavy rain, a cheer went up as the cross beam was placed in position.

By half past six the whole of the Lawnmarket and High Street were crowded - to the house tops. By Glasgow standards for such an occasion, the crowd of 35000 was not large - but Edinburgh did not have a Green.

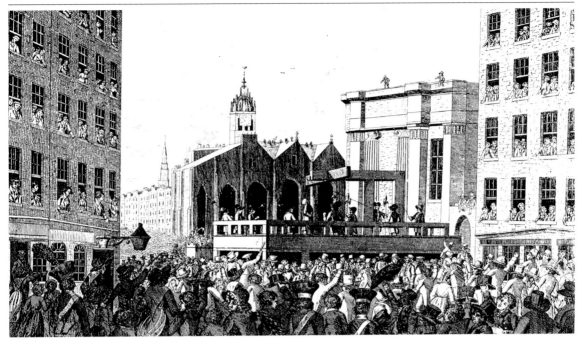

Burke's Execution   (*Edinburgh City Libraries*)

By half past seven, as his fetters were being knocked off, the impatient crowd began a series of loud and long shouts - they wanted Burke.

At precisely eight o'clock, led by the city officers with their Lochaber axes, the procession moved off up Libberton Wynd from the lock-up. The Magistrates followed, with Burke, dressed in a new suit of black clothes and white neckcloth, supported by two priests, coming next. The shouts grew to a cry of exultation, mixed with groans and hissing.

Burke's sure step became more and more faltering and he would not open his eyes again till he was on the scaffold. But once there, his defiant stare redoubled the crowd's noise.

As the rope was being adjusted, a vehement cry, 'Burke him!', 'Burke him!', 'Burke him!', was raised. And when the cap was pulled over his face the mob wanted it left off.

The drop fell, but the rope, whether by design or otherwise, was too short. He struggled many minutes, taking deep breaths.

Now came the cry for his accomplice; 'Bring out Hare!', 'Now for Hare!', which was sustained intermittently until Burke was cut down at nine o'clock. Three cheers were called, 'for humanity', and a shout for 'one more cheer', was answered.

After remaining suspended for exactly 45 minutes, the body was lowered down, placed in a coffin, and carried shoulder high back to the Lock-up-house.

Many who wanted a piece of the rope settled for a shaving of wood out of the rude coffin, and with the dispersing crowd ebbed fears of a riot.

But the spectacle was not quite over yet - there was still the dissection to be carried through. Overnight Burke's body was removed to Dr Munro's classroom, where next day it was exposed and partly dissected. The brain, as was to be expected in an executed criminal, was soft.

Regular students of the college were overwhelmed by the mob which besieged the class room door from an early hour. By two o'clock the police had become targets for stones and snowballs, and by the time reinforcements had arrived, most of the windows in the college had gone.

Shortly afterwards, parties of 40 or 50 were allowed entry to view the body, and peace was restored.

Executioner; Thomas Williams
Edinburgh

May 20th; **Edward MOORE** Glasgow

A labourer from Stonelaw near Rutherglen, hanged for the murder of his pregnant wife, Mary MacAvoy, in November 1828. His body was given for dissection.

Executioner; Thomas Young
Glasgow

August 19th; **John STEWART** Edinburgh
Catherine WRIGHT

Tried at Edinburgh on 14th July 1829 for 'having on the previous 15th December, on board the *Toward Castle* steamboat, in a voyage between Inveraray and Glasgow, administered to Robert Lamont, merchant and farmer at Balligirton on the Island of Ulva, a quantity of laudanum, mixt up with porter or ale, in consequence of having drank which the said Robert Lamont lingered in a state of insensibility until the morning of 16th December 1828, when he died'.

Born at Stoneykirk in the Rhinns of Galloway in 1803, Stewart's true name was Broadfoot. At 20, after marrying 'a respectable young woman of wealthy (and disapproving) parents', he enlisted in the Marines at Chatham. On her death in 1825 he was granted leave to bring their child to Scotland - when he deserted.

A dexterous pickpocket and veteran gambler he next met and married Catherine Wright at Dumfries.

On the road between Edinburgh and Biggar they met an old companion of Stewart - on his last housebreaking expedition. He had found a more profitable and less dangerous way of obtaining money. By administering stupefying drugs in drink to the unsuspecting, their pockets could be plundered with impunity. Lamont was to be the first fatal result for Stewart and Wright.

Their execution, which passed without incident, was carried out in driving rain.

Executioner; Thomas Williams
Edinburgh

October 29th; **John CRAIG** Paisley
James BROWN

Hanged in County Square for stouthrief, having broken into the house of William Robertson, a bleacher at West Foxbar the previous June, with an accomplice, Robert Stewart, who was outlawed for not appearing in court. The trio assaulted Robertson and his sister before ransacking the house.

In their efforts to make peace with the world before departing it, Craig and Brown were granted the unusual privilege of an audience with Robertson,

when they implored his forgiveness.

On the scaffold Brown dropped the handkerchief in seconds and both died with a few faint struggles.

Brown, who left a widow and nine children, had kept an inn at Newtonards in Ireland before coming to Scotland in 1827.

Although his inseparable companion, Craig had been in the Johnstone area some nine years, the source of his income was a mystery. When not dealing in forged notes, he acted as a glazier 'but is said to have generally stolen at night those panes of glass he put in during the day'. He left a wife and three children.

Executioner; Thomas Young
Glasgow

1830

January 6th; **William ADAMS** Edinburgh

A slater by trade, 20-year-old Adams was executed for robbing Michael Firnie of £1.4.6 and a tin snuff box, on the stairway leading from Kirkheuch to Parliament Stairs in Edinburgh the previous September.

Executioner; Thomas Williams
Edinburgh

March 17th; **Robert EMOND** Edinburgh

Emond was not, as an initial newspaper report suggested - 'A sort of non-descript merchant, who dealt in groceries, haberdashery and sundry other wares' - but a brutal killer, who murdered his sister in law, Mrs Franks and her daughter Madeline, in their walled garden cottage at Abbey of Haddington, with a kitchen knife. He was motivated through Mrs Franks holding a bill over part of his wife's property.

On the scaffold, in the company of his brother, he is reported to have changed colour frequently when the hangman commenced his duties.

His body was given for public dissection.

Executioner; Thomas Williams
Edinburgh

May 12th; **William PORTER** Glasgow
John HILL

Condemned for assaulting and robbing 76-year-old William Marshall on the Glasgow to Keppoch Hill road on 19th December 1829. Felling him with repeated blows to the head, they robbed him of his shoes, spectacles, an old silk handkerchief and 7s in money.

A petition to save them from the scaffold failed,

although it was signed by a number of the jury.

Executioner; Thomas Young
Glasgow

August 18th; **James THOMSON** Edinburgh
David DOBIE

With the imminent death of George IV, the trial of the 'Gilmourton Carters' for the rape and murder of Margaret Paterson was postponed from 1st to 12th July.

As in all cases of rape, their trial was conducted behind closed doors, and the public only admitted once the jury had retired. They returned a verdict of guilt.

Resigned to their fate, they appeared on the scaffold dressed in blue coats and black trousers.

There is no explanation as to why their bodies were not given for public dissection until November, or where they were kept.

Executioner; Thomas Williams
Edinburgh

September 29th; **William McFEAT** Glasgow

Although admitting the murder of his wife, Maxwell McKinley, McFeat denied using a weapon. He claimed to have kicked her to death.

After borrowing a suit of black clothes for a funeral and soiling the neckcloth, he sent Maxwell with it to a washerwoman, but she sold it instead.

On the evening before his execution, his two children, the eldest about 12 years, were admitted to his cell. As orphans they became the responsibility of the parish.

Executioner; Thomas Young
Glasgow

September 30th; **John HENDERSON** Cupar

A hand loom weaver, hanged for the murder of his employer, James Millie, at Whinny Park the previous June.

The crowd of 15,000 gathered on the rising ground to the rear of Cupar Jail where the scaffold was erected, would have agreed with the press description of Cupar's first execution since 1743 as, 'a novelty of no common description'.

In his last days he wept bitterly, and during the building of the scaffold (which he heard distinctly in his cell) all his efforts at composure were spent.

Executioner; Unknown

October 8th; **Catherine DAVIDSON**
Aberdeen

Condemned for murdering her husband James Humphrey, a butcher, Davidson was the first woman hanged at Aberdeen since Elspet Reid in 1785.

The Humphries kept a public house 'in a lower quarter of the town', becoming over the years drunkards in a constant state of feuding. From the trial evidence, Davidson was the aggressor, several times coming close to cutting his throat.

After a particularly bitter fight on the night of Friday 16th April 1830, she took her chance when Humphrey fell asleep and poured oil of vitriol (concentrated sulphuric acid) into his mouth. He died on the Sunday morning, refusing to blame her.

Her final days were troubled by the memory of being at Jean Craig's execution in 1783, when she was struck on the breast by the rope, which it was then customary for the hangman to throw into the crowd.

Her body was given to Dr Charles Skene, Professor of Medicine at Marischal College.

Executioner; Unknown

1831

January 27th; **David LITTLE** Glasgow

In 1825, as an 18-year-old, Little and a gang of 'disguised ruffians' forced entry into Gartloch House at Calder, assaulted and maltreated the occupier, and stole all they could carry.

Little fled to his native Ireland, enlisted in the army, deserted, and settled as a cotton spinner in Manchester, where he met a girl. They intended to marry, but piqued after a quarrel, she reported his past to the police.

Five years after the crime, aged 23, he was tried and condemned at Glasgow for stouthrief.

Executioner; Thomas Young
Glasgow

May 16th; **James CAMPBELL** Glasgow

In 1822 Campbell was condemned at Glasgow for theft by housebreaking, but had the sentence commuted to transportation for life. If fact he was not transported, and served his sentence aboard the hulks on the river Thames.

Released in August 1830, he returned to his old haunts and habits, which again brought him to the Circuit Court at Glasgow on a charge of theft by housebreaking. This time, aged 36, there was no respite.

Executioner; Thomas Young
Glasgow

August 11th; **George GILCHRIST** Glasgow

Everything Gilchrist put his hand to prospered - except robbery. Proprietor of the Inn of Hillend on the Airdrie road, he was also a partner in a stage coach company plying between Edinburgh and Glasgow. When his estate was wound up his 50 horses sold for £1,100.

But avarice proved his undoing when, along with William Gilchrist and James Brown, he was charged with having abstracted from a box in the Prince Regent coach from Glasgow to Edinburgh, on 24th March 1831, £5712 6s, belonging to the Commercial Banking Company.

Evidence revealed that Gilchrist, dressed as a woman, and his accomplices passed themselves off as travellers and gained access to the coach boot.

The case against William Gilchrist and Brown was found not proven.

On the scaffold he collapsed and had to be supported by two attendants.

Executioner; Thomas Young
Glasgow

October 6th; **James BYERS** Glasgow
Mary STEEL

James Martin was too drunk to notice the laudanum in his last glass of porter in James Rennie's spirit cellar in Glasgow's High Street, and already dead when the Byers carried him into his lodgings in nearby Steel Street.

After condemnation, Steel confessed to purchasing and administering the laudanum and taking four 30s Irish banknotes from Martin's pocket, but denied any intention to murder him. Byers affirmed his innocence to the end, denying knowledge of the plan.

Standing on the platform Byers looked thin and haggard beside his stout, portly and very good looking wife who appeared bold and fearless.

Executioner; Thomas Young
Glasgow

October 19th; **Thomas ROGERS** Jedburgh

Executed in front of the Castle for the murder of Neil McKiernon, an Irishman, at Sharpitlaw Annan in the August, by striking him with a bludgeon.

To the end he denied knowledge of the crime, being 'quite unconscious of having stained his hands in the blood of a fellow creature'.

A prisoner in Jedburgh Castle when Robison was hanged in May 1822, he purchased the rope from the jailer, and, reports the Kelso Mail, had his portrait painted a few days before his own execution.

Executioner; John Murdoch
Glasgow

October 20th; **William HEATH** Glasgow

On Sunday, 26th December 1830, 42-year-old Heath entered Watson's Bank in Virginia Street, Glasgow by false keys or picklocks and made off with over £6,000 in banknotes.

Captured in London, without the money, he was returned to stand trial with an accomplice, Elizabeth Crowder or Thurnley.

Circumstantial evidence told of them taking lodgings in Warwick Street, with Thurnley posing as his sister. In fact they were fellow brothel keepers in London. Witnesses spoke to the sound of hammering in their room - where the windows were always screened - and to the key blanks later found in it. They were seen in the vicinity of the bank and seated next to the bank porter in church.

At 7.20am on the second day of their trial the jury returned their verdict. She was dismissed - he was condemned.

An attempt to barter the money for his life won him a 14-day reprieve, but failed to save him.

His wife took the body to London for burial.

Executioner; Thomas Young
Glasgow

October 24th; **Hugh McLEOD** Inverness

When the impecunious McLeod met the packman Murdoch Grant at Drumbeg in Sutherland in March 1830, it seemed the answer to a prayer. The youngest son of a cottar at Lynemeanach, Assynt, he had recently given up teaching, and a schoolhouse at Lochbroom, and was heavily in debt.

With a promise to buy all his goods, Grant agreed to met McLeod the following day in the hills above Drumbeg.

The day's events were related by McLeod in his confession:

> 'At length we got near Loch Torr na h Eigen - I was going first - suddenly I turned round and with a violent blow under the ear, felled him to the ground. He lay sprawling in great agony - but never spoke. I took money out of his warm pockets and put it into mine - about £9 in all.
>
> 'I gave him 2 or 3 violent blows and then dragged his body into the loch as far as I could with safety, and placed a large stone on the breast.
>
> 'Even then life was scarcely gone, for water kept bubbling up from the mouth. It was evening but not dark.
>
> 'I threw the hammer into the loch and

rifled the pack - I took most portable things such as stockings and silk handkerchiefs, then carried the heavy goods and sunk them in a moss loch farther into the moor.

'I saw the body every day in passing the loch, but had not the courage to take it out and bury it.'

Grant was missed, but his body lay undiscovered for four weeks. Evidence pointed to murder and soon pointed to McLeod.

A tailor named Kenneth Fraser, 'The Dreamer', reported having witnessed the murder in a dream, and described a cairn where the pedlar's pack would be found. The pack was not there but some of Grant's possessions were.

Incarcerated in Dornoch Jail to await trial, McLeod also had a dream.

Meeting his father in a churchyard, he had never been in before, both stood by a newly opened grave, with a coffin by its side. His father said, 'Hugh, that is your grave, you will now be placed in it, but you will be allowed twelve months yet, but at the end of that period you must occupy that grave'. McLeod presumed that as the dream was speaking of 12 months hence, he would be acquitted at Inverness. But that was not how it would turn out.

The trial was set for September 1830, but due to insufficient jurymen, the diet was deserted till the Spring of 1831. Come April, the absence of a material witness brought another postponement, before the trial finally proceeded on 26th September 1831 - the dream of 12 months earlier in Dornoch Jail, was to become a reality.

At 1.30pm the execution party left the prison, with McLeod dressed in a long black cloak, made for the occasion, and a white nightcap. To ensure the hangman's presence, he too had been secured in the jail, but now he walked behind McLeod, holding the end of the halter which hung from the culprit's neck.

On the gallows McLeod addressed the 8,000 strong crowd in Gaelic, and was still singing the psalm, in a clear voice, as he threw the signal and the drop fell.

His body was given to Edinburgh University for anatomical dissection.

Executioner; Donald Ross
Inverness

December 2nd; **James GOW** Edinburgh
Thomas BEVERIDGE

The extent of domestic violence in 1830s Edinburgh is indicated by the execution of three men in a single month, for murdering their spouses.

Gow, condemned for killing his wife with a shoemaker's knife, also stabbed a neighbour who came to her rescue. To one of the clergymen he confessed that, 'so ungovernable were his passions when under the influence of liquor, that he could only compare himself to the maniac among the tombs'.

Due to intemperance, Beveridge and his wife lived, 'very uncomfortably', in Little Jack's Close. On the night of the murder (Sunday 16th October 1831) cries of murder were heard but ignored, due to their frequency.

Executioner; Thomas Williams
Edinburgh

December 19th; **John McCOURT** Edinburgh

Condemning McCourt for murdering his wife Catherine by violent kicking, in their home in Rattray's Court, Cowgate, the Lord Justice Clerk strongly remarked on the prevalence of the crime as proof that the country was fast approaching the bottom of the scale of nations in religion and morality.

Catherine's drinking over the previous four years had ruined a comfortable home. Only three of their eleven children survived to any age.

Executioner; Thomas Williams
Edinburgh

1832

January 18th; **William LINDSAY** Glasgow

Originating in 'the demon spirits of party politics', Lindsay was hanged for the murder of William Mason at Shotts the previous November.

Sitting over drinks, Mason proposed a toast to the Reform Bill, then passing through Parliament, and Lindsay took offence. Words led to blows and blows led to Lindsay stabbing the proposer with a large knife.

A 35-year-old mill wright from Dunbartonshire, Lindsay's body was given to Dr John Burns, Professor of Anatomy at Glasgow College, for dissection.

Executioner; Thomas Young
Glasgow

January 19th; **Samuel WAUGH** Ayr

Parliament's second reading of the Reform Bill in

Memorial Stone to Alexander Ross   (*Author's Collection*)

April 1831 brought jubilation to many towns, including Girvan in Ayrshire. Two thirds of the town's 6,000 population were Irish, and many of them Roman Catholics, who saw the Bill as a harbinger of political emancipation. They were wrong - its purpose was, 'to sweep away existing abuses and extend the right to vote to Persons of Property and Intelligence'.

The jubilation slid into rioting between Irish Roman Catholics on one side and Irish Orangemen on the other.

Spring passed into summer and as the Orangemen's annual 12th July march drew closer, Girvan's magistrates grew anxious. The Girvan lodge had invited brethren from Maybole, Crosshill and Dailly.

The magistrates sought help and advice from Sheriff Substitute William Eaton at Ayr, but he told them there was no law to prevent the march, and should it get out of hand it was their responsibility.

However, he negotiated a compromise. The guest lodges, on arriving at the north of Girvan, would take a peripheral route to the meeting place at the south of the town and hence avoid confrontation in the town centre,

This agreed, the force of 150 special constables took their oath and their batons and went out to face the incoming marchers at the Kilgrammie road end. They had not long to wait before the procession came into view - numbering two or three hundred, 'some with guns, some with swords, some with pikes, and a considerable number with pistols'.

The Orangemen stopped and two constables went forward to inform them of the detour. The leader agreed to the proposed new route, but was immediately damned, and told to march on. Confusion broke out as part of the march took the prescribed route, whilst others marched on.

A crowd of women and children, disappointed at the lack of action, now showered the Orangemen with stones, and a mêlée broke out.

At this point, Waugh stepped from the ranks, raised his gun, and fired at a group of special constables, killing Alexander Ross. It was a signal for the Orangemen - who now charged towards the town, bludgeoning and cutting down all who came in their path with sword, pike and bayonet.

Sheriff Eaton, being on hand, was able to mount an immediate investigation. Within 48 hours 31 Maybole men were imprisoned at Ayr. Waugh was arrested at Newton Stewart.

Waugh, described as 'a thin looking man past middle age, with his head bound up to support a broken jaw', and the march leader John Ramsay were indicted at Ayr Autumn Circuit for the murder, and five others for mobbing and rioting.

In the interests of impartiality and fairness, their defence counsel successfully contested the trial venue - Ayr being only 21 miles from Girvan, and fresh indictments were served for Edinburgh.

On Thursday 28th December 1831 the *Ayr Advertiser* stopped the press to report that the Marquis of Hastings coach had just arrived with news that Waugh would be hanged at Ayr. The jury had been divided - nine supported a conviction for murder and six for culpable homicide.

When told there would be no reprieve, Waugh replied that had they not been stoned there would have been no violence, 'his own blood and that of Alexander Ross lay upon the people of Girvan'.

Waugh was still suspended as the *Ayr Advertiser* went to press with its report of his execution. It had little to report. The execution passed without incident before a crowd of 5,000, and next morning his body was taken to Edinburgh for dissection.

Constable Ross was not forgotten in Girvan, where two stones, one at the place of the murder and one over his grave, were raised. The murder spot at the junction of the Kilgrammie road has now been lost to road development and the stone re-sited.

Over his grave in Girvan Old Cemetery, a rectangular pedestal surmounted by a pyramid is inscribed;

ERECTED
by
500
of the inhabitants of
GIRVAN
to the memory
of
ALEXr ROSS
who
while discharging his
duty as a constable
was shot
by
an Orangeman
on the 12th of July
1831.

Executioner; John Murdoch
Glasgow

January 21st; **John HOWISON** Edinburgh

On the morning of his execution for murdering an elderly widow, Matty Geddes, at 'The Long Row' on the Barnton West Gate to old Cramond Bridge road, Howison astounded his carers by confessing to eight previous murders.

A stout 40-year-old common beggar of forbidding appearance, he had a weak intellect and a strong preponderance for drink. His first murder had been four years earlier and the last about twelve months past.

In a house near Lauder at harvest time 1829 he had murdered a labourer named Jamieson after a quarrel. The following year after quarrelling with a labourer at Whittingham near Morpeth, he murdered him with a stick.

The other six murders had been committed in Edinburgh; two boys and a girl in the West Port, two boys in the Cowgate and another boy at the head of the Canongate. After killing the children, he said, he 'took no more thought of them'.

He died denying the murder of Matty Geddes.

Executioner; Thomas Williams
Edinburgh

1832

October 31st; **John CHISHOLM** Perth

Hanged for the murder of his second wife, 76-year-old Chisholm was a devout church attender and a special constable, and had been a merchant in Perth's South Street for 40 years. He also had an ungovernable temper.

His first wife frequently reproached him, 'for his unkind usage' and warned, 'he would be hanged though she would not live to see it'.

Executioner; John Murdoch
Glasgow

November 7th; **George DOFFY** Glasgow

Indicted for murdering his wife, Helen Broadly, by throwing her on the house fire. Although severely burnt about the back, belly and legs she lingered from 14th May till 9th June 1832, when she died.

He should have appeared at the Glasgow Autumn Circuit on 20th September, but with the country in the grip of a cholera epidemic the court was adjourned until 16th October.

On 6th September the following figures for the epidemic in Glasgow were published:

> 'Total, from 12th February 1832, in the whole district, (Population 202,426) viz. - Royalty, all the Townships in Barony Parish, and the whole Barony of Gorbals:- Cases 5146. Deaths 2467. Recoveries 2611.'

The outcome of the trial was unaffected by the three week delay - 45-year-old Doffy was found guilty and condemned.

Buried in the north courtyard of the prison, a tablet was affixed to the wall opposite the Felon's Gallery:

> 'Buried in the centre of this Court, George Doffy, hanged for the murder of Helen Broadly, his wife, on 7th November 1832'.

Executioner; Thomas Young
Glasgow

1833

February 7th; **Henry BURNETT** Glasgow

Within months of returning from a sentence of transportation, Burnett assaulted and robbed Mr

Handyside, an elderly man, in Glasgow's Wellington Street, in October 1832.

Despite the ferocity of the assault, his sentence was respited 14 days for enquiry, but his nerve was such that he expressed no alarm when the appeal was rejected.

He confessed to a number of other similar crimes whilst in prison and walked to the scaffold unflinchingly.

Executioner; Thomas Young
Glasgow

October 2nd;   **Robert TENNANT**   Stirling

Executed in front of the Court House in Broad Street for robbing and murdering William Peddie near Beaucross, Falkirk the previous August.

Only after the signal, did Williams notice 21-year-old Tennant's neckcloth. He had hoped to shorten his suffering by leaving it on, and implored mercy whilst the hangman removed it.

When leaving for Edinburgh, Williams was chased and stoned by a crowd, and lucky to escape with his life.

Executioner; John Williams
Edinburgh

1834

20th January;   **Hugh KENNEDY**   Glasgow

A 'boots' at Glasgow's Buck's Head Inn, 27-year-old Kennedy was hanged for attempting to murder James Goodwin by throwing a mixture of sulphuric acid and sand on his face whilst the man was asleep. Goodwin had refused to advance his wages.

Convicted on circumstantial evidence, he was the only person in Scotland to suffer under Lord Ellenborough's Statute (10 Geo IV c 38) which made attempt to murder a capital offence.

Executioner; Thomas Young
Glasgow

April 2nd;   **Mannes SWINEY**   Greenlaw

Executed in front of Greenlaw's County Hall for assaulting and robbing John McFee on the road between Lauder and Stow the previous September.

There are no adverse reports on Williams' performance at this execution - but perhaps the good people of Greenlaw were less critical than the mobs which thronged Libberton's Wynd.

Executioner; John Williams
Edinburgh

May 31st;   **William NOBLE**   Elgin

Tried at Inverness for the murder of William Ritchie on the road near Lhanbryde the previous December. During a drink-fuelled argument Noble felled his adversary with a stick.

Following condemnation he declared, in a manner typical of a 20-year-old army deserter, with perhaps a little help from the clergy; ' ... the judge, jury, witnesses and others who were the means, under the direction of Almighty God, who never slumbers or sleeps, of bringing home the guilty actions to me, all acted honestly and justly in convicting me of this offence'.

Executioner; Unknown

October 23rd;   **John BOYD**   Greenock

A respectable hat dealer in Greenock, Boyd was condemned at Glasgow of murdering his wife, Sarah McLachlan, in their home in Harvey Lane.

Executioner; Thomas Young
Glasgow

1835

May 30th;   **Mark DEVLIN**   Dundee

'A smart little man, rather good looking than otherwise, and about 26 years of age', Devlin was executed in front of the Town House for a rape committed on 13-year-old Ann McLachlan of Small's Wynd, Dundee, on the evening of Sunday 15th February 1835, at the back of a hill called 'The Law'.

Disturbed about 1.00am by joiners erecting the scaffold, he soon fell asleep again.

Executioner; Unknown

July 13th;   **James BELL**   Edinburgh

The execution of 26-year-old Bell, for the murder of Sergeant Major Moorhead, was the first and last in the city by its bungling hangman John Williams.

While he was pinioning Bell's arms, the city officials first witnessed his incompetency. On the scaffold he cried like a child - as did Bell. He could not adjust the rope, and mindful of the riot at Johnstone's execution in 1819, the Superintendent of Works pushed Williams aside and did the job for him. Stones came from the crowd, sympathetic to the culprit's plight, but stopped when the drop fell.

Williams was stoned as he escaped down Libberton's Wynd, and next day resigned.

Executioner; John Williams
Edinburgh

August 3rd;   **Elizabeth BANKS**   Edinburgh

As a child, Elizabeth Banks repeatedly declared that she would one day die by the hands of the executioner. Aged 54 the day came, after poisoning her second husband, Peter Banks, in their home at Dewarton in Borthwick parish.

A brute of a man who subjected her to frequent beatings, she spent tuppence of a shilling given her as charity, on the arsenic, which she administered in his salts and water.

Executioner; John Scott
Edinburgh

September 29th; **George CAMPBELL**   Glasgow

Hanged for the murder of Mary Harlin or Watters, a widow, in her house in Deacon's Close, Calton, the previous 6th June.

Executioner; Thomas Young
Glasgow

October 10th;   **John ADAM**   Inverness

Before burial in Inverness Jail, Adam's head was examined by a phrenologist, who found the culprit's conscientiousness to be deficient, but his secretiveness and amativeness to be strong.

Phrenology was the 'would-be science of mental faculties supposed to be located in various parts of the skull and investigatable by feeling the bumps on the outside of the head.'

When the body of Janet Brechin was found half buried in a ruined hut at Millbuie, in the Black Isle, her husband of seven months, known as John Anderson, was arrested. He proved to be 31-year-old Adams. Giving up her shop, she disappeared with life savings of £113 - £75 of which was found on Adams.

He was executed at the Longman, and buried, upright, under the flagstones in Inverness Jail. Since then he has been moved several times and now lies, or stands, under the Police Headquarters at Perth Road, Inverness.

Executioner; Unknown

1836

April 4th;   **Charles DONALDSON**
Edinburgh

Complaining of the cold and faintness, Donaldson had three tots of brandy in his last hour, and the arm of a stout porter on his way to the drop.

Condemned for murdering his wife, he was 46 years old but had all the appearance of a decrepit man.

Executioner; John Scott
Edinburgh

1837

April 8th;   **Alexander MILLAR**   Stirling

Condemned at Edinburgh on 18th March for the murder of William Jarvie at Dennyloanhead, 19-year-old Millar was disappointed when returned to Stirling in the Soho Coach. Hoping to go by steam boat, he had intended throwing himself and his shackled escort, into the sea.

The prison governor asked the wright who came to measure him for his coffin to measure a broken pane of glass - and guess Millar's height. 'Oh', said Millar, 'there is no use for that way of bringing him in. I know what he wants, I will stretch myself out, and let him measure me'.

As his behaviour spoke of trouble on the scaffold, he was taken out wearing a halter, held by the hangman, to face the 9,000 strong crowd. The prophesy of an old woman in Denny, whom he had accused of being a witch, came to mind - and pulling off his shoes threw them into the crowd. He would not after all die with his shoes on.

After a plaster cast was taken of his head he was buried within the prison.

The unknown hangman wore a black wig and disguise.

Executioner; Unknown

1838

October 18th;   **William PERRIE**   Paisley

A 38-year-old tobacco spinner, and native of Glasgow, Perrie was hanged for murdering Mary Mitchell, his wife of eight months in a fit of jealousy. His first wife had died two years before.

He appeared on the scaffold dressed in black, where:

> 'The executioner having adjusted the rope, Perrie then engaged in prayer for 8 or 10 minutes. During the time he had been on the scaffold the most solemn silence prevailed, until the moment he dropped the handkerchief, when a low mournful sound rose simultaneously from the crowd, the

bolt was immediately drawn, and one unit of humanity was blotted from the sum of human existance.'

The rope was a new one, and when the drop fell it began to untwist itself, making the body twirl about.

After a phrenologist had taken a cast of his head, he was buried within the prison

Executioner; John Murdoch
Glasgow

1838

May 21st; **Elizabeth JEFFREY** Glasgow

Tried and condemned at Glasgow for two murders committed in her home at Carluke in Lanarkshire.

On 4th October 1837 she poisoned Ann Newall or Carl by adding arsenic to a 'medicine' of meal, water and whiskey. And on 28th October attempted to murder Hugh Monro, a lodger in her house, by putting arsenic in porridge. Monro survived the porridge, but not the rhubarb.

She confessed that Ann Carl's murder had been an experiment to test the probable effects of the poison on Monro, to whom she owed six pounds.

For the scaffold she dressed in a black merino gown, a tartan woollen shawl and mourning cap.

Executioner; John Murdoch
Glasgow

1839

March 25th; **Arthur WOOD** Dundee

Tried at Edinburgh with his wife Henrietta Young or Wood for the murder of John Drew Wood, his son by a previous marriage, in their house in Thorter Row, Dundee, in the early hours of Sunday 5th August 1838. After dashing his head against a wall they strangled him with rope. The case against Henrietta was found not proven, but Arthur was condemned.

He was the first to be executed outside the newly-built prison in Bell Street.

Executioner; Unknown

1840

April 16th; **James WEMYSS** Edinburgh

In Autumn 1839 Wemyss, an umbrella maker, and his wife, Sally McRavey, deserted their wandering tinker life and settled in a low lodging house in Edinburgh's Plainstane Close. With their goods and chattels came their intemperate habits and quarrels.

Early in the morning of 28th January 1840 words led again to wallops - with a brickbat and then a stool. She died with her head between his knees as the blows rained down. He put her to bed and made his escape.

Described as 40 years of age, 6 feet tall, stout made, fair hair, full-faced, a stooping walk and a Paisley accent, he was soon after traced, tried and condemned.

On the drop, with the rope adjusted and the cap pulled down, the executioner drew the bolt - but nothing happened. Presuming the mechanism to have jammed, Scott tried to release it by stamping on it, but this only increased the groans and hisses from the crowd.

When an official spotted that Scott had drawn the wrong bolt Wemyss was finally launched into eternity.

Executioner; John Scott
Edinburgh

May 27th; **Thomas TEMPLETON** Glasgow

Condemned at Glasgow Spring Court for murdering his wife in their East College Street home, Lord Cockburn, the presiding judge, had this to say of the 45-year-old bookbinder:

> WEST CIRCUIT - 1840
> Bonaly, 11th May 1840.
> ' ... when I went to Glasgow ... We had five days work, from nine in the morning till six or seven in the evening, having been liberated, how-ever, on Saturday the 9th in time to reach home that night.
> There was nothing particular in the cases, the great mass of them being aggravated thefts, followed by seven years transportation, ad nauseam. There was one capital conviction for murder. But even this was common-place; the common Scotch case of a brute, excited by his own liquor, and pretending to be provoked by that of his wife, and finding himself alone in his own house with his helpless

victim, proceeding to beat her to death. This man seemed to think it a sort of defence that it was a Saturday night, when, "he was always worst, it being his pay day". His wife was perfectly sober, and though "she could take a dram", was not of dissipated habits generally, and was never known to show any violence towards her husband. Yet though the proof could not have been clearer if the jury had seen him murder her, they unanimously recommended him to mercy on the grounds of provocation, of which there was not a tittle, either in evidence or in truth. Such is the modern aversion to capital punishment. His name was Thomas Templeton.'

In this case, Cockburn's distaste for the 'modern aversion', was shared, and Templeton did hang.

It was certainly a period of moral confusion, as the *Glasgow Chronicle* report shows:

'during the time of the execution, a practical proof of the efficacy of capital punishment, in improving the morals of the community, was exhibited in the police dragging some juvenile black-guards to the police office, for picking pockets in the crowd.'

Executioner; John Murdoch
Glasgow

1841

May 14th; **Dennis DOOLAN** Bishopbriggs
Patrick REDDING

Tried at Glasgow on 23rd April 1841, along with James Hickie, for the murder of John Green, a ganger on the building of the Edinburgh to Glasgow railway, Doolan and Redding entered the dock with a good deal of animation:

'The former nodded familiarly to his counsel, and looked around with a confidential air, a smile playing on his countenance. He was dressed in a coarse blue frock coat and moleskin trousers; Redding in a blue coat and light moleskin trousers; and Hickie had what is called a slop, a waistcoat with white sleeves made like the

sleeves of a shirt, over which he had a ragged plush vest.'

The indictment was read:

'... on the 10th day of December 1840, upon a wooden bridge at and over that portion of the line of the Edinburgh and Glasgow Railway ... at or near Crosshill, near Bishopbridge ... the prisoners did ... violently, wickedly, and feloniously attack and assault John Green, then a ganger or super-intendent over labourers ... with an iron poker, and with an iron bar or rod, or some other heavy and lethal weap-on, inflict several blows upon the head and other parts of the body of the said John Green, and did fell him to the ground, and did repeatedly jump upon and kick him while he was lying on the ground ... and he was mortally injured, and reduced to a state of insensibility, and soon there-after died, and was thus murdered by the said prisoners, or one or more of them.'

Doolan and Redding said simply, 'Not Guilty, my Lord.', while Hickey replied, 'Not guilty of bating him', and the trial proceeded, 'in a court crowded to suffocation'.

Green had taken charge of Doolan and Redding's gang on 8th December, and next day sacked Doolan. In their lodgings that night Doolan had said, 'I'll leave him (Green) so that he will not sack any body again'.

All three were found guilty and condemned; Doolan and Redding unanimously, but Hickie, not as an actor, but art and part. He was later reprieved.

Condemning them, Lord Moncrieff proposed that the execution:

'... for an example to the country, should take place at or near to such place adjoining Crosshill, in the parish of Cadder, and county of Lanark, as the Sheriff of said county shall ad-judge'.

The scaffold was knocked together in front of the jail the previous evening, and taken out to Bishop-briggs by Stockwell Street, Glassford Street, Ingram Street, North Albion Street, George's Street and High Street. Its lumbering progress became an object of interest and attraction, and by the time it came to the head of High Street, there was a moving mass accompanying it.

At exactly 8.00am next morning, the chained culprits, decently dressed in black, were placed in a former parcel van, which took its place in the procession:

Cavalry - a body of the 1st Dragoons
City Marshall
Cavalry
Sheriff Allison
Culprits
Strong Guard of Cavalry
Executioner
Magistrates of the City

From leaving the Jail, neither lifted his head, until their arrival at the scaffold, when Doolan gave one glance towards it - then reverted to his former posture.

The scaffold was erected in a large field, long since lost, overlooking the bridge on which the murder was committed. They mounted it with the greatest composure.

On being thrown off, Doolan struggled with dreadful violence, but Redding appeared to die instantaneously.

Murdoch later spoke of difficulty in adjusting Doolan's rope. On account of it being too stiff, the noose had not caught him in the proper place, which accounted for his violent struggle. However, he observed, 'The other rope came down kindly enough'. He was paid £24 for his work.

The purpose of having the execution at Crosshill failed for, due to a boycott, very few, if any, of the railway navvies were in the 50,000 crowd.

The authorities, however, had been well prepared. In addition to an unspecified number of police, there were 500 of the 58th Regiment of Foot, a detachment of the 1st Royal Dragoons, and a body of the 4th Royal Dragoons from Edinburgh ... and three pieces of artillery.

Whilst Green was interred in the Old Aisle cemetery at Kirkintilloch, Doolan and Redding were buried within the precincts of the South Prison.

Executioner; John Murdoch
Glasgow

1843

May 18th;   **Charles MACKAY**   Glasgow
Condemned for murdering his wife, Catherine McKechnie, in their house in Old Wynd, Glasgow on 18th December 1842, by punching and kicking,

and finally stabbing her in the femoral artery with a knife. Both were addicted to drink - both possessed violent tempers.

Lord Cockburn, the trial judge, writes of Mackay:

> '... a brute, who after fatiguing by beating his half-drunk wife, at last sharpened a knife on the hearthstone, and stabbed her, all because she would not give him breakfast, which his blows made her incapable of doing ... . She was an intolerable wife, in-somuch that he had often said that "one of us would certainly swing for the other". This scene occurred on a Sunday; a day sacred, with part of our population, to whisky and brutality.'

Written at his dictation, Mackay left the following letter:

> 'Condemned Cell, South Prison,
> 'Glasgow, 17th May, 1843.
> 'My Lord, - Believing that some explanation of the circumstances which led to the commission of the awful crime for which I have been condemned to suffer death is necessary, the more especially as I do not intend to speak upon the scaffold, I take the liberty of addressing you for that purpose.
> 'I was born in Bridgegate Street of Glasgow in October, 1817. My parents, one of whom (my father) is still alive, were very poor people. Unfortunately for me, they either wanted the means or the inclination to give me any education. My mother died when I was very young. I learned the alphabet when about twelve years of age, through the kindness of a companion, who took me with him to school, but having continued only about a week, I got no further. When committed to prison I could neither read nor write.
> 'I was eighteen years when I became first acquainted with my late wife. We lived together nearly six years before being married. When sober, we never quarrelled, it was always under the influence of drink we fell out. I always entertained a sincere regard for my wife ....'

Executioner; John Murdoch
Glasgow

1843

October 4th;   **Allan MAIR**   Stirling

Condemned for murdering his 85-year-old reputed wife in their home at Candie End, Muiravonside, 84-year-old Mair was the oldest person executed in Scotland.

Bent with age and suffering, he was carried onto the scaffold - 'his whole appearance indicating the utmost degree of human frailty, borne down with the intense idea of grief, struggling to bear up against what he considered the greatest injustice'.

His address to the crowd was unprecedented in its venom, as he harangued minister, Sheriff, Fiscal and witnesses:

> 'The meenister o' the paarish invented lees against me. Folks, yin an' a, mind I'm nae murderer. I ne'er committed murder, and I say as a dyin' man who is about to pass into the presence o' his Goad. I was condemned by the lees o' the meenister, by the injustice of the Sheriff and Fiscal, and perjury of the winesses. I trust for their conduct that a' thae parties shall be overta'en by the vengeance of Goad, and sent into everlasting damnation. I curse them with the curses in the Hunner an' Ninth Psalm - "Set thou a wicked man o'er them" - an haud on thee, hangman, till I'm dune - "An' let Satan stand at their richt haun. Let their days be few, let their children be faitherless, let their weans be continually vagabonds'; and I curse them a ...'

But Murdoch had heard enough and drew the bolt.

Executioner; John Murdoch
Glasgow

1844

April 3rd;   **James BRYCE**   Edinburgh

On the evening of 26th December 1843 Bryce called on his brother-in-law, John Geddes, at Blaw Wearie, West Calder seeking money to pay for a son's wedding - telling him one of his children was dead and he had no means to bury it.

When Geddes refused him money, '... he had just put the pot on the fire, and was turning round, when it came into my heart to murder him'. After killing him with fire tongs, Bryce took six pounds in silver and two bad half crowns from a chest and ran from the house.

The morning of his execution was wet and uncomfortable for the 30,000 who watched his decently dressed figure mount the scaffold and drop into eternity.

Executioner; John Murdoch
Glasgow

1847

October 5th;   **Thomas LEITH**   Dundee

Executed on an elevated platform outside the jail in Bell Street for the murder of his wife, Leith, a former Primitive Methodist and abstainer, had been a successful tradesman in the city.

Executioner; Unknown

1848

May 19th;   **James ROBERTSON**   Forfar

Following Robertson's conviction at Perth Spring Court for murdering his illegitimate child, Lord Cockburn wrote in his diary:

> 'Perth, Sunday Night, 23rd April 1848. - Getting on slowly, and dull, commonplace work. The audience was relieved yesterday by a murder. But it was a poor one. An infant suffocated in its clothes by its natural father. He was condemned, but won't be hanged.'

A petition from the town of Brechin, seeking a reprieve, brought the following response from London:

> Whitehall
> May 15, 1848.
>
> Sir,
> Secretary Sir George Grey having had under consideration the memorial which you transmitted in behalf of James Robertson, who was convicted of murder at the Perth Circuit Court, holden in April last, and sentenced to death, I am directed to aquaint you, that he has given the most careful consideration to this case, and that he has personally communicated on the subject with Lord Cockburn who

presided at the trial; but he deeply regrets that he has been unable to discover any sufficient ground on which to recommend the prisoner to the mercy of the Crown; and it does not appear to Sir George Grey that he could do so, without encouraging the expectation the deliberate murder of a child by its own father was not to be capitally punished.

I am &c.

Denis Le Marchant

Executioner; Unknown

October 26th;   **James McWHEELAN**   Ayr

After murdering sixteen-year-old James Young on the Old Rome Road, south of Kilmarnock, in the early hours of Saturday 27th May 1848, McWheelan made for Beith, where he pawned the boy's watch for 25s.

Before nightfall he was in Paisley Jail for robbing Lochwinnoch tollhouse, when the police investigation tied him to the pawned watch and the murder in Ayrshire.

Condemned at Ayr in September, the prison authorities found him ungovernable - incessantly battering his cell door and roaring like a maniac. Although heedless to religious instruction, he would argue that like Cain he should be released with a mark on his forehead.

The scaffold by the prison's west wall was only just ready as the magistrates entered the prison at 7.15am, to find 32-year-old McWheelan in the care of a Reformed Presbyterian minister. He had accepted religion in his final two days.

At 8.15am the burgh officers, bearing halberds, led the procession out to the platform and McWheelan was placed on the drop. 'In height he would be about five foot ten inches tall; his forehead was ample and white and crowned with jet black hair; bushy whickers; an Italian like complexion and visage; and large lambent eyes'.

His prayer, 'O Lord, do not let my guilty soul die in sin, O Lord take me to thyself', audible to those near the scaffold, was repeated again and again and again. Five, ten, fifteen minutes passed, but still he held the signal napkin.

As the crowd grew restless, Provost Miller's perplexity grew. He had little experience of executions, let alone one where the culprit was so reluctant to go. After a further fifteen minutes he gave the command, 'Do your duty executioner!', which brought the instant crash of the drop.

Later that day McWheelan was buried within the prison.

In 1813 the *Ayr Advertiser* reported James Merry's execution in six lines - McWheelan commanded as many pages, including 'poetry':

> 'Twas on Kilmarnock Fast and Glasgow Fair,
> Was the day McWheelan was hanged at Ayr'.

THE MURDERER
> 'Today I've seen a murderer - Start not
> With fear and loathing at that dreadful name,
> Nor call to your mind's eye grim images
> Of direst horror ... '

and so on for 79 lines.

Executioner; James Murdoch

Glasgow

1849

May 22nd;   **James BURNETT**   Aberdeen

A 44-year-old farm servant from Tyrie parish in Aberdeenshire, condemned for murdering Margaret Murray or Burnett, his wife of 26 years, by arsenic poisoning. Several years older than him, she was confined to bed, paralysed on one side following a stroke.

His execution, 'accomplished with fewer revolting features than is usual', was attended by a crowd of 12,000, who assailed the hangman with cries of execration.

Executioner; Unknown

May 29th;   **John KELLOCHER**   Perth

Indicted at Perth for the murder of Janet Anderson in her cottage at Buttergask, Dunblane, the previous November.

Although he had not visited her for some time, the impecunious Kellocher knew from the days when he lodged with her, that Old Janet had money in the house. He would call on her.

Her warm welcome unnerved him, and after an hour, he left. 'But the devil again entered my heart', and returning, picked the axe from its place by the door, and struck her twice on the head. He then stole £12 15s from the house.

Standing erect and defiant whilst sentence was pronounced, he afterwards poured a volley of the grossest abuse upon the court - calling the judges, 'nasty beasts' - 'and much more of a greatly worse complexion'.

His execution outside Perth Prison passed without event. He was 27 years old.

Executioner; John Murdoch
Glasgow

October 16th; **James ROBB**   Aberdeen

In a trial conducted behind closed doors, 22-year-old Robb was accused of murdering and raping 63-year-old Mary Smith, in her cottage at Redhill, Auchterless.

Robb, a country labourer and known criminal, had left Badenscoth Fair the worse of drink, avowing to gratify his passion on somebody before he slept. Mary Smith's cottage lay on his homeward path. Refused entry, he climbed to the roof and came down the chimney - the soot on his clothing and a button torn from his jacket, helped convict him. Miss Smith died of heart failure.

Executioner; William Calcraft
London

October 25th;   **Thomas WILSON**   Jedburgh

It was 7.15am on a dull and rainy morning as the 200 strong, baton-armed Burgh Guard, mustered by the town drummer, marched to the open ground fronting Jedburgh Castle. As they formed a cordon, a black flag fluttered on the castle flagstaff and a death bell tolled.

At 8.00am the Provost, magistrates and the prison governor led Wilson out from jail to the scaffold and ascended the platform.

The previous July at St Boswell's Fair Day in Kelso, whilst navvies were attempting to rescue a prisoner from police custody, a shepherd named William Lauder was beaten to death. The resulting riot was finally quelled by the 2nd Dragoons from Piershill.

Thomas Wilson and John Brady were apprehended and condemned for the murder at Jedburgh Circuit Court.

On the platform he reiterated his innocence, claiming to have been mistaken for another man.

Murdoch tottered up to the scaffold on his stick, and pulling the rope from his pocket, fastened it to the beam and adjusted it around Wilson's neck.

He next put the signal handkerchief in Wilson's hand - which he instantly dropped - and moved to the trigger. Only after the drop fell was the cap drawn over the face.

The body was cut down at nine o'clock, when it fell like the carcase of a sheep, into the arms of attendants below the scaffold.

The *Kelso Chronicle* reports that Brady, who was still under respite and only later reprieved, was much affected, as he and some other of the rioters carried Wilson's corpse back into the jail. The crowd of 3,000 dispersed without trouble, and Murdoch left with his £20 fee.

The *Chronicle* also reported; 'There were several parties from Hawick, but, as they richly deserved, they were all mostly too late.'

Executioner; John Murdoch
Glasgow

1850

January 31st;   **Margaret LENNOX or HAMILTON**   Glasgow

At Glasgow's first execution in seven years, Margaret Hamilton was hanged for the murder of Jane Hamilton with arsenic on the night of 7th June 1849, in the deceased's home in Kirk Street, Strathaven.

She was also found guilty of stealing a bank receipt from the house and cashing it by forging the deceased's signature.

Executioner; John Murdoch
Glasgow

August 16th;   **William BENNISON**   Edinburgh

A native of Portadown, 33-year-old Bennison was accused first of bigamy, having on 5th November 1838, at Tavanagh, near Portadown, married Mary Mulling, and while she was alive, on 5th December 1839 entered into a matrimonial connection with Jean Hamilton (now deceased), who resided in Storey Street, Paisley; and, secondly, of murder, having on the 12th or 13th days of April last, within the house in Stead's Place, Leith Walk, near Edinburgh, wilfully, wickedly, and feloniously, and with intent to murder, mixed with some porridge, or oatmeal, a quantity of arsenic; and his wife, Jean Hamilton, having partaken of the same, did immediately become ill, and, after lingering in a state of great suffering, died about the second or third day thereafter.

Suspicion fell on Bennison when a neighbour's dog died after eating what Jean had left of the porridge.

After hearing 15 of the 66 Crown witnesses, the jury took only 20 minutes to reach its unanimous verdict.

For Edinburgh's first execution in six years, the very roofs held some of the 20,000 spectators. Bennison appeared in the procession wearing a frock coat, coloured vest and white neckcloth - and an expression of coolness and serenity, which did not forsake him.

On the platform, Murdoch was reprimanded by a bailie for his unnecessarily harsh treatment of Bennison - but things went speedily, and with the words, 'The Lord Jesus have mercy on my soul', the drop fell at 8.20am.

At 9.20am the body was in a coffin for burial in Calton Jail and by 10.30am the scaffold was removed, although groups congregated around the spot for most of the day.

Lack of public sympathy for Bennison was reflected in the support for a commutation petition. Of 160 men employed at Shotts' Iron Foundry, where he had worked, only 23 signed.

The Scots Black Kalendar quotes the following street ballad:

'Great was the throng to see him hung
For crimes that were so vile.
To Edinburgh upon that day
They tramped for many a mile.
They led him out all clad in black -
Black coat and vest so white -
A mocking smile was on his lips,
He wore a nosegay bright.'

Executioner; John Murdoch
Glasgow

1851

October 24th;   **Archibald HARE**   Glasgow

T M Tod in *The Scots Black Kalendar* states, 'Hare was believed to be a nephew of William Hare, of the Burke and Hare atrocities', whilst contemporary newspapers say of him, 'The particulars that can be relied on ... are very brief, and present no features of interest'.

Even after conviction, for mortally stabbing Ronald McGregor during a drunken brawl in Blantyre's Main Street in August, 25-year-old Hare displayed courage and self possession. He ate heartily and with relish, and enjoyed undisturbed sleep.

When thrown off, a low suppressed cry rose from the 10,000 strong crowd, which soon afterwards dispersed peaceably.

Executioner; John Murdoch
Glasgow

1852

July 5th;   **Michael SCANLANE**
                   Peter SCANLANE   Cupar

Leaving their mother in Banbridge Workhouse, County Mayo, 25-year-old Michael and 22-year-old Peter, had come to Scotland and found work at Hilton of Forthar Lime Works in Fife.

On the night of Saturday 15th February 1852, with an accomplice Thomas McManus, they broke into the home of 66-year-old Margaret Maxwell at Hilton, and murdered her for a pittance of money and a few trinkets.

Condemned at Edinburgh on 14th June, they were returned to Cupar to wait out their final three weeks. The scaffold, too, came from Edinburgh.

Twenty two years had elapsed since Cupar's last execution, and that fact coupled with the prospect of seeing two brothers hanged drew a crowd of 10,000.

As Fluthers Green lay some 600 yards from the prison, an omnibus was hired to convey them, along with Calcraft and the officials.

On arrival, 'Both brothers leaped quickly out of the van, which was close to the scaffold, and running as fast as possible up the stairs, at once took their places on the drop facing each other, with the utmost composure and firmness ...'.

The *Fifeshire Journal* reports the silence being rent by the cry, 'Oh! Mike! Mike!', and Michael Scanlane's response, 'Oh, there's Margaret!', as the drop fell.

Fears of an attempt to rescue the brothers dissolved in a thunderstorm, and after hanging an hour their bodies were taken back to the prison for burial.

Executioner; William Calcraft
London

1853

January 13th;   **George CHRISTIE**   Aberdeen

Hanged for the brutal murder of Barbara Ross, an elderly cow-feeder and her 5-year-old grandson, with an axe, in her cottage at Sunnybank near Kittybrewster Toll Bar on the outskirts of Aberdeen, on the evening of 4th October 1852.

Knowing the old lady to have sold two of her pigs, the impecunious Christie left with the money and a few trinkets. When arrested that night he had 14s 6d in his pocket. The house resembled a slaughterhouse.

His defence counsel offered no evidence, and the Edinburgh jury unanimously found him guilty.

Although considerably emaciated, he walked to the scaffold with a firm step and mounted the platform unassisted; 'Do you have anything to say?'. 'No, nothing'. 'Are you ready?' 'Yes, quite ready'.

He was laid to rest beside Burnett and Robb.

Executioner; William Calcraft
London

March 14th; **John WILLIAMS** Greenlaw

A 27-year-old American, whose shipwright father had left Dundee for Boston in the 1820s, Williams led a short nomadic life. Starting at an early age; he worked on the Newfoundland cod fishers; sailed with a Baltimore slaver; served on the *Pennsylvania*, then the largest ship in the American Navy; and deserted a merchantman at Greenock about 1847. In Northumberland he picked a precarious living between the herring seasons before settling at Wislaw Mill in Berwickshire as a manservant.

His way to the scaffold was by Cleekbimin Toll Bar after robbing and murdering the toll-keeper Andrew Mather, the previous December.

The *Kelso Chronicle* of 14th March 1853 describes the morning of his execution:

'From an early hour numbers of people ... were seen wending their way to the scene of death, notwithstanding the threatening appearance of the atmosphere. A heavy leaden mist lay motionless over the cold and dreary moors, and the snow, stretching in long lines on the surrounding heights, looked like white fringes to a funeral pall.

'Shortly after 11 the rain fell fast, and the crowd, about 800, sought shelter in the commodious stables and coach-house of the Castle Inn, full in front of the drop.'

'Held in a small room in the County Hall from 6.00am until a quarter to twelve when the Sheriff Substitute, Procurator Fiscal and clergy had assembled, Williams was brought in. The clank of his chains as they struck every step in the vestibule, announced his approach.

'By 11.55am, still dressed in prison garb of coarse flannel jacket, vest and trousers, he was on the platform with the rope on his neck and the cap on his head.'

'The handkerchief dropped from his hand and at the doleful sound of the bolt he shivered and passed from this world.'

Executioner; William Calcraft
London

August 11th; **Hans Smith McFARLANE**
Helen BLACKWOOD Glasgow

On the morning Thursday 21st July 1853, McFarlane and Blackwood, with Mary Hamilton and Ann Marshall or Young were placed at the bar of the High Court in Edinburgh charged with murder.

'... On 12th June 1853, within the house in Croiley's Land, New Vennel, Glasgow, occupied by McFarlane and Blackwood, by administering to the now deceased Alexander Boyd, ship-carpenter, a quantity of whisky, mixed with snuff, or other deleterious substance, and assaulting him with a chamber pot, whereby he was knocked down, and after being stripped and robbed was thrown out of the window, 23 feet high, and killed.'

The principal prosecution witnesses were 11-year-old William Shillinglaw and his 9-year-old brother, James, pupils of the Ragged School, but their presence in the house required explanation. Following the death of their father, their mother married Hans McFarlane's father, by whom she had a child, which had died the week before. She was now homeless, 'necessitating her poor boys to seek refuge at night under the bed of their desperate relative Blackwood'. The brothers witnessed the unfolding tragedy from under the bed, quite unnoticed by the company.

The four accused, the deceased and a fellow ship-carpenter, James Law, had been, 'on the spree' and returned to McFarlane's house, where Law immediately fell asleep.

Whisky was produced and Boyd was given a cupful to which snuff had been added. He drank it down, and collapsed gasping, appearing to get sick and 'stupid-like'. Rising, he lunged at Blackwood, who struck him with a water-pot, and he fell back his full length, striking his head on a stone foot stool. The stone, weighing about 2 cwts, was produced in court.

Stripped of his clothing he was dropped out of the window, whilst Ann Marshall stood wringing her hands and wailing, 'Oh, ma man's deid - ma man's deid; he went tae the windae an' fell o'er it'. The company then left the house, leaving Law, who was still asleep across the fireplace.

Following the evidence and summaries, the jury returned their verdicts in 20 minutes; McFarlane and Blackwood guilty as libelled; Marshall also guilty, but recommended to mercy; and Marshall not proven.

On a hazy August morning, 25-year-old McFarlane from Partick, and 30-year-old Blackwood from Gorbals, paid for their crime before a crowd of 40,000

The last press mention of the case concerned James Law:

> THE LATE NEW VENNEL TRAGEDY. - The man who, in a state of intoxication and insensibility, lay on the floor while his companion was thrown over the window and murdered, and for which the perpetrators were executed recently in Glasgow, after having gone abroad, has since died. It is said that he was so much affronted at his exposure that he would not face any of his companions. He was a carpenter to trade, and wrought some time in the building yard of Messrs Robert Steele & Co., Greenock.
>
> *The Glasgow Examiner.*

Executioner; William Calcraft
London

1854

January 25th;   **William CUMMING**   Edinburgh

Executed for the murder of his wife at Leith, the previous October, Cumming displayed a calmness and composure approaching bravado.

Addressing the crowd of 10,000, half the number which turned out for Bennison four years earlier, he repeated his innocence - his wife had fallen down the stairs whilst drunk, and he had asked a neighbour to help carry her into the house. His affections for her were unbounded. He had walked no fewer than six times from Glasgow to Edinburgh to see her - once from Bristol to London - and from London to Leith, which took him fourteen days.

The crowd responded with cheers, hootings and cries of 'Shame!'

Calcraft then adjusted the rope, but on placing the white cap on culprit's head, Cumming raised it, to uncover his eyes as the bolt was drawn.

Executioner; William Calcraft
London

May 11th;   **Alexander CUNNINGHAM**   Ayr

Hanged for murdering his wife, Janet McCulloch, by shooting her with a fowling piece through the window of the cottage where she worked as a weaver in Piedmont Street, Girvan, on the evening of Thursday 22nd December 1853.

Executioner; William Calcraft
London

1855

May 23rd;   **Alexander STEWART**   Glasgow

Seventeen-year-old Stewart, or 'Collier Stewart' as he was known, was a loafer, drunkard and inveterate thief:

> 'He appears to have been altogether uneducated; was idle, loose, dull and morose ...'

On Sunday 26th November 1854 he was in No. 1 Clayband Pit bothy at Maryhill coal pits with a number of cronies, begging tobacco from the old watchman John Welsh. As the others left they warned Old Welsh to be careful - it was the last they would see him. Two hours later he was found dying from head wounds inflicted with a pick axe.

Twenty thousand turned out for his execution, or stopped on their way to work, but the public interest in either him or his fate was such, that few lingered after the drop fell.

Executioner; William Calcraft
London

1857

February 2nd;   **Peter McLEAN**   Linlithgow

Executed on a raw and hazy morning in front of the County Buildings for the murder of Thomas Maxwell on the Whitburn road between Bathgate and Durhamtown, the previous mid-November.

Led out a few minutes before 8.00am, he addressed the three or four thousand spectators; 'Good people, take warning by me. Avoid evil company and drink, and keep the Sabbath'. One of the last gallows

Calcraft's letter, accepting the execution of Alexander Cunningham   (*Ayr Carnegie Library*)

speeches, it would have been recognised by spectators back through the centuries.

Executioner; William Calcraft
London

October 21st;   **John BOOTH**   Aberdeen

A crowd of 1,800, 'composed mainly of the lower classes', assembled to witness Aberdeen's last execution for 106 years as Booth mounted the scaffold in Castle Street. The 37-year-old tinker was paying for the frenzied murder of his mother-in-law at Oldmeldrum on 21st July.

Drinking cronies had alluded to his wife's unfaithfulness, on which, when he returned home, he challenged her. Denials increased his exasperation to the point where, taking up a large hunting knife, he lunged at her, cutting her arm.

She ran to her parents' home followed by Booth, who arrived to find her mother on the street calling out, 'Murder! Murder!' Falling upon her with the knife, he stabbed her six or seven times before striking the heart. She died instantly.

Executioner; William Calcraft
London

1858

January 14th;   **John THOMSON**   Paisley

Billed as, 'A Match For Miss Smith's Case', Thomson's trial came five months later at Glasgow, in December 1857.

(Madeleine Hamilton Smith was tried at Edinburgh in July 1857 for the murder of her erstwhile lover, Pierre Emile L'Angelier. The jury's verdict on the three charges of poisoning were: not guilty; not proven; not proven)

The indictment served on Thomson set forth:

'First, that the accused, John Thomson, alias Peter Walker, did, on 13th September 1857, in a house at Eaglesham, administer prussic acid, in beer, to a woman named Agnes Montgomery, a reeler in the Eaglesham Mill, in consequence whereof she soon died, and was thus wilfully murdered by the pannel, and, Second, that the accused did, on the 25th or 26th September 1857,

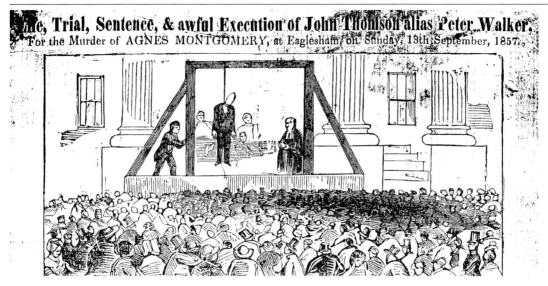

Life, Trial, Sentence, & awful Execution of John Thomson alias Peter Walker,
For the Murder of AGNES MONTGOMERY, at Eaglesham, on Sunday, 13th September, 1857.

Woodcut from Thomson's Execution Broadside   (*Paisley Library*)

administer prussic acid, in whisky, to Archibald Mason, and his wife Agnes Stenhouse or Mason, with intent to murder them, in consequence whereof they suffered grievous bodily harm, and their lives were endangered.

There were 50 productions and 91 witnesses. The Smith trial had 214 productions and 65 witnesses. But unlike the Smith trial, the jury, after a 20 minute absence, brought in a guilty verdict.

Whilst the Clerk of the Court was writing out the sentence, a band of music was heard most incongruously playing, 'Will ye no come back again?', outside the building.

Before passing sentence, the Lord Justice Clerk, his voice choking with emotion and tears running down his cheeks, impressed upon Thomson that, '... he had now walked to the foot of the scaffold - and the fearful consequences of meeting the Great Judge with an impenitent heart'.

Twenty thousand turned out on a cold and stormy morning for his execution, which was carried through without difficulty until Calcraft's manner of taking down the body drew shouts of deprecation.

Executioner; William Calcraft
London

1861

January 18th;   **Patrick LUNNAY**   Dumbarton

Executed at the County Buildings, for murdering James Cassidy, a fellow Irishman, in their lodgings at Bank Street, Alexandria, on 10th October 1860, following an argument.

Convicted at Glasgow, he appeared on the scaffold, before a crowd of 2,000, ' ... not of the earth, but rather like a pale bloodless inhabitant of the grave, revisiting once more the glimpses of a wintry morn'.

Executioner; William Calcraft
London

1862

April 29th;   **Mary REID or TIMNEY**
Dumfries

Convicted of the cold murder of 40-year-old spinster Ann Hannah at Carsphad Farm, 5 miles north of New Galloway, in the picturesque Glenkens Valley, Kirkcudbrightshire, on the morning of Monday 13th January 1862.

Timney, who lived with her husband and children

in an adjacent cottage, had sworn to take her victim's life following a quarrel the previous month. Hannah had refused to lend her money, or allow her to gather firewood from the farm.

Seen coming from the farmhouse with a blood-stained mallet, her bloodstained clothing was later found in the rafters of her cottage.

Reports of her execution reflect a change in press coverage. No longer moralistic sermons, they chronicle the full horror of the event.

After learning there would be no reprieve, her strength diminished as her hysteria increased, and she ate little or nothing. The *Glasgow Herald* reporter wrote:

> 'While we were in prison, with the Provost and Magistrates, when the death warrant was being formally handed over, about twenty minutes before the hour - eight o'clock - fixed for the execution, we heard the loud and prolonged moanings of the wretched being resounding through the building, telling of the extremity of her misery'.

The wailing continued as she came to the steps of the scaffold, 'Oh, my puir weans! my weans! my puir weans!'

On the drop, there was one last scream as she felt the platform jerk and fall from her feet. Incapable of giving the signal, the decision was taken for her.

The crowd of 2,500 soon after dispersed and in mid-afternoon she was interred within the prison.

The Hannah's farm was lost under the waters of Carsphad Loch, formed by the building of a hydroelectric dam.

Executioner; William Calcraft
London

1864

May 16th;   **John RILEY**   Glasgow

'A fairer morning the eye of a condemned criminal never looked upon', reported the *Daily Mail* on Riley's execution:

> 'The first comers, who congregated at dawn, were obviously those whose use and wont it was to merge night into morning - dissolute women, thieves attendant, partly on business and partly, one might say, on pleasure,

and these with their like formed for a while a distinctive element in the crowd. By seven, however, many of a better class, drawn thither by a prevalent morbid curiosity, had swollen the mass'.

'Looking across the square, the eyes beheld a multitudinous array of white faces, with gaze upturned towards the gallows, and stretching away into the Green. Women, girls of tender years, lads, from the mere infant upwards, rowdy-looking young men, labourers, mechanics, with breakfast can in hands, arrested seemingly, on their way to work, and we can also add, respectabilities old and young, whose presence at such a scene could scarcely have been anticipated, formed the motley crowd.'

The centre of focus for the 30,000 strong crowd was 'Sodger' Riley due on the scaffold at 8.00am for murdering and robbing 57-year-old Mrs Laffy of Legbrannock, near Bothwell, the previous December.

At 3.00am work had started on the scaffold, which for the first time in Glasgow was curtained by a 3'6" black cloth screen, to prevent the public witnessing the death struggles - a recent innovation at London and Liverpool.

Minutes after 8 o'clock Riley, with the officials and Calcraft in train, came onto the platform. Three minutes of prayer - the signal - and the drop fell - two feet. The customary Calcraft 'short drop' left Riley to struggle for nine minutes.

At three o'clock that afternoon he was at rest under the stones of the South Prison courtyard.

Executioner; William Calcraft
London

June 21st;   **George BRYCE**   Edinburgh

Hanged at the head of Libberton Brae for murdering Jane Seton, a 23-year-old nursery maid to a family near Ratho, whom Bryce believed responsible for a maidservant in the same household jilting him. After stalking her for a fortnight, 30-year-old Bryce rushed into her employer's house and cut her throat with a razor.

Although praised by the press for his manner in dispatching Bryce, Askern's use of the short drop left Bryce to struggle for several minutes.

Bryce is said to have been an uncle to James Bryce, executed at Edinburgh on 3rd April 1844 for murdering a brother-in-law.

Jane Seton was the first burial at the newly opened cemetery in her native North Queensferry:

Jane Seton, 23
I know, O Lord, that thy judgments
are right. Into thine hands I commit
my spirit. Thou hast redeemed me,
O Lord, God of Truth. - Psalm XXXI,
verse 5.

Erected by the children to whom she was a
nurse,
as a mark of love.

The headstone is no longer extant, and the inscription is taken from *The Scots Black Kalendar*.
Executioner; James Askern
Maltby

1865

July 28th;   **Edward William PRITCHARD**
Glasgow

Of Glasgow's three causes célèbres of the nineteenth century; Madeleine Smith, Jessie McLachlan and Edward William Pritchard, only Dr Pritchard came to the scaffold, for Glasgow's final public execution.

At the conclusion of a four day trial at Edinburgh on 7th July, 40-year-old Pritchard was condemned on two charges of murder:

1) Between 10th and 25th February 1865, in the house at 249 Sauchiehall Street, Glasgow, administer to Jane Cowan or Taylor (his mother in law) tartarised antimony, aconite and opium, in food, resulting in her death on 25th February

2) Between 22nd December 1864 and 18th March 1865, in the same house, administer to his wife, Mary Jane Taylor or Pritchard, quantities of tartarised antimony and aconite, as a result of which she died on the latter date.

Dr Edward William Pritchard   (Mitchell Library, Glasgow)

Mrs Jane Pritchard   (Mitchell Library, Glasgow)

An anonymous letter to the Procurator-Fiscal at Glasgow, suggested both women died, 'under circumstances at least very suspicious', and Pritchard was arrested at Glasgow's Queen Street Railway Station on 20th March, after taking his wife's body to Edinburgh for burial the following week in the Grange Cemetery.

Pritchard sat up to a late hour on his final night, reading and writing, but was calm and composed when awakened at 5.30am.

Through the night, not only was the scaffold set up, but the west end of the Green cleared of showmen's booths - it was Fair Fortnight - and four sets of barricades erected.

At precisely 8.00am the magistrates took their seats in the court, and Pritchard was brought to the table at the foot of the bench. He was attired in deep mourning, wearing the clothes in which he had been apprehended. Asked if he had anything to say, he replied, 'I acknowledge the justice of the sentence', and bowed.

Mrs Jane Taylor (*Mitchell Library, Glasgow*)

So packed was the courtroom, that the procession to the scaffold broke into a shambles, and Pritchard was on the drop before everyone was out.

His appearance created a commotion - 'How well he looks!' 'He's very pale!' 'That's him!' and 'Hats off!'.

Calcraft adjusted the cap, and putting aside the long hair and beard, placed the rope and tied the legs - and at 8.10am the drop fell.

He suffered a good deal.

> '... as he shrugged his shoulders more than half a dozen times, his head shook, the whole body trembled and swung round and round; and it was only after Calcraft went below and pulled the legs that it was brought to stillness.'

At 8.45am the body was taken down, but so carelessly that the bottom was knocked out of the plain pauper coffin, which then had to be repaired. At 1.00pm he was laid to rest in the jail yard beside John Riley.

With the renovation of the Justiciary Buildings in 1910, the bodies interred in the jail were exhumed for burial elsewhere. In reality their remains were gathered in a herring box borrowed from the adjacent fish market. Pritchard's body was well-preserved, and a report on the condition of his skull was published in *Glasgow Medical Journal* of 1912.

His elastic sided boots, which were also in good condition, were stolen.

Executioner; William Calcraft
London

1866

January 31st;   **Andrew BROWN**   Montrose

When brought to trial at Edinburgh for the murder of John Greig, on the schooner *Nymph*, off the Forfarshire coast on 6th September 1865, 25-year-old Brown's defence counsel tendered a plea of insanity. It was not accepted.

Heading for London with a cargo of flooring timber, the schooner had left Montrose earlier in the day, with Captain John Greig, Brown and two seamen named Pert and Rae. Hours out of Montrose and two and a half miles off the coast, Brown attacked the skipper with an axe, striking two fatal blows to the head. Pert saved Greig from a third blow, and his own life, by wresting the axe from Brown and pitching it overboard. When he later asked Brown what had come over him, the latter replied, 'Well, Jock, I'm going stark mad, out of my mind.'

Taking command of the vessel, Brown steered north for Stonehaven where his mother lived, and where he was later arrested.

Ignoring the question of insanity, the jury unanimously found him guilty, with a minority recommendation to mercy.

On his final day he penned the following letter:

> Forfar Prison
> Jany. the 30th, 1866.
> Before I leave this world I desire to acknowledge the justice of my sentence ... I ask the forgiveness of my captain's friends for the great loss and sorrow I have caused them. I never meant to say that I did it because I had a grudge at him, although I was tempted to say it. It came into my head all at once, like the shot of a gun; but it was no sooner done than I would have given all the world to have gotten him to live again, and I have sincerely grieved for him ever since. I wish to die in peace with all men. What I may have said about my shipmates at any time I ask their forgiveness, as I hope for pardon myself...'

He was held in Forfar Jail and brought by special train on the final morning for the first execution at Montrose since Shuttleworth in 1822. An orderly crowd of 3,500 gathered around the scaffold outside the police office in George Street, where he was held until the appointed hour.

Executioner; William Calcraft
London

May 22nd;   **Joseph BELL**   Perth

A noted poacher, Bell was executed for murdering Alexander McEwan, a baker's vanman, with a borrowed shotgun, the previous December on the road near Vicars Bridge, Blairingone, Perthshire, and robbing him of £5 10s.

Executioner; William Calcraft
London

1868

May 12th;   **Robert SMITH**   Dumfries

Despite the Capital Punishment Amendment Act being only 17 days from the statute book, the Magistrates of Dumfries were refused leave to execute Smith, 'The Cummertrees Murderer', in the privacy of Dumfries Jail.

On 1st February 1868, the 19-year-old labourer had ravished, murdered and robbed 9-year-old Thomasina Scott, daughter of John Scott, shoemaker and grocer at Burnside Cottage in Croftheads Plantation near Cummertrees. On her way to buy provisions for her mother, she had 9s 11d in her purse.

Realising that Mrs Jame Crichton of Longfords Cottage had seen him with the girl, he attempted to murder her.

Although a second choice, due to Calcraft being unable to attend, Askern from Maltby in Yorkshire proved equally competent.

This last public execution attracted little interest in the town, with only 500 or so spectators - mainly young lads, mill girls and labourers. Having shaken hands with the Magistrates, Smith mounted the scaffold, where the Yorkshireman at once pulled the cap over his face, placed the noose around his neck, and tied his feet with rope. Then, dissatisfied with the position of the rope, he took it off, worked it in his hands and replaced it before putting the signal into the culprit's hand.

The release of the bolt drew cries from girls in the crowd.

Executioner; Thomas Askern
Maltby

1870

October 4th;   **George CHALMERS**   Perth

Forty-five-year-old Chalmers' hanging, the first private execution in Scotland, followed his condemnation for murdering John Miller, keeper at Blackhill Toll Bar near Braco on 21st December 1869.

Miller was found in the ransacked house next morning with a crowbar by his shattered skull. Clothing, a watch and money had been stolen, and cast off clothing left by the murderer pointed to him being a vagrant. News that Chalmers had been released from Alloa Jail a day or two before, led to a hue and cry.

He evaded capture until May 1870, when he was

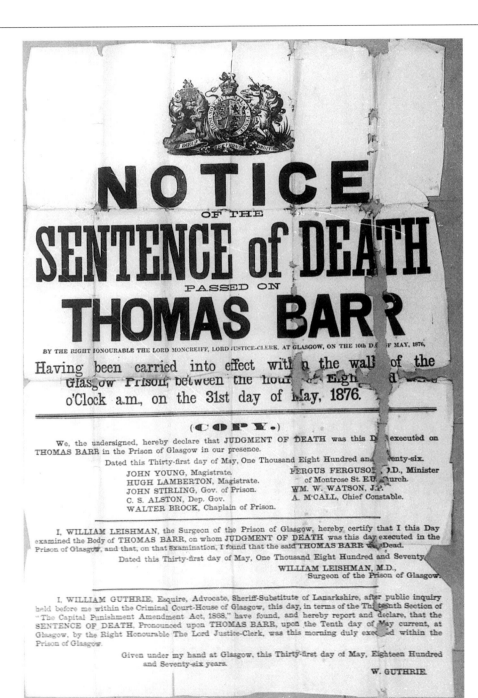

Notice of Sentence of Death — Thomas Barr   *(Ayr Carnegie Library)*

arrested in Dundee - still wearing some of Miller's clothing. He was found guilty by a majority of 13 to 2, and condemned.

Hanged within the old County Prison, his last utterance was, 'Farewell for evermore; thank God I am innocent'.

Executioner; William Calcraft
Middlesex

1875

October 5th; **Patrick DOCHERTY**   Glasgow
Condemned for murdering John Miller with a garden hoe during a brawl at Rutherglen Bridge the previous May.

Also on the court cause list, also condemned for murder was a man named Middleby who was later reprieved, albeit his murderous act had been more deliberately accomplished.

There was a belief that, due to a mix-up in the system of review for reprieve, 21-year-old Docherty was hanged in error.

Executioner; William Marwood
Horncastle

October 19th; **David WARDLAW**   Dumbarton
A 56-year-old shoemaker from Bonhill, Dunbarton-shire, Wardlaw ended thirty years of troubled marriage by murdering his wife, Mary Brown, with a hammer. Inebriated, he had no recollection of the crime.

A Poor Relief Application in September 1853, when he was 34, and living in Burn Street, Bonhill, reveals that he came from Fife around 1838. The eldest of their five children, 11-year-old David, was off work with a severe burn to his arm, and his wage of 2s 6d per week had been lost. Matters did not improve with the passing years - the public purse paid for the black suit he wore on the scaffold.

The jury added a recommendation of mercy to their verdict, but neither it, nor three petitions, saved him.

Erected by the prison's back wall, the Glasgow scaffold, built only two weeks earlier to hang Docherty, was a 50-yard walk from the condemned cell. For half this distance it was in Wardlaw's full view. He kept his eyes to the ground.

With his legs pinioned - and cap pulled down - the lever was pulled - and the drop fell with a loud grating sound.

Executioner; William Marwood
Horncastle

1876

May 31st;   **Thomas BARR**   Glasgow
In October 1874, as a 34-year-old widower with four young children, Barr married 22-year-old Margaret Sloan and set up home at Eastfield in Rutherglen. His suspicious and jealous nature made life difficult.

In February 1876 she returned to her mother's house in Glasgow's Gallowgate - for the last time. Hearing of her being in company with two male lodgers in the house, he called there on Wednesday 1st March, and when refused entry, forced his way in. He murdered both mother and daughter with a knife, and fled.

The search concentrated in Aberdeenshire where he had connections, and when the constable at Belhelvie, 12 miles east of Aberdeen, read Barr's description, and recalled him passing through the village, he tracked him to Ellon. Barr was soon on his way back to Glasgow and the constable on his way to part of the £100 reward.

In returning their verdict, the jury neither regarded his plea of insanity at the time of the crime, nor recommended him to mercy.

Executioner; William Marwood
Horncastle

1878

May 31st;   **Eugène Marie CHANTRELLE**
Edinburgh
Born at Nantes, France in 1834, Chantrelle studied medicine until the French Revolution of 1848 ruined his father's shipping business - and his hopes of a profession.

His communist sympathies led him to join the Republicans in the Parisian coup d'état of 1851, where he received a sabre wound to the arm, but the success of the Napoleonic Party forced him out of France.

After a period in America he came to Britain, settling in Edinburgh in 1866, where he hoped to finance the resumption of his medical studies by teaching. Besides French, he was fluent in German and proficient in Latin and Greek and his French text books were adopted in many schools.

At Newington Academy he met Elizabeth Cullen Dyer, then a fifteen-year-old student. When they married on 11th August 1868 she was seven months pregnant. The unhappy marriage ended with Elizabeth's death on 2nd January 1878 from opium poisoning.

Eugène Marie Chantrelle

Elizabeth Chantrelle

Having insured her life the previous year for £1,000 against accidental death, he fractured a gas pipe in her bedroom and gave her lemonade and pieces of orange laced with opium. The post mortem dissection was inconclusive, but traces of the poison were found in vomit on the bed clothes.

The four day High Court trial concluded with a unanimous verdict of guilty, which surprised no one but Chantrelle. He asked leave to address the court, and was well into a chemistry lesson on opium and morphia, before being stopped and instructed to have his counsel take the matter to the proper quarter.

His execution, on a genial summer morning, was the first in Edinburgh since George Bryce in 1864, and the first within Calton Prison. The thousands drawn to Calton Hill hoping to catch a glimpse of his walk to the gallows, were disappointed due to screening which had been erected.

At eight o'clock Marwood pinioned him, and the procession walked the 50 yards to the scaffold in an outhouse, where Chantrelle eyed the apparatus with interest, and took his place. The Lord's Prayer was interrupted by a click and Chantrelle disappeared from view. Marwood had given him a drop of eight feet.

Before burial, a plaster cast was taken of his head for the Phrenology Museum.

Executioner; William Marwood
Horncastle

October 3rd; **William McDONALD** Cupar
Although almost certainly mad, McDonald, a fisherman from St Andrews in Fife, was executed for murdering his wife, in what he claimed had been a pact to end their miserable lives. He turned the gun on himself, but survived.

Repeated appeals to the Home Secretary failed, and the sentence was carried out in the gardens of the old prison at Cupar.

Executioner; William Marwood
Horncastle

1883

May 23rd; **Henry MULLEN** Glasgow
Martin SCOTT

Both active poachers, Mullen and Scott were hanged for the murder by shooting of two game-keepers at Port Glasgow, on 3rd February 1883.

Coming directly from a double execution at Taunton, Marwood was on his last visit to Scotland before his death in September.

Executioner; William Marwood
Horncastle

1884

March 31st; **Robert Flockhart VICKERS**
William INNES Edinburgh

In the early hours of Saturday 15th December 1883 James Grosset, head gamekeeper on Lord Rosebery's estate by the Moorfoot Hills, Midlothian with two assistants, John Fortune and John McDiarmid, was out hunting poachers. The morning was frosty clear under a full moon.

About 3.00am the keepers came upon two armed men, who answered a call to surrender by shooting Fortune and McDiarmid. Grosset, lucky to escape, raised the alarm, and from his description, Vickers and Flockhart, two miners from the neighbouring village of Gorebridge were arrested. They were both noted poachers.

Removed to Edinburgh Royal Infirmary, Fortune died on the Tuesday following, and McDiarmid on 8th January 1884.

Following their condemnation at the High Court, Berry's application to execute them, was accepted by the city magistrates. It was his first in a long career.

In his book, *My Experiences as an Executioner*, Berry gives an account of the proceedings in Calton Jail that Monday morning:

'... At 7.45 the living group wended their way to the prison, and into the doctor's room, ready for the last scene of the drama. The prisoners were brought face to face for the first time since their conviction. They kissed each other; and the scene was a very painful one, to see mates going to meet their end on the gallows. ... I was called to do my duty. I was handed the warrant, which was made out by the judge who condemned them to die. I

then proceeded to pinion the prisoners, previously shaking hands, bidding goodbye to this world ... Both prisoners walked without assistance to place of execution; they was at once placed under the beam on the drop, where everything was done as quick as lightning, and both culprits paid the highest penalty of the law.'

Executioner; James Berry
Bradford

1889

March 11th; **Jessie KING** Edinburgh

A baby farmer in the Stockbridge area of Edinburgh, 27-year-old King was convicted of murdering two of the children in her care. Another charge was found not proven, and there may have been many more.

Expecting only a short term of imprisonment, she groaned and shrieked and finally collapsed when sentence was passed, and had to be carried from the courtroom.

The finding of a large pin and a length of rope in the condemned cell were suggestive that she contemplated suicide.

Born in the Anderson district of Glasgow, she was employed there as a mill worker, before moving to Edinburgh where she was a laundry worker at Causewayside.

She was the first woman to hang since Mary Timney in 1862.

Executioner; James Berry
Bradford

April 24th; **William Henry BURY** Dundee

'I'm Jack the Ripper, and if you go to my house you will find the body of my wife, which I've cut up and put in a box'.

The constable at Dundee police office may have been the first to hear such a claim, the final Ripper murder in London having been only three months earlier, but he was not the last. In the late 1970s, police were still getting messages which opened, 'I'm Jack ...'.

Whatever the veracity of 29-year-old Bury's opening claim, the mutilated remains of his wife, Ellen, were found in a packing case at 113 Princes Street, Dundee, and he was arrested.

Fabricating a letter from a prospective employer,

he brought her to the city to murder her for a £300 inheritance, telling friends they were going to Australia.

From the condemned cell he wrote to the Home Secretary, confessing to the Whitechapel murders. Although he had left London's East End shortly after the last 'Ripper' murder, that of Mary Jane Kelly in Miller's Court on 9th November 1888, no notice was taken of his confession.

Executioner; James Berry
Bradford

1890

September 23rd; **Henry DEVLIN**   Glasgow

Hanged for murdering his wife at Benhar, near Shotts, on 22nd June, the 45-year-old father of seven had to be carried the 90 yards from the condemned cell to the drop.

At the inquiry following the execution, Dr Sutherland, the prison-surgeon, stated that the spine had not been fractured, and death had been due to asphyxia.

Executioner; James Berry
Bradford

1892

January 11th;   **Frederick Thomas STOREY**
Greenock

When at Greenock with a travelling circus, Storey learned that his infatuation for Mrs Elizabeth Harmstone or Stewart, known professionally as Miss Pastor, was not reciprocated. His response was that of a vindictive man.

Purchasing a four-inch bladed sailor's knife, he accosted her on Argyle Street, Greenock, on the night of Saturday 14th November 1891, and stabbed her in the left breast.

As she ran shrieking across the street and into a shop, where she died, he walked away. Meeting an acquaintance he presented him with the knife and finished the night drinking. He was arrested some hours later.

He was executed outside the County Buildings and buried within the prison.

Executioner; James Berry
Bradford

1893

January 18th;   **William McKEOWN**   Glasgow

McKeown and a friend Thomas McNeilly spent the evening of Monday 10th October 1892 on a drinking spree in Glasgow, returning to the house, West Lodge in Maxwell Drive, Pollockshields, with 'a common woman of the town', Eliza Connor. The previous owner of the house, ex-Bailie Wilson of Glasgow, had recently died and McKeown was employed as resident caretaker.

All were drunk, and on reaching McKeown's room, McNeilly lay on one of two beds, 'to sleep off his debauch' - whilst McKeown and Connor occupied the other.

About six o'clock the following morning, the trio was aroused by the arrival of the gardener. He cooked his breakfast in the room, but on being told to come back at nine o'clock, he left. McNeilly then woke - realised he was late for work - and left.

Between then and nine o'clock when the gardener returned, Connor was killed, her body cut up, and buried in three separate holes in the garden. The gardener found blood in the courtyard and the room, but no sign of McKeown.

In the early afternoon he was seen crossing East Henderson Farm, between Glasgow and Paisley, by two gamekeepers who gave chase. They found McKeown with a severe laceration to his throat, and a scribbled note in his pocket, 'I am put to do this; may the Lord have mercy on my soul'.

He spent several weeks in hospital, but was fit to stand trial at Glasgow, with McNeilly, on 27th/28th December 1892. McNeilly was discharged, and despite tendering a plea of guilty to culpable homicide, McKeown was condemned.

He claimed to have struck the woman a fatal blow after she took his watch, and only afterwards dismembered her body. The prosecution claimed he murdered her by cutting her throat.

As the black flag appeared above wall of Duke Street Prison, a suppressed sigh passed over the immense multitude in Drygate.

One old Irish woman seemed to gloat over the tragic event, if one was to judge from her hearty ejaculation when she saw the black flag - 'The Divil an' all has got howld of him now.'

Executioner; James Billington
Farnworth

1897

June 7th;   **George PATERSON**   Glasgow

The Culprit — George Paterson

Condemned at the High Court in Edinburgh for the murder of Ann McGuire, his 27-year-old common law wife, on the night of Saturday 20th February 1897, in his house at 46 Milton Lane, Cowcaddens, Glasgow. He was aged 31.

Returning home the worse of drink and finding Annie to have taken 5s from his pocket (to pay the rent) he beat her with a red hot poker. There were 50 burns about her head and body. On the Tuesday he consented to her being seen by a doctor, who admitted her to the Royal Infirmary. Next morning she succumbed to peritonitis.

His defence counsel tendered a plea of temporary insanity, caused by the influence of drink on a mind weakened by sunstroke. He had spent six of his eight year army service in India.

The press described crime as:

> '... a tragedy as may at any time be the
> outcome of the terrible life that is lived
> in many squalid houses in our city ...'

He fully expected a reprieve, and there were circumstances in his favour: his exemplary army service; the jury returning a verdict of guilty to murder and not culpable homicide by a majority of one, and their recommendation to mercy; his efforts to save Annie's life after the assault; and it being the year of Queen Victoria's Diamond Jubilee.

When told it was not to be, he sat speechless, and almost collapsed.

Executioner; James Billington
Farnworth

1898

March 12th;   **John HERDMAN**   Edinburgh

Despite the support of a petition of 11,000 signatories, 52-year-old printer's machineman Herdman, was hanged for the murder of his common law wife, Jane Calder, in their house in Milne's Close, Edinburgh.

Sir Henry Littlejohn, the police surgeon, described her wounds, which Herdman inflicted by kicking and stabbing, as the worst he had seen.

Executioner; James Billington
Farnworth

1902

November 12th; **Patrick LEGGETT**   Glasgow

After fatally stabbing his wife, Sarah Jane, in the neck at 98 Wylie's Back Land, their home in Glasgow's Whiteinch, on Saturday 13th September 1902, Leggett attempted to drown himself in the River Clyde - but was rescued.

Condemned at Glasgow he was executed in the joiner's shop of Duke Street Prison.

Executioner; William Billington
Bolton

July 26th;   **Thomas GUNNING**   Glasgow

When handed over to the magistrates who would see through his execution for the drink-frenzied murder of his paramour, Agnes Allan, in their house in Green Street, Bridgeton, Glasgow, the previous April, he was asked simply, 'Are you Thomas Gunning?'. 'Yes', he replied.

Without further ceremony, he was walked through the canvas-covered passage to the scaffold in the joiner's shop.

Executioner; William Billington
Bolton

1905

November 14th; **Pasha LIFFEY**   Glasgow

A 20-year-old native of Mafeking, Basutoland, who toured the country with travelling shows, Liffey was convicted at Glasgow for the rape and murder of 64-year-old Mary Jane Welsh in Dykehead Road, Larkhall, the previous 11th August.

He was executed by Harry Pierrepoint, on his first visit to Scotland.

Executioner; Henry Albert Pierrepoint
Huddersfield

1908

March 5th;   **Joseph HUME**   Inverness

Condemned at Aberdeen for the murder of 48-year-old John Barclay Smith, a road contractor to Elgin County Council, in Smith's house at Lhanbryde, Morayshire, the previous September.

Smith was seen returning home with Hume, to whom he had given work and shelter, on the afternoon of Saturday 24th September. He was very drunk whilst Hume, a penniless 24-year-old army deserter from Fort George, was sober.

Once in the house Hume struck his benefactor repeatedly about the head with a roadman's hammer, and stole a gold watch and money.

In Edinburgh, with the money gone, an attempt to pawn the watch roused the broker's suspicions, and led to his arrest in Stirling.

This first capital sentence in the Highland capital since John Adam in 1835, irked the magistrates, who would have had it carried out at Aberdeen. But neither their objections nor the 7,000 signatories to a petition for a reprieve could move the Home Secretary.

However, in response to an objection from residents surrounding Porterfield Prison, the prison bell was not tolled, although the black flag was hoisted.

The scaffold was borrowed from Glasgow.

Executioner; Henry Albert Pierrepoint
Huddersfield

August 19th;   **Edward JOHNSTONE**   Perth

An obsessively jealous man, Johnstone murdered his common law wife, Jane Wallace Withers, in their lodgings at Saline, Fife, on 7th June 1908, after seeing her kiss a fellow lodger. Catching her round the neck in feigned affection, he cut her throat with a razor. A special plea of insanity at the time of the crime failed, and the jury found him guilty.

Perth Prison had no condemned cell, but despite being held in the warder's duty room by the main gate, he was oblivious to the preparations for the execution.

Joiners, building the scaffold in a shed by the prison's southern wall, came and went, as did two corporation labourers who dug his grave in stony ground.

Nor did he notice the delivery of the thin dealwood coffin, draped in black, by a local undertaker. Wider than the usual, to accommodate the quicklime, it had neither handles nor winding sheet.

Learning of the failure of the appeal for clemency, to which he had originally objected, he remarked, 'I have borne it well. I will not show the white feather now'. Nor did he.

Executioner; John Ellis
Rochdale

1909

July 6th;   **Alexander EDMONSTONE**
Perth

Executed for the murder of 16-year-old Michael Swinton Brown, in the School Wynd public lavatories, East Wemyss, on 19th February 1909.

A clerk with the linen manufacturers, G & J Johnstone, Brown was returning from Buckhaven with the company payroll money, when Edmonstone lured him to the toilets. The boy was left dying of his head wounds, as Edmonstone ran with the leather bag and the £85 payroll.

Arrested four weeks later in Manchester, his landlady claimed the £100 reward.

At 8.02am a crowd of 1,500 watched the raising of the black flag.

Executioner; John Ellis
Rochdale

1913

October 2nd;   **Patrick HIGGINS**   Edinburgh

On a perfect October morning, the crowd of 500 men, women and children on Calton Hill overlooking the jail, were entertained by a street fiddler, whose repertoire included 'The Lost Chord'.

In the jail, handling its first execution in 15 years, the atmosphere was tense. Due to lack of experienced staff, the press would be excluded from the execution chamber.

A widower, with previous convictions for child neglect, 38-year-old Higgins had been condemned for murdering his two sons, aged 4 and 7, by throwing them into the disused quarry at Niddry Mains Farm, between 25th October 1911 and 1st January 1912. On 8th June 1913 their bodies, tethered together, were found floating in the water.

'Of the labouring class', the press wrote, 'he slept out at night and cooked his food in his working shovel'.

Resigned to his fate, he offered no resistance on coming onto the platform. The scaffold was over a well, and the rope attached to an overhead beam.

A warder appeared atop the prison's eastern tower - attached the black flag to the rope - and stood. When he hoisted the flag to half mast at three minutes past eight, Higgins had gone to his doom.

Executioner; John Ellis
Rochdale

1917

May 16th;   **Thomas McGUINNESS**
Glasgow

Before finally murdering him on 8th March 1917 in the house at 101 Blackburn Street, Govan, Glasgow, McGuinness subjected five-year-old Alexander Imlach, the son of his common law wife, to months of ill-treatment.

In a house, ' ... of the poorest description, with squalid and meagre furnishings', the boy was repeatedly assaulted with blows and punches, and burns from cigarettes.

Executioner; John Ellis
Rochdale

1919

November 11th; **James ADAMS**   Glasgow

Hanged in Duke Street Prison for murdering Mary Kane or Doyle, by cutting her throat with a razor, in her house at 29a Cameron Street, Glasgow on 1st August 1919.

The pair had co-habited until Doyle decided to return to her husband on his demob from the army in Egypt.

Executioner; John Ellis
Rochdale

1920

May 26th;   **Albert James FRASER**
          James ROLLINS   Glasgow

Twenty four-year-old Fraser and 23-year-old Rollins had a scheme. Posing as prostitutes in Glasgow's city centre, their paramours, Gladys White and Elizabeth Stewart, would decoy men for them to rob.

On the evening of Tuesday 3rd February 1920, 35-year-old Henry Senior was accosted by Gladys White in Hope Street, and taken by tram to Queen's Park Recreation Ground, a popular spot on the south of the city for courting couples.

As Gladys settled on the grass and Senior pulled a ten shilling note from his wallet - Fraser and Rollins came out of the darkness.

The discovery of the body next day sparked a massive police hunt which led to Belfast and the arrest of the foursome.

The High Court in Glasgow heard that Senior's face was bruised, lacerated and disfigured, and that both lower and upper jaws were shattered. Taking his coat, shoes, watch and a small amount of money, they left him to die. Gladys and 18-year-old Stewart, sealed the men's fate by speaking for the prosecution.

After seeing the scaffold, Ellis was of a mind to hang them separately, 'lest the swinging of the bodies together might interfere with his arrangements', but finally decided on a double execution.

Standing back to back on the double trap door, the white caps over their faces, and the ropes on their necks, they bid each other farewell.

The last utterance, 'Cheer up, Jimmy', came from Fraser as the drop fell.

Executioner; John Ellis
Rochdale

1922

February 21st;   **William HARKNESS**   Glasgow

Although condemned with his wife Helen, for killing 14-year-old Elizabeth Benjamin, Harkness went to the scaffold alone, following her reprieve.

On 31st October 1921 the young Jewess had called at the Harkness's home at 67 George Street, Whiteinch, Glasgow, collecting for her father's credit drapery business. After murdering her with a blunt instrument, they robbed her of 40s.

In answer to two shrill whistle blasts ringing through the silent prison, the black flag was raised.

Executioner; John Ellis
Rochdale

EXTRACT OF AN ENTRY IN A REGISTER OF DEATHS 1861 - 1965

kept under the Registration of Births, Deaths and Marriages (Scotland) Act 1965

DC 029196

No.	Name and Surname, Rank or Profession, and whether Single, Married or Widowed (1)(2)	When and Where Died (3)	Sex (4)	Age	Name, Surname, and Rank or Profession of Father; Name, and Maiden Surname of Mother (5)	Cause of Death, Duration of Disease, and Medical Attendant by whom certified (6)	Signature and Qualification of Informant, and Residence, if out of the House in which the Death occurred (7)	When and Where Registered and Signature of Registrar (8)	
776	Albert James Fraser / Plumber (Single)	1920 May Twenty-Sixth 8h 0m a.m. H.M. Prison Duke Street, Glasgow (U.R. Glasgow)	M	24 Yrs		Dislocation of Cervical Vertebrae from hanging as Cert by Gilbert Garrey M.D. D.P.H.	A.D. Drysdale Governor H.M. Prison, Duke Street, Glasgow Present	1920 May 28th at Glasgow (Signed) William Potter Registrar	

EXTRACTED from the Register of Deaths for the District of Dennistoun
in the Burgh of Glasgow this 23rd day of February 1990

ATTENTION IS DIRECTED TO THE NOTES OVERLEAF

R.Ketvin Registrar
Glasgow District

Death Certificate — Albert James Fraser *(Registrar, Glasgow)*

EXTRACT OF AN ENTRY IN A REGISTER OF DEATHS 1861 - 1965

kept under the Registration of Births, Deaths and Marriages (Scotland) Act 1965

DC 029197

No.	Name and Surname, Rank or Profession, and whether Single, Married or Widowed (1)(2)	When and Where Died (3)	Sex (4)	Age	Name, Surname, and Rank or Profession of Father; Name, and Maiden Surname of Mother (5)	Cause of Death, Duration of Disease, and Medical Attendant by whom certified (6)	Signature and Qualification of Informant, and Residence, if out of the House in which the Death occurred (7)	When and Where Registered and Signature of Registrar (8)	
775	James Rollins / Engine Driver (Army Pensioner) (Married to Hannah Lennox)	1920 May Twenty-Sixth 8h 0m a.m. H.M. Prison, Duke Street Glasgow. (U.R. Glasgow)	M	23 Yrs	John Rollins Cabinetmaker Elizabeth Ann Rollins M.S. Slain (deceased)	Dislocation of Cervical vertebrae from hanging as Cert by Gilbert Garrey M.D. D.P.H.	A.D. Drysdale Governor. H.M. Prison, Duke Street, Glasgow Present	1920 May 28th at Glasgow (Signed) William Potter Registrar	

EXTRACTED from the Register of Deaths for the District of Dennistoun
in the Burgh of Glasgow this 23rd day of February 1990

ATTENTION IS DIRECTED TO THE NOTES OVERLEAF

R.Ketvin Registrar
Glasgow District

Death Certificate — James Rollins *(Registrar, Glasgow)*

1923

June 11th; **John Henry SAVAGE**
Edinburgh

A 50-year-old marine fireman, Savage was executed on a scaffold erected in the well of a stone stair near his cell in Calton Jail for the murder of Mrs Jemima Nicholson or Grierson, by cutting her throat with a razor, in her home at 25 Bridge Street, Leith on 14th March 1923.

An alcoholic, deserted by her husband, Grierson was no more than a companion to Savage, who also had a drink problem. Methylated spirits rendered him irresponsible.

Executioner; John Ellis
Rochdale

October 10th; **Susan McALLISTER or NEWELL**
Glasgow

Newell's murder of 13-year-old Johnnie Johnstone in her lodgings at 2 Newlands Street, Coatbridge, Lanarkshire cannot be explained; nor can her

John and Susan Newell in the Dock at Glasgow   (*The Daily Record*)

decision to wheel his body the 11 miles to Glasgow in a child's go-cart, the following day.

On Wednesday 20th June 1923, after weeks of quarrels, her husband John had left 28-year-old Newell and his eight-year-old step-daughter, Janet McLeod. He too was arrested for the murder, but acquitted.

Coatbridge held its Cattle Show that day, and Johnnie had earned 2s 3d selling newspapers, when he disappeared. Newell strangled him in the Newlands Street house.

Next morning, heading for Glasgow with her daughter and the go-cart containing Johnstone's body, she was given a lift in a lorry which dropped her, ironically, in Duke Street. Her intention had been to dump the body in a back court, but when lifting the go-cart from the lorry, the bundles slipped, revealing the body. The police were informed and Newell was arrested.

At her trial in September, a plea of insanity at the

time of the crime was refuted, and she was found guilty - although the jury recommended her to mercy.

With a crowd not exceeding 200, mostly women, standing outside the prison, Ellis walked her to the scaffold:

> 'Only once through the terrible ordeal did she betray the nervous strain which the awful situation imposed.
> 'That was when, pinioned and standing on the fatal platform, the executioner deftly slipped the customary white cap over her head and face.
> 'Involuntarily she shuddered, and gave utterance to a brief sentence, which the group of official witnesses construed as a plea for the removal of "that thing".'

Scarcely had the words crossed her lips when the lever was drawn, and the body shot into the depths.

Executioner; John Ellis
Rochdale

October 30th;   **Philip MURRAY**   Edinburgh

A newspaper vendor, Murray lived off the £7.00 per week immoral earnings of a Mrs Catherine Donoghue in her house at 40 Jamaica Street, Edinburgh

On the night of 23rd June 1923, Donoghue returned to the house with William Ronald Cree, a Dunfermline man, to find Murray very drunk and argumentative. Taking umbrage at Cree, he struck him with a smoothing iron and threw him out of the first floor window - killing him.

No black flag was hoisted to mark the execution.

Executioner; Robert Baxter
Hertford

1925

September 24th; **John KEEN**   Glasgow

Condemned at Glasgow for murdering Noorh Mohammed, an Indian pedlar, by striking him with a piece of coal, on the stairway at 5 Clyde Street, Port Dundas (described by the contemporary press as, 'a dingy hinterland') on the night of 16th May 1925.

The incident involved three others, John McCormack, Robert Fletcher and William Dayer, in a multiplicity of charges including other assaults and the theft of 24 jumpers, 36 scarves and two dresses. Only Keen was condemned.

John Johnstone   (*The Daily Record*)

His execution broke a precedent; Mrs Bell of Glasgow became the first female magistrate to attend an execution, and as at Edinburgh two years before, the black flag was not flown.

Executioner; Thomas Pierrepoint
Bradford

1928

January 24th;   **James McKAY**   Glasgow

When interviewed by police regarding the disappearance of his mother, Agnes Arbuckle or McKay, from her home at 213 Main Street, Southside, Glasgow, McKay answered:

'She is dead. She died about ten days ago. I put part of her in the Clyde; the rest is in the bunker.'

The officers' enquiry had started the previous day when part of Mrs McKay's dismembered body was found in the river at Polmadie. The remainder was found in the coal bunker at her home, and McKay was charged with murdering her between 27th September and 16th October 1927. His motivation lay in an inheritance of £100

Executioner; Robert Baxter
Hereford

August 3rd;   **George REYNOLDS**   Glasgow

Tried for the murder of his friend Thomas Lee of 28 Cathedral Street, Glasgow, 41-year-old Reynolds lodged a plea of self defence.

Reynolds was regularly at Lang's Bakery in Wesleyan Street, where Lee worked as a boiler fireman, but on the night of 21st March 1928, when Lee awoke from a drunken sleep to find Reynolds stoking the fire, he accused him of trying to take his job.

Words led to a scuffle, and picking up a branding iron, Reynolds struck him with it. Lee fell dead.

The jury also found him guilty of two lesser charges of stealing a small amount of money and a suit of overalls.

A reprieve extended his life from 18th July to 3rd August, when he became the last culprit to be hanged in Duke Street Prison.

Executioner; Thomas Pierrepoint
Bradford

August 13th;   **Alan WALES**   Edinburgh

Executed for murdering his wife, 24-year-old Isabella

Hain or Wales, in her parents' home at 17 Pirniefield Place, Leith, where they resided, on 5th June 1928. They had married in December 1926.

This, the first execution at Saughton Prison, would be the last in Edinburgh until September 1951.

Executioner; Robert Baxter
Hereford

1946

February 8th;   **John LYON**   Glasgow

For the first execution in Glasgow since 1928, and the first to be carried out at Barlinnie Prison, Lyon was sentenced to death for the murder of John Thomas Brady, a 19-year-old demobilised sailor, in a gang fight in Washington Street, Glasgow on the night of Saturday 20th October 1945.

Also condemned, at the end of a five day trial, but later reprieved, were his brother-in-law, Alexander Crosbie (on his 18th birthday) and 25-year-old John Alexander Lennie.

Leaving the prison the night before the execution, his father carried a letter:

'Everything is alright. Don't worry yourselves. I don't want you to hold a grudge against the Secretary of State for Scotland, Mr Westwood. He is just doing his job, and it happens to be me.'

Executioner; Unknown

April 6th;   **Patrick CARRAHER**   Glasgow

Described as, 'aught but a rat', Carraher was tried twice for murder.

Aged 31, with convictions for assault and crimes of dishonesty, he was tried at Glasgow in September 1938 on two charges; one for assault by brandishing a knife, and:

'that on 14th August 1938, at the junction of Ballater Street and Thistle Street, both in Glasgow, you did assault James Sydney Emden Shaw, 3, Ballater Street, aforesaid, and did cut or stab him in the neck with a knife or other sharp instrument, and did murder him; and you have been previously convicted of assault.'

At the end of the two day trial the jury foreman announced to the court:

'Our verdict on the first charge of assault is not guilty; a unanimous

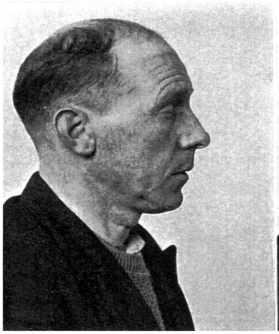

Patrick Carraher in 1945

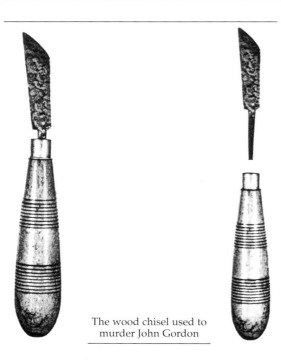

The wood chisel used to
murder John Gordon

verdict. On the second charge our verdict is guilty of culpable homicide, by a majority.'

Carraher was sentenced to three years penal servitude.

On Thursday 28th February 1946 when Carraher appeared before the Glasgow February Circuit, again for murder, the charge against him had a familiar ring:

'Patrick Carraher, prisoner in the Prison of Barlinnie, Glasgow, you are Indicted at the instance of the Right Honourable George Reid Thomson, His Majesty's Advocate, and the charge against you is that on 23rd November 1945, in Taylor Street, Glasgow, near McAslin Street, you did assault John Gordon, junior, 240, Aitken Street, Glasgow, and did stab him on the neck with a wood chisel or other similar instrument and you did murder him, and you have been previously convicted of crime inferring personal violence.'

Tower Cottage

The jury was enclosed at 11.35 am on the third day of the trial, returning 20 minutes later with a unanimous verdict, 'guilty of murder as libelled'.

Executioner; Unknown

August 10th;   **John CALDWELL**   Glasgow

From Fielden Street, Bridgeton, Glasgow, 20-year-old Caldwell was hanged for the murder by shooting of ex-Detective Sergeant James Straiton, who disturbed him and a fifteen-year-old youth breaking into a house at 524 Edinburgh Road, Glasgow, on the night of 26th March 1946.

Arrested on 1st April, he was also tried on two charges of attempted murder and four of theft by housebreaking.

His execution excited little public interest.

Executioner; Unknown

1948

February 6th;   **Stanislaw MYSZKA**   Perth

Condemned at Perth in January 1948 for the murder of Mrs Catherine McIntyre of Tower Cottage, Tombuie Estate, between Aberfeldy and Kenmore in Perthshire, the previous September.

Leaving the nearby Polish Army Resettlement Centre at Taymouth Castle, 23-year-old Myszka came upon Tower Cottage, where finding Mrs McIntyre alone, battered her to death with the butt of a shotgun and stole £80.

Executioner; Unknown

1950

October 30th; **Paul Christopher HARRIS**
Glasgow

With his 30-year-old brother, Claude Milford Harris, 28-year-old Paul was condemned for murdering Martin Dunleavy in a brawl at 151 Neptune Street, Glasgow.

Dunleavy, who had intervened in the fight, was severely lacerated about the face with a broken bottle and later died in the Southern General Hospital.

Claude was reprieved two days before the execution.

Executioner; Albert Pierrepoint

December 16th; **James Ronald ROBERTSON**
Glasgow

Thirty three-year-old Robertson had served five years with the City of Glasgow Police, when he was condemned for the murder of 40-year-old Catherine McClusky, on 13th November 1950.

Examination of her body, which was found on Prospecthill Road near Aitkenhead Road, Glasgow, in the early hours of 28th July, showed her to have been bludgeoned and afterwards run over several times by a vehicle.

Enquiry yielded Robertson's name, and his association with her.

He was the first British police officer to be executed since PC George Cook of London in 1893.

Executioner; Unknown

1951

September 16th; **Robert Dobie SMITH**
Edinburgh

At Edinburgh's first execution since 1928, Smith was hanged for murdering William Gibson, a 44-year-old Sergeant with Dumfries and Galloway Constabulary, at Dumfries on 22nd May 1951.

A 30-year-old electrician, and ex-Royal Navy sailor, Smith was twice mentioned in despatches before his demob in 1946. His killing of Gibson with a shotgun in Bank Street, Dumfries, was motiveless.

Executioner; Unknown

1952

April 12th; **James SMITH** Glasgow

Condemned at Glasgow High Court for the murder of 34-year-old Martin Joseph Malone, whom he stabbed with a dagger during a fight at Hibernian Hall, Royston Road, Glasgow the previous November. He was 21 years of age.

Executioner; Unknown

May 29th; **Patrick Gallagher DEVENEY**
Glasgow

On 26th February 1952, the night before his predecessor on the gallows at Barlinnie was condemned, Deveney, a 42-year-old labourer, strangled his wife Jeannie Todd in their house at 115 Blackburn Street, Glasgow.

Executioner; Unknown

1953

January 26th; **George Francis SHAW** Glasgow

Accused with 22-year-old George Dunn of the robbery and murder of Michael Conly or Connelly, on or about 17th August 1952.

A local character, the aged Connelly, known as Old Mick, had lived the life of a hermit in his hut on Huntlygate Farm, by the Lanark - Carstairs road since the 1930s.

Dunn, with a mental age of eight, was found guilty of culpable homicide and committed to the institute for mental defectives at Carstairs, whilst 25-year-old Shaw was condemned.

Executioner; Unknown

1954

April 23rd; **John LYNCH** Edinburgh

A 45-year-old Irish labourer, Lynch was condemned for the murder by strangulation of four-year-old Lesley Sinclair, and three-year-old Margaret Johnson, in a lavatory at 5 Marshall's Court, Greenside, Edinburgh, the previous 11th December.

Executioner; Unknown

June 23rd; **George Alexander ROBERTSON**
Edinburgh

Hanged for murdering his former wife, Elizabeth Greig or Robertson or McGarry, by stabbing her in the house at 57 Tron Square, Edinburgh, and the killing of his 18-year-old son George Alexander Roberson at 42 Tron Square.

Executioner; Unknown

1958

July 11th; **Peter Thomas Anthony MANUEL**
Glasgow

For the 18 days from 12th May 1958, the national press kept 31-year-old Peter Manuel where he wanted to be, in the public eye, as they covered, 'The Trial of the Century'.

The indictment was an appalling catalogue: murder and thefts by housebreaking spanning two years:

1) On 2nd January 1956, in Capelrig Plantation, East Kilbride, murder 17-year-old Anne Kneilands, by striking her repeatedly on the head.
2) Between 12th and 15th September 1956, break into the house at 14 Douglas Drive, Bothwell, and steal articles, and maliciously discharge a firearm into a mattress.
3) Between 15th and 17th September 1956, break into the house at 18 Fennsbank Avenue, High Burnside, and steal articles.
4) On 17th September 1956, break into the house at 5 Fennsbank Avenue, High Burnside, and murder Marion Hunter McDonald Reid or Watt, Margaret Hunter Reid or Brown and 17-year-old Vivienne Isabella Reid Watt, by shooting.
5) On 25th December 1957, break into the house at 66 Wester Road, North Mount Vernon, and steal articles.
6) On 28th December 1957, on the footpath between Mount Vernon Avenue and Kenmuir Avenue, Mount Vernon, murder 17-year-old Isabella Wallace Cooke, by strangulation.
7) On 1st January 1958, break into the house at 38 Sheepburn Road, Uddingston, and murder Peter James Smart, Doris Hall or Smart and 10-year-old Michael Smart, by shooting.

Had Manuel managed to escape a capital conviction on these charges, a Northumbrian

Manuel's victims (right)

Anne Kneilands

Mrs Brown

Mrs Watt

Vivienne Watt

Isabelle Cooke

Michael Smart

Mr Smart

Mrs Smart

DE GAULLE TO LEAD

(SEE BACK PAGE)

The Bulletin
and SCOTS PICTORIAL

43rd Year. No. 128 Friday, May 30, 1958 Price 2½d

CLOUDY

All Scotland—Cloudy, with occasional scattered showers and sunny periods early in the West.
TO-MORROW—Changeable

NOW IN CONDEMNED CELL AT BARLINNIE
TO AWAIT EXECUTION ON JUNE 19

MANUEL TO HANG

Jeers and boos as the van drives off

Report by Malcolm Nicolson

PETER Thomas Anthony Manuel, sentenced to death after being found guilty of murdering seven people, left with jeering and booing ringing in his ears as he made his last exit yesterday from the High Court in Glasgow, which had been the scene of his historic 16-day trial.

The derisive calls came from a crowd of about 100—mostly women—gathered near the back entrance to the court buildings as he was driven away in a "black maria."

Guarded night and day

More booing pursued the van as it swept away through streets near-by, on its way to Barlinnie Prison.

There, last night, Manuel slept in the condemned cell, where he will be kept — under guard night and day — for the three weeks until the date fixed for his execution, June 19.

Standing erect between two policemen with drawn batons in the dock of the High Court, 31-year-old Manuel stared fixedly at the Judge, Lord Cameron, as at 4.58 p.m. yesterday the death sentence upon him was pronounced.

Lord Cameron, with black tricorn on head, was visibly moved as he uttered the last ominous words of the sentence, "Which is pronounced for doom."

Manuel flushed at this moment of climax in the 16-day drama at two minutes to five after he had been found guilty of two capital murders. These were Watt murders and the Smart murders—both by unanimous verdicts of the jury.

He was also found guilty, unanimously, of murdering 17-year-old Isabelle Cooke, but the jury did not find him guilty of the capital charge in this case.

The sentence of death by hanging will be carried out in Barlinnie Prison, Glasgow, between 8 a.m. and 10 a.m. on June 19.

Manuel's final exit

After the sentence was passed Manuel, still flushed, turned and walked down the steps from the court.

This was his final exit from the vivid drama which has been enacted in the colourful High Court for almost three weeks.

It came after nearly two and a half hours of suspense as the jury considered their verdicts.

Turn to Back Page

Anne Kneilands **NOT GUILTY**

The Watts **GUILTY**

Isabelle Cooke **GUILTY**

The Smarts **GUILTY**

● Peter Manuel . . . he flushed as he was sentenced to death for the murders of the Watts and the Smarts.

How one newspaper saw Manuel's sentence

detective officer was waiting to apprehend him for the murder of Sydney Dunn, a Newcastle taxi driver on 8th December 1957.

On the ninth day of the trial Manuel dismissed his counsel - three years earlier he had defended himself at Airdrie Sheriff Court on a charge of rape, and won a not proven verdict. His ego again drove him centre stage, although at the conclusion of the proceedings, the trial judge, Lord Cameron, commended him for conducting his defence, 'with a skill that is quite remarkable'.

Through the forest of allegation, accusation, alibi and prevarication offered by Manuel, the jury emerged with a verdict of guilty to seven of the murders. Due to lack of direct evidence he was found not guilty of killing Anne Kneilands.

With his appeal rejected, he confessed to three more murders, one as early as September 1954 in London. It is believed there were others. He also attempted suicide by drinking disinfectant.

He spent his final three weeks in silence.

Executioner; Harry Allen
Preston

1960

December 22nd; **Anthony Joseph MILLER**
Glasgow

The charges against 19-year-old Miller and his co-accused James Douglas Denovan, bore similarities to those against Rollins and Fraser 40 years earlier. Both pairs had lured men to Queens Park Recreation Ground for the purpose of robbing them. Miller and Denovan, however, had preyed on homosexuals.

On 6th April 1960 John Cremin was murdered by a blow to the head, and robbed of his bankbook, watch, knife and £67 of money.

At their trial in November, both were found guilty, although 16-year-old Denovan was saved from the gallows.

Executioner, Unknown

1963

August 15th;   **Henry John BURNETT**
Aberdeen

At Aberdeen's first execution since Booth in 1857, 21-year-old Burnett became the last culprit hanged in Scotland.

An affair with 24-year-old Margaret Geujan ended with Burnett shooting her husband, Thomas, a 27-year merchant seaman, at 14 Jackson Terrace, Aberdeen. When charged by the police, Burnett replied, 'I gave him both barrels'.

The crowd of 300 outside Craiginches Prison were told at 8.25 am that no notice would be posted and quietly dispersed.

Executioner; Unknown

4

The Executioners

Prior to 1750, many communities had an executioner - there were witches as well as criminals to be punished - but over the years as costs increased their numbers dwindled, until by the mid-eighteenth century only the circuit towns could afford the luxury.

But these, too, were depleted, leaving John Murdoch, nominally based in Glasgow, as the last in the country. On his death in 1856, Scotland became reliant on English hangmen, starting with William Calcraft, an employee of the Sheriff of Middlesex.

Although 'finishers of the law', were known universally as hangmen or executioners, Edinburgh had its Dempster or Doomster, Stirling its Staffman, and the others their Lockman.

Wanted,

FOR THE BURGH OF AIR

A LOCKMAN.

Apply to A. Murdoch, Town-Clerk.
Town-Clerk's Office. }
Air, 19th Aug., 1823. }

Advertisement — Ayr Advertiser - 21 August 1823
(*Ayr Carnegie Library*)

The Dempster was, ' ... the officer of a court who pronounced doom or sentence as directed by the clerk or judge'. The duty could fall upon the hangman, as at the High Court of Justiciary in Edinburgh, where he received a salary from the Exchequer.

The press report that at the condemnation of John Dow Cameron at Perth in October 1753:

'When the Dempster or Hangman came in order to pronounce the

Sentence he (Cameron) struck him with his hands and fists and would not allow him to come near him'.

The practice later fell into disuse, although the title survived.

The title Staffman was unique to Stirling. J S Fleming in his 1898 publication, *Old Nooks of Stirling*, writes:

'The name "Staffman", given by the community of Stirling to this functionary, is purely a local term, no dictionary or encyclopaedia (including Jamieson's *Dictionary of the Scottish Language*) contain it. The name was attributable to the staff, or insignia of office, with which on being appointed, he was presented or invested'.

The word is contained in the *Concise Scots Dictionary* (pub AUP 1985), where it is defined:

Staffman - the BURGH hangman, la17th-e18th. Stirling.

'Lockman' was widely used, even in advertisements for the post, and derived from the hangman's perquisites. The *Scottish National Dictionary* gives the following:

'Lockman - hangman, so called from the small quantity of meal (Scottice, lock) which he was entitled to take out of every boll exposed to market in the city. In Edinburgh the duty has been very long commuted; but in Dumfries, the finisher of the law still exercises, or did lately exercise, his privilege, the quantity taken being regulated by a small iron ladle, which he uses as the measure of his perquisites. [see W McDowall, *Hist Dumfries* (1873) 581].'

It is difficult to obtain a true picture of the early hangmen of the period through the apocryphal writings of the Victorians. Their practice of writing to amaze or amuse often left truth behind.

On appointing a new executioner, the burgh or city magistrates would frame a contract on the lines of the following example from Perth:

'IT IS AGREED Betwixt John Caw, Esquire, present Provost of the Burgh of Perth ... and William Robertson Late residing in Anstruther Easter on the other part as follows; The said William Robertson hereby covenants and agrees Binds and obliges himself to enter upon the date hereof into the Town of Perth's service as their Executioner of the Law and thencefurth to continue in that office during his Natural Life, and faithfully, diligently and Submissively to serve and obey the present Magistrates of Perth and their Successors, in the said office of Executioner in every part thereof and at all times as he shall be commanded, and that he shall never desert the service of the town of Perth nor fail in or neglect his duty, under such Penalty and punishment as the Magistrates for the time being shall find just to inflict upon him, and in case of his desertion it Shall be lawful to the Magistrates to cause apprehend his person wherever he can be found and carry him back to the Town of Perth there to underly the foresaid penalty and punishment and again to sett about the duties of his office if the Magistrates shall think fitt to re-admit him thereto, and on the other part the said Magistrates bind and oblige themselves ... to make payment and satisfaction to the said William Robertson of the sum of Seven Shillings Sterling of Wages weekly ... whereof five shillings Sterling is to be paid him weekly for his subsistence, and the other two shillings Sterling is to run in arrears to be applied for clothes and other necessaries ... of all other perquisites allowed to former Executioners in this Burgh ... he shall have no Title or Claim.

And the said William Robertson is to have and possess the Executioners dwelling house free of Rent. As also he is to have Ten Merks Scots for every Criminal he shall hang and two shillings and sixpence Sterling for every Criminal he shall whip or put on the pillary upon Sentence of the Lords of Justiciary or by the Magistrates ...'.

Alexander Lowson, in *Tales, Legends, and Traditions of Forfarshire*, writes of a hangman's induction ceremony, but fails to give the town or the period:

'A very curious ceremony took place when the hangman was appointed. He was taken into a hall, where the oath of office was administered to him. On the table in the hall lay an axe, well sharpened, the same as that used for the beheading of traitors, - a pair of leg irons, handcuffs and other fetters - a small coil of ropes, and a pair of white caps. The magistrates made him repeat the following oath;
'I swear to hang, or behead, and to draw or quarter, or otherwise destroy all felons or enemies to the peace of our Lord the King, and of his subjects duly sentenced according to law, and I will do the like unto father, or mother, sister, or brother, and all kindred whatsoever. So help me God.'
'Thereupon a black veil was thrown upon him at his rising, when he was conducted out of the court amid the groaning of the assembly, the tolling of the dead bell, and the horrifying words of the magistrate grating in his ear, 'get thee hence wretch'.

What brought men into the profession? Money? Status? Probably a bit of both.

In the 1790s when a carpenter was earning 2s per day, a hangman could earn 2s 6d, plus one, three or five guineas per execution. And in purely physical terms, the carpenter who had to erect the gallows, was harder working than the executioner who operated upon it.

Status too was an enticement. The hangman was provided with a rent-free house, a uniform, coals and clothing. The Glasgow executioner had a conspicuous uniform of blue coat, yellow buttons, and a scarlet collar neck. John Sutherland, however, would not wear it, as it pointed him out to the finger of scorn.

Although there was the danger of assault at an execution, by and large the incumbents were left in

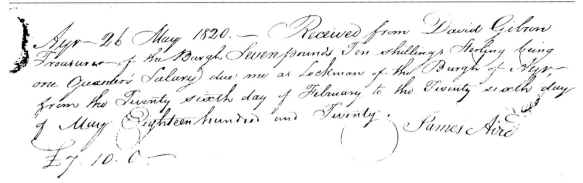

Salary Receipt — James Aird   (*Ayr Carnegie Library*)

peace. Intemperance was an occupational hazard, for all and sundry would buy the executioner a drink - just to hear his tales. The murder of William Taylor at Elgin in 1811 and John Scott at Edinburgh in 1847 were exceptions.

Some took the post to avoid debt, imprisonment or transportation. Both John Milne at Aberdeen and John High of Edinburgh were said to have been thus recruited.

As we see from Robertson's agreement at Perth,

their duties also included whipping and pillorying, and Thomas Young at Glasgow worked as a general labourer about the Jail.

The passing of the callous octogenarian John Murdoch, brought another in the same spirit, William Calcraft - humanity had not yet come to the scaffold. Only with James Berry, and those who followed, would the science of the drop be understood and strangulation give way to instantaneous death.

JAMES AIRD   Ayr

From the Ayrshire village of Tarbolton, Aird was appointed in December 1815, on a salary of £30 per annum and a fee of £3.6.8 per execution.

The local historian James Paterson in his 1864 book, *Reminiscences of Auld Ayr*, writes of him being shunned by the townspeople, and treated as an imbecile:

> 'Being beyond the pale of human society, he was forced to seek companionship in animals; birds, rats and mice. ... With every man's hand against him, he never bought bread twice from the same baker, and for the same reason never drew his water from the same spring.'

Early nineteenth century Ayr surely had many bakers and a surfeit of wells.

At his death in August 1823, an obituary in the *Air Advertiser* (14th August 1823) paints a very different picture. He certainly kept animals about his apartments in the Old Wallace Tower in High Street, but did 'good services' for his neighbours, ridding their houses of vermin - for no recompense.

> 'To poverty in his fellow creatures', reports the *Advertiser*, 'he opened his hand liberally and to all behaved with a respect and modesty seldom or perhaps never combined with the office. In the execution of his horrible duty he happily combined steadings of purpose with great humanity to the suffering object.'

He had launched eight culprits into eternity.

On Saturday 9th August 1823, whilst watching a cargo of wood unloaded at Ayr Harbour, he ventured onto the deck where he was struck by a capstan handspoke. He left uncomplaining, but in great pain.

When next morning, Sunday, the Wallace Tower bell, which it was part of his duties to toll, was silent, the door was forced and he was found dead on the stairway. He was 47 years of age.

An unknown bard had the last word on him:

> 'The burglars now may loudly crow
> and doers of misdeed
> No more the bad ones he'll throw off
> Tis true - the Hangman's dead.'

The Magistrates paid his outstanding salary to a brother in Galston, Ayrshire – for onward transmission to his widow and children 'who were somewhere in England'.

ROBERT AITKEN   Perth

Deserting his previous occupation as a barber at Pathhead of 'Kircaldie', Aitken contracted himself executioner at Perth on 25th October 1792. Nothing further is known of him.

JAMES ALEXANDER   Edinburgh.

Following the departure of David Drummond, Alexander was appointed on 8th March 1749, on a salary of £200 Scots, paid quarterly, from the previous Candlemas (2nd February), on the following conditions as noted in the Council Minutes:

> ' ... £12 Scots for his Yuill Ox, Twenty Merks Scots for every execution at the Gallow Lea and a Crown for Ropes. Ten merks Scots for every execution att the Grassmarket and half a crown for ropes, and forty shillings Scots for every drumming and scrouging every person through the City and one pound Scots for scrouging every person at the Correction House.'

The *Scottish National Dictionary* does not mention Yuill Ox, but refers to 'yule goose', amongst others. In modern terms it was a Christmas gift.

On 27th October 1762 the City Council granted his widow £4.3.4, being his last salary.

THOMAS ASKERN   York

Appointed at York in 1856 when 40-years-old and a prisoner in the Castle for debt, Askern worked throughout the north of England and Scotland - initially as a second choice to Calcraft.

The press report of Bryce's execution at Edinburgh in June 1864 concludes:

> 'This is the first occasion on which Askern has done duty as an executioner in Scotland; and from the quiet, unobtrusive and solemn manner in which he did his disagreeable work - contrasting favourably with his rival Calcraft - it is probable it will not be his last occasion. He is about forty-five years of age, six feet in height, dark complexioned, and with a profusion of hair about the face.'

Another report, which relates the rope being too short and Bryce being left to struggle, agrees with the more general opinion that he was a bungler.

At his last execution, at Armley Jail, Leeds in 1877,

the rope, which it was his duty to supply, snapped and the culprit fell.

He died in his native Maltby in December 1878, aged 62.

ROBERT BAXTER
Hereford

Baxter spent most of his career as assistant to both Ellis and the Pierrepoints. In May 1928 he carried out his first execution before coming to Edinburgh to hang Alan Wales on 13th August 1928.

In December that year at Swansea, his assistant Alfred Allen fell into the pit with the culprit when Baxter pulled the lever. The prison governor remarked that he was, 'quicker than anyone I have seen'.

JAMES BERRY
Bradford

James Berry

On the death of William Marwood in September 1883, Berry and some 1,400 others applied to the Sheriff of London for the vacant post. He was placed on a short list of twenty and called to the Old Bailey for interview - but was unsuccessful.

Born at Heckmondwike by Dewsbury, West Yorkshire, in February 1852, he was a shoe salesman and a constable with Bradford Borough Police before resigning in 1882.

In March 1884, his application to the Magistrates of Edinburgh to execute Vickers and Innes was accepted, and his career opened. He came to Scotland four more times in his nine-year career, finishing with Storey at Greenock in January 1891.

Speaking of the execution of Jessie King at Edinburgh on 11th March 1889, he said in reference to executing women, 'It always made me shiver like a leaf'. It was his opinion that she would be the last woman hanged.

He may, or may not, have been as competent as his ghosted autobiography, *My Experiences as an Executioner*, would indicate.

He died at Bradford on 21st October 1913, aged sixty one.

JAMES BILLINGTON
Bolton

A native of Bolton, Lancashire, Billington's first execution was at Armley Jail, Leeds, in 1884, when aged 27. With the retirement of Berry in 1892, he became senior executioner. He first came to Scotland the following year, to hang McKeown at Glasgow - coming again in 1897 and 1898, for Paterson and Herdman.

The last of his 147 executions in a 27-year career, was at Strangeways Prison on 3rd December 1901. He died ten days later, aged 54.

WILLIAM BILLINGTON
Bolton

In 1901, the Home Office list of approved executioners included three Billingtons, James and his two sons, Thomas and William. On their father's death in 1901, William became the preferred successor. In November 1902, he executed Patrick Leggett at Glasgow, returning once more, in July 1904, with brother Thomas as his assistant to perform the duty on Thomas Gunning.

The following year he was imprisoned for one month, with hard labour, for failing to maintain his estranged wife and their two children. He died in March 1934, in his early 60s.

ANDREW BOYLE
Edinburgh

A one-time weaver in Angus, Boyle took up his post on 1st July 1767, fresh from the 1st Regiment of Foot, on the same conditions as his predecessor John Liddle. However, in February 1768, the Magistrates were obliged to publish the following advertisement:

> By the honourable the Magistrates of Edinburgh,
>
> WHEREAS, on the evening of the 24th of February instant, ANDREW BOYLE, late common Executioner in this city, who was lately committed to the city guard, on suspicion of having committed sundry thefts in and about the city, found means to escape out of the guardhouse, disguised in his wife's cloaths, who had been admitted to see him there. The Magistrates hereby promise a Reward of Five Guineas, to any person or persons, who shall apprehend and secure the said Andrew Boyle in any prison in Scotland, within three months of this date.
>
> Boyle is a man about five feet eight inches high, smooth faced, of a dark swarthy complexion, has black hair, and is supposed to have carried off with him a coat of a light blue and white mixture, in which probably he is now dressed.

In May 1768 he was convicted at Stirling of stealing two shirts at Airth, and banished to the Plantations for life.

On 27th July 1768, the City Chamberlain paid £4.9.6 to John Clerk, which, with the 10s 6d previously paid, made to £5 his reward for apprehending Boyle.

WILLIAM CALCRAFT London

Born at Baddow near Chelmsford in 1800, Calcraft was the first English hangman to work in Scotland after the passing of John Murdoch, when hired to dispatch the Scanlane brothers at Cupar in July 1852. And between then and the execution of George Chalmers at Perth in 1870 he missed only two, which went to Askern of York.

Although a quiet and respectable looking man, at least in his younger days, with a wife and two young sons, he was like Askern, incompetent and bungling. At Glasgow in 1864, Riley struggled for nine minutes at the end of a two foot rope before dying. In later life he was to became scruffy and surly.

He, however, was perfectly at peace with his work. The report of the execution of McLean at Linlithgow in 1857, speaks of him, '... in skullcap and slippers smoking his pipe in apartments in the new prison.'

CALCRAFT, THE HANGMAN

William Calcraft

The last salaried executioner, he died at home in Hoxton on 13th December 1879, his last execution having been at Newgate Prison on 25th May 1874.

DONALD CAMERON Edinburgh

On 3rd July 1776, Cameron replaced Edward Hay who had served since March 1768. Whereas in Perth executioners bound themselves to the post for life, Cameron was only asked, 'to give at least three months premonition before he quit the said office'. He was followed by John High.

JOHN CHAPMAN Ayr

In June 1815 Chapman was accepted by the Town Council for the post of Lockman, on a salary which was £30 per annum, with perquisites. These included an allowance for coals, a suit of clothes, a pair of shoes, and two apartments in the Old Wallace Tower in High Street. The Treasurer reported to the same meeting that he had already paid £2 15s for the suit of clothes and 6s for the shoes.

Chapman resigned in the August without fulfilling any duties.

JOHN CUTHILL   Stirling.

The only extant record of Cuthill is in Ayr Burgh accounts when he was hired in November 1781 to execute Robert Dun.

JOHN ELLIS   Rochdale

John Ellis

When Ellis applied to the Home Office for a post as executioner, his father, 'played hell all round and cut him off without a farthing'.

After a week's training at Newgate Prison in 1901, he become an assistant to the Billingtons. On New Year's Day 1907 he carried out his first execution - at Warwick - and in August 1908, first came to Scotland, for Edward Johnstone at Perth.

In 23 years he carried out 203 executions - including some of the most infamous: Crippen, Seddon, George Joseph Smith and Sir Roger Casement.

The 8th of January 1923 was the beginning of the end - with the execution of Edith Thompson at Holloway. The end came in Duke Street Prison, Glasgow the following 10th October.

> 'It is often rumoured', he said, 'that my retirement in 1924 was the outcome of the Mrs Thompson case. It was nothing of the kind. My reasons were altogether different. Mrs Thompson was the first woman I actually hanged, and it was my most upsetting experience, but there was another after that - Mrs Newell at Glasgow.'

In August 1924 he appeared before the magistrates court for attempted suicide.

On Tuesday 20th September 1932, having returned home drunk, he was sitting at table with his wife and daughter, when he rushed to the kitchen - coming back with a razor. Threatening to kill his wife, and cut his daughter's head off, they rushed from the house. His son arrived in time to see him sink to the floor with two severe lacerations to his throat. When the police arrived, Ellis was lying dead in an enlarging pool of blood.

ISAAC GIBBS   Edinburgh

When noting Gibbs appointment in the Council Minutes of 10th December 1762, the clerk left a blank for the ex-soldier's regiment - it remains blank. He resigned in December 1765.

PETER GRANT   Ayr

Taking his post in February 1783, Grant was paid £4.6.8 per annum with allowances of £7.16.2.

A diarist in Ayr writes the only known reference to him, outwith official records:

> 'Friday 4th May 1792.
> The two lads Thomson and Gilmore, sentenced at last Circuit to be whipt and banished, underwent the former today - but their friends having Bribed the Executioner (Peter Grant) to feign sickness, they got little or no punishment, the hangman having been carried in a cart.'

Perhaps Grant's sickness was not feigned, for his death is recorded in the Council Minutes of 28th August 1793.

He had performed one execution: Mossman, Means and Barns in May 1785.

LAUCHLAN GRANT — Ayr

A collier from Kilmarnock, 22-year-old Grant was appointed in August 1793, but remained only a few months, without performing any duties.

EDWARD HAY — Edinburgh

As with so many hangman, Hay was an ex-soldier, having served with 68th Regiment of Foot, before taking the Edinburgh post in March 1768. He remained until July 1776, when Donald Cameron was appointed, 'in room and place of Edward Hay'.

JOHN HIGH — Edinburgh

Better known as 'Jock Heich', High was appointed on 15th August 1778. In his book, *Traditions of Edinburgh*, Robert Chambers writes:

> 'High had been originally induced to undertake this degrading duty in order to escape the punishment due to a petty offence - that of stealing poultry.'

This is unsubstantiated.

On 3rd May 1780 he petitioned the Town Council, stating that as his appointment had not been recorded in the Council Record he was not receiving the additonal salary due from the Honourable Court of Exchequer, for his duty as dempster. The Council acceded.

A good servant to Edinburgh, where he hanged over 40 culprits, he is only mentioned again in council minutes when awarded a wage increase. Nothing is known of his antecedents.

He was buried in Greyfriars graveyard on 22nd October 1816 - and had the Magistrates known what would come with his successor - John Simpson - they might well have wept.

ROBERT JAMIESON — Ayr

Appointed in time to execute David Edwards at Ayr in June 1758, for which he was paid 20 Merks (£1.11), the records show his quarterly salary of £1.1.8, but give no indication of his term in office.

JAMES KIER — Perth

An ex-marine aboard His Majesty's Fleet, Kier was appointed on 13th May 1785, on a weekly wage of 7s, but vanishes thereafter from the records.

JOHN LIDDLE — Edinburgh

Appointed on 11th December 1765, Liddle, a discharged soldier, replaced Isaac Gibbs, and carried out two executions; Margaret Adam in 1766 and Robert Hay the following March. In July 1767 his post was taken by Andrew Boyle.

WILLIAM MARWOOD — Horncastle

William Marwood

A cobbler to trade, Marwood was the first to apply 'science' to the craft of executions, when he realised that 'strangulation' could be eliminated by using a longer drop.

Between 1875 and 1883 he was called to Scotland six times, for five single and one double execution, including that of Chantrelle in May 1878. His last, Mullen and Scott at Glasgow in May 1883, was deferred for one week as he was in Dublin executing the Phoenix Park murderers.

He died in September 1883 after a short illness.

ARCHEY McARTHUR — Glasgow

Following the death of the scurrilous John Sutherland in 1803, Glasgow's Magistrates took care with the wording of the advertisement for his successor:

> 'Wanted, for the City of Glasgow, an Executioner.
> The bad character of the person who last held the office having brought upon it a degree of discredit, which it by no means deserves, the Magistrates are determined to accept none but a sober well behaved man. The emoluments are considerable.
> Applications will be received by the

Lord Provost, or either of the Town-Clerks.
Council Chambers,
Glasgow, 13th April 1803.'

The successful applicant was thirty-year-old McArthur, or 'Buffy', a good natured and inoffensive creature, but an inveterate tippler.

From an account published in the *Glasgow Herald* at the death of his successor, John Murdoch, we find that Buffy was about 5' 2" in height, stout and rotund in body (hence the nickname Buffy), with short bandy legs and a big bullet-shaped head.

His first gallows duty came in June 1803 when he assisted John High of Edinburgh to execute the thief William Cunningham. The following year, when executing the Glasgow forgers Scott and Adamson, he acquitted himself with the sang froid he would display throughout his career.

He had married early, but had only one child, a hunchback boy, who died in the Infirmary just before himself.

At his death, in 1813, he was honoured in a broadside poem, entitled, 'ELEGY - on the death of the late Executioner'. Its eighteen doggerel verses of six lines gives some facts on his life:

'Ah! fatal death what brought you hither,
To slay poor Archey in a fever,
An' leave the finishers altogether
    To mourn with pain,
Thinking they will ne'er get a brither
    Like him again.'

We learn that on returning to his native Glasgow after a free discharge from the army , where he had served as a pioneer in France and Holland, he took to selling fish on the streets.

'When's stock was sold then with his dear
'To D_____d Jock's he fast did steer,
'And drank large draughts of whisks and beer
Till they got fu'
'And then at last gaed hame, as I did hear,
But ne'er did rue.'

There is doubt as to his true name. Being so large, Glasgow City Council's administration treated the city's executioner like any other employee, and did not name him. From the above 'Elegy', we learn that his name was Archey, and only with the obituary of John Murdoch (*Glasgow Herald*, 26th March 1856) comes the full name 'Archey McArthur' - 40 years after his death. However the following entry appears

in the Gorbals Register of Death (1807-1824):

1814
18 Jan Archibald McArthur   50
Consumption

In 1809, when Ayr Town Council hired the Glasgow functionary to execute Dornan and Smith, the account from Glasgow contained the item:

'Gratuity to Archd. McLauchlane the Executioner by agreement,
        £5.5/-'.

JOHN McDONALD   Aberdeen
Appointed 1803-04. Died March 1805.

ARCHEY McLAUCHLANE   Glasgow
See McARTHUR, Archey.

JOHN MILNE   Aberdeen
Convicted in April 1806 of stealing beehives at Corse, Milne accepted the post of hangman in lieu of seven years transportation, on a salary of £7 10s per half year,

He inflicted many whippings, before his first execution - Andrew Hosack in June 1810, and remained in office until his death in 1818-19 when he was earning £19 per annum.

In October 1831, his wife, Christian was in the news. *The Aberdeen Journal* reported:

'Christian Waters or Milne, relict of the late hangman, was once more brought before the Police Court on Wednesday charged with committing a breach of the peace at Hangman's Brae, and breaking a pane of glass in the house of her husband's successor. She was sent 60 days to the Bridewell.'

Seaton's engraving 'View of Castle Street' dated 1806, shows him as a squat unkempt figure in a Tam O'Shanter bonnet.

JOHN MURDOCH   Glasgow
A baker by trade, Murdoch came to Glasgow from the north about 1830, and within a short period was acting as unofficial assistant to Thomas Young, despite being in his early 60s.

Free from the chains of an official appointment, he was in the habit of going the rounds of the Circuit Court until, 'some business came up'.

In October 1832, when the Magistrates of Perth had to execute the murderer John Chisholm, the town clerk, knowing Murdoch to have hanged Samuel

Waugh at Ayr the previous January, wrote his counterpart there for an opinion as to his competence. Ayr replied that:

> 'Murdoch discharged with great propriety the painful duty of Lockman ... and great must be the change indeed if he does not do the duty at Perth with coolness. He seems to be no novice at the trade.'

From an obituary published in the *Glasgow Herald* of 26th March 1856, we learn that he was a very different man from Young, and not one to seek companionship, or happily converse about his duties. Indeed as he became better known about Glasgow, he removed himself to anonymity in Paisley, Motherwell and Kilmarnock. In May 1849 he was at 3 Garthland Street, Paisley.

Soon he was following the Court around Scotland and the north of England, presenting himself and credentials to circuit town magistrates when necessary.

He held reprieves in 'moral detestation', blaming weak government, 'for doing him out of the best job he was ever likely to have'.

As a late starter, he was advanced in years when his career and reputation were at their peak. Reporting the execution of Thomas Wilson at Jedburgh in 1849, the *Kelso Chronicle* wrote of him:

> 'He is an old man and we would think should be giving up such kind of work now'. He had 'tottered up to the scaffold with the aid of a stick'.

His last execution was of the murderer Archibald Hare at Glasgow in October 1851, when he was 83 years old and crippled with rheumatism. Hirpling along behind Hare with the aid of a staff, it was not until he was on the scaffold that the spark of old returned and put life into him.

With his death, Scotland was without an executioner, and dependent upon hangmen from England.

JOHN NEWALL   Kirkcudbright

The *Times* newspaper of 25th December 1835 reports the death of Janet Newall, aged 84 years, the last of the family of John Newall, 'who held the respectable situation of hangman in the town of Kirkcudbright'.

Newell had been, 'Common Whipper of the town and Stewartry' until John Greig was condemned at Kirkcudbright in June 1750 - and Newell refused to act as executioner.

The Town Council minutes show that on 5th June 1750:

> 'The Magistrates and Council recommend to baillie Freeland, with all possible diligence in his own prudent way, to cause apprehend the person of John Newall, and to incarcerate him within the tolbooth of Kirkcudbright, there to remain till he be treated and agreed with by the Magistrates and Council, for puting in execution the sentence of the Stewart Depute, against Henry Greig, tinker, and thereafter to continue therein till the execution of said sentence be performed'.

Three weeks later Newall accepted the post of executioner 'of all corporal and capital punishments'. He would receive £20 Scots annually and a rent free house and yard.

For his first and last execution he was paid five guineas - and four pence per day for the time he spent in the tolbooth.

ALBERT PIERREPOINT   Huddersfield

'I hanged John Reginald Christie, the monster of Rillington Place', Albert Pierrepoint once wrote, 'in less time than it took the ash to fall off a cigar I had left half smoked in my room at Pentonville'.

Born on 30 March 1905 in the Bradford district of Clayton, the young Pierrepoint knew from the age of nine years he would following in the footsteps of his father Harry and Uncle Tom Pierrepoint

In 1931, after a successful interview and one week intensive training at Strangeways Prison, he was placed on the Home Office list of executioners.

The turning point in his career came in 1940 when, as principal hangman, he executed a gangland murderer at Pentonville in London.

During the Second World War he hanged two saboteurs at Gibraltar and 15 spies in Britain; and at its end was appointed an honorary lieutenant-colonel for the duty of executing Nazi war criminals. He once hanged 27 of them in one day.

Although at the war's end his career as an executioner still had ten years to run, he opened a pub, *Help the Poor Struggler*, at Hollinwood, between Oldham and Manchester. No doubt his renown helped promote the business.

In his twenty five year tenure he hanged over 400 people, including Ruth Ellis, the last woman executed in Britain.

His resignation in February 1956 left the Home

Office list of executioners without a Pierrepoint for the first time in 50 years. The family name was almost synonymous with the post.

HENRY ALBERT PIERREPOINT   Bolton

When appointed assistant to Billington in 1901, 25-year old Harry started a tradition which would see a Pierrepoint (his son Albert and brother Tom) on the Home Office list of executioners until 1956.

He held the number one position on the Home Office list from 1905 until 1910 when he was overtaken by Ellis. His weakness for alcohol may have played a part.

He resigned in 1914, having performed over 100 executions, and died in December 1922 at the age of 48.

THOMAS WILLIAM PIERREPOINT
                                              Huddersfield

Trained by his brother Henry, six years his junior, Thomas was steadier, stronger in character and the more reserved of the two.

Despite being on the Home Office list over 40 years, and becoming senior executioner on the retiral of Ellis in 1924, he neither wrote memoirs, nor contributed to a biography.

On his retiral in 1943 he was credited with over 300 executions.

JOHN RANKINE   Stirling

Public records on Rankine, apart from an entry in Stirling Town Council Minutes ordering his dismissal on 2nd February 1771, are scant. The entry reads:

'Act Dismissing Rankine as Staffman.
'The Councill Considering, That John Rankine the present Staffman, Is not only upon occasions when necessity Calls unable to execute his Office, But also that he and his wife keep a Bad house in the Night time by entertaining Tinkers and Vagabonds and having quarrels with them to the great annoyance and disturbance of the Neighbourhood, They therefore Dismiss him as Staffman, And appoint the Treasurer to give him Ten Shillings Sterling money for paying the expence of Carrying him and his Wife to Glasgow or elsewhere.'

To sack a town official for 'great annoyance and disturbance to the Neighbourhood' seems drastic, and there may well have more than the official record admits to.

William Drysdale in his book *Old Faces, Old Places and Old Stories of Stirling*, published in 1899, writes of Rankine:

'A native of Ayr, where his father had been executioner, he came to Stirling as successor to Tam Garland, the encumbent during "the '45".'

WILLIAM ROBERTSON   Perth

From Anstruther East, Robertson was appointed on 1st April 1789. On 27th August the magistrates applied to the Sheriff of Perth for an apprehension warrant following his desertion. It is unknown whether he was ever traced.

DONALD ROSS   Inverness

Meeting on 19th December 1833, Inverness Town Council decided to dispense, immediately, with Ross's services - but allow him occupancy of his house until the following Whitsunday.

Ross had gained the post through an advertisement in the *Inverness Journal* of 1st February 1811, following the murder of William Taylor at Elgin:

EXECUTIONER WANTED
THERE is an EXECUTIONER wanted for the Town of Inverness. Besides a comfortable house and ample allowance for firing, there are many considerable perquisites annexed to the office, which would enable any sober man who holds it to live comfortably. Particulars will be learned by applying at the Town Clerk's Office.
Inverness, 30th January 1811.

He was appointed on a salary of £16 per annum.

It was not until his dismissal, however, that the enormity of his perquisites, 'his bites and nibbles at the public purse', became known. Through the *Inverness Courier*, they were reported the length and breadth of the country;

1. He was provided with a house, bed and bedding.
2. He was allowed 36 peats weekly from the tacksman of the petty customs.
3. He had a bushel of coals out of every cargo of English coals imported into the town.
4. He was allowed a piece of coal, as large as he could carry, out of every cargo of Scotch coals.
5. He had a peck of oatmeal out of every hundred bolls landed at the shore.
6. He had a fish from every creel or basket of fish brought to the market.

7. He had a penny for every sack of oatmeal sold at the market.
8. He had a peck of salt out of every cargo.
9. He was allowed every year a suit of clothes, two shirts, two pairs of stockings, a hat and two pairs of shoes.

Added to these fixed and regular sources of income, Donald levied blackmail on the lieges in the shape of Christmas boxes. He was paid £5 for each execution.

JOHN SCOTT — Edinburgh

On 28th July 1835, Bailie McLaren announced to the town council that John Williams had left the city, after only four months in the post. However, the bailie also reported that John Scott, late executioner at Aberdeen, had offered himself.

Little is known of his days in Aberdeen, but he was credited with the execution of Catherine Davidson on 8th October 1830. At least he was experienced.

Scott's demands were readily agreed to. He wanted 12s per week, a free house, 21s for each execution and 10s 6d for each whipping as well as the usual allownce from the Court of Exchequer for the post of dempster.

In early December 1840 his request to be furnished with coal and gas in his house in the Old Fishmarket Close was refused.

But even experienced executioners could have bad days. Scott's came on 16th April 1840 when he had to hang James Wemyss. The *Caledonian Mercury* takes up the story as Wemyss dropped the signal:

> 'An awful pause ensued - the executioner drew a bolt which turned out to be the wrong one. A groan of execration and hisses rose from the crowd. The executioner, evidently in desperation, tried by stamping with his heel to put the machinery of death in motion; but in vain.
> The commotion was increasing, when one of the officials in attendance ran up the steps of the scaffold and, withdrawing the bolt, an end was put to the agonies of the miserable man, and he was launched into eternity.'

On 12th August 1847, Scott became the first executioner to be murdered since William Taylor at Elgin in 1811. Standing at the corner of Old Fishmarket Close, and a few yards from his home, he was attacked by James Edie, a drunk, after a short altercation. Knocking Scott to the ground with repeated violent blows to the chest, Edie continued the attack as Scott was rescued and carried into a shop. A blow to the head produced insensibility, and a few minutes later Scott was dead.

Eleven days later, when his death was formally announced to the magistrates, they granted his widow two weeks wages and occupancy of the house until the following Whitsun (15th May 1848).

He was the last executioner in Scotland to be employed directly by a council.

JOHN SIMPSON — Edinburgh

Appointed on 23rd November 1816 following the death of John High. For his first execution, John Black in December 1816, the Magistrates hired Thomas Young of Glasgow to assist him. His next gallows duty came on 30th December 1818 when he made such a hash of the execution of Robert Johnstone, that he was dismissed next morning.

He is reported to have settled in Perth in early 1819, and taken the post of executioner under the alias John Foster. He may also have died there of typhus in October 1819.

JOHN SUTHERLAND — Glasgow

Of all Scotland's executioners, Sutherland or 'Hangy Jock' 'a poor silly creature, pitted by the smallpox, and with the countenance of a cadaver', was the most reviled.

In his book, *Glasgow, Past and Present*, Senex Reid writes of him;

> 'He was ordinary of stature, but lank and shrivelled, with a small head, having a white and wizened countenance, spindle like legs, which when he was in full dress were adorned with white stockings; he had also buckles to his shoes and at the knees. His clothes were of blue cloth, including a long coat, with a collar, cuffs and facings of scarlet, and a cocked hat with white edging. At times he showed frills from his wrists, reaching to the knuckles of his skeleton like fingers, which wielded the cat o' nine tails. Altogether Jock's aspect was such that had he lived when it was the fashion in Scotland to drown wrinkled old women who were accused of witchcraft, he might have been burned as a warlock.'

In his duties, he was incompetent, and so nervous that whilst on the scaffold, he frequently trembled from head to foot. At the execution of John McMillan in 1798 he was unable to draw the bolt, and it took the hand of Lord Provost John Dunlop to launch McMillan into eternity.

When advertising the post of Executioner following his death in 1803, the Magistrates were anxious to appoint a sober, well-behaved man, 'The bad character of the person who last held the post having brought upon it a degree of discredit, which it by no means deserves'. Their prayers were answered in the application of Archey McArthur.

JOSEPH TAIT   Dumfries

Appointed in January 1787 whilst incarcerated for a debt which the town council paid. In 1789, 'after many complaints that his present salary from the Town is too small and that he cannot subsist himself and his family', he was paid £10.

He continued in the post until it was abolished in 1808 by which time he was paid £18 per annum.

WILLIAM TAYLOR   Inverness

Little is known of Taylor except his demise. In November 1810, he was hired to hang Alexander Gillan at Spey and 'by some means incurred the displeasure of the Morayshire people'. Some time afterwards he received false word of an execution in Aberdeen, and passing through Elgin was set upon by a crowd.

At the top of Ladyhill he was put in a cart which was then pushed down the hill. He escaped, but was caught again, and next morning found dead in a shack at Drumduan.

The *Aberdeen Journal* of 20th March 1811 reports:

> 'We understand a precognition is going on before the Sheriff of Elgin, regarding certain circumstances which are said to have occasioned the death of the miserable creature who acted as executioner in Inverness, when on his way through Elgin to Aberdeen. From his well known habits, it is highly probable that his death is more to be ascribed to the effects of drunkeness and cold than to inhumanity on the part of the people of Elgin.'

Despite their high opinion of the good people of Elgin, the *Journal* did not baulk at reporting the Inverness Spring Circuit:

> 'James McCurroch and John Dawson, shoemakers apprentices, from Elgin, accused of assaulting, stabbing and

otherwise maltreating William Taylor, late executioner at Inverness, while at Elgin, were found guilty, and sentenced to be transported beyond seas for seven years'.

Taylor was buried in 'Hell's Hole' on Cluny Hill.

JOHN THOMSON   Ayr

Within three weeks of James Aird's death in August 1823, the Magistrates had Thomson as his successor. A poor choice, he became a thorn in their flesh, and carried out only one duty, the execution of Anderson and Glen in December 1823.

In November 1825 he presented a petition, stating that with a large family to support he could not afford the new suit he needed to attend divine service. This was refused, and following a similar request, and similar refusal in July 1827, he resigned.

With his final salary he was granted £4, 'to remove himself and his family to some distant place'.

The post of Executioner left Ayr with him.

ROBERT WELSH   Aberdeen

Immediately following his appointment on 30th December 1773 the city council agreed to increase his salary to 13s 4d per month. By 1800 this had risen to 21s 7d. He was succeeded by John McDonald.

JOHN WILLIAMS   Edinburgh

On 16th March 1833 (confirmed at a council meeting on 27th March), John, an ex-soldier with the 25th Regiment of Foot, was appointed in place of his deceased father, Thomas Williams. With a wage of 10s per week he was also promised £1 for each person executed and 10s for every whipping.

After the execution of Robert Tennant at Stirling in October 1833 he was chased out of the town by, 'a low disorderly mob, who had become quite outrageous'. Abused and assaulted in a garden near Castlehill Bridge, he ran to the river followed by the crowd, who showered him with stones. Swimming to the opposite bank he was rescued by constables and lodged safely in the jail.

Two men were later charged with being actively engaged in the assault.

His one execution in Edinburgh, James Bell on 13th July 1835, was a fiasco. The *Edinburgh Courant* reports that, even when pinioning Bell in the Jail he cried like a child. On the scaffold, he was pushed aside by the superintendent of works, who adjusted the rope for him. Not unusually for Edinburgh, the crowd were close to riot, and Williams was lucky to escape. On 28th July the council learned that he had left the city, carrying off his effects, and leaving his house keys with a neighbour.

THOMAS WILLIAMS   Edinburgh

Appointed on 18th December 1819 to replace John Simpson, his appointment was confirmed at a council meeting on 29th March 1820. In the June, when granted his 'Doomster's' allowance from the Exchequer, and given a free house, his wage was reduced from 14s to 12s per week.

On his death in 1833 he was succeeded by his son John Williams.

ROGER WILSON   Dumfries

Said to have been, 'a respectable man, if such a term can be applied to a hangman', Wilson was appointed on 17th April 1758 on a salary of £6.0.0 per annum, a house-rent allowance of £1.13.4. and the universal right to a lock or ladleful of meal, barley, peas etc. out of every bag exposed in a town's market.

Although this universal right must have been resented, it does not appear to have been questioned - except in Dumfries. The year 1781 was one of scarcity, and levying his dues in Dumfries market, Wilson was challenged by John Johnstone and refused his 'right'. The action led to Johnstone being imprisoned, then released, whilst legal advice was sought.

This confirmed that the hangman was following an established custom which could be enforced if necessary. Johnstone raised an action in the Court of Session for wrongful imprisonment, and a Declarator, that the magistrates were acting unlawfully in allowing their executioner his 'rights' in the weekly market.

The actions were eventually dismissed and Johnstone went back to prison - being unable to pay his costs.

He retired four weeks before his death on 21st September 1785 and was succeeded by Joseph Tait.

Ironically, Wilson's wife is alleged to have committed suicide by hanging.

THOMAS YOUNG   Glasgow

With the death of Archie McArthur in 1813, Glasgow was again reliant on the Edinburgh finisher, until Young's appointment in December 1814.

His first duty, in February 1815, was not in Glasgow but in Ayrshire, when the Commissioners of Supply for the County hired him to hang the robber John Worthington at Symington Toll.

Through 23 years, until his death in 1837, Young was an asset to his adoptive city, and frequently, as

the years progressed, to other places where the post of executioner was being abolished. Although credited with executions, one as early as 1807 at Inverarary, which he did not perform, he did execute 56 culprits in Glasgow and some 14 elsewhere.

By his indentures he bound himself, 'for and during all the days of his natural life', to serve the city as its Common Executioner, and to put into full execution the sentences of the Magistrates and the Lords Commissioners of Justiciary, 'whether the same be Capital or shall consist of whipping Criminals, putting them in the pillory, or in the Stocks, or exposing them upon the platform.'

Between these duties he served as a labourer in and around the Jail for a of salary of £50 per annum, paid at 30s per fortnight and the residue in two equal sums in June and December. In addition, he was provided with a free house, 'Coals and Candles', a pair of shoes twice a year - and one guinea for each execution. For the execution of Hardie and Baird at Stirling in September 1820 he was paid £40 plus expenses.

So much for Young the Executioner, what of Thomas himself. Following his death on Thursday 9th November 1837, *The Scots Times* published an obituary.

Discharged from the Berwickshire Regiment of Volunteers, he worked as a labourer in Glasgow, before applying for the post of Executioner. Attached to his application was a reference from the commanding officer of the Volunteers.

Although 'by no means a drunkard', he could, with glass in hand, speak animatedly about his duties, and minutely describe the prompt disposal of the poor wretches who were his business on the scaffold.

There are few reports of him acting inhumanely on the gallows, where he carried executions through swiftly and efficiently. Only once was he assaulted, despite his regular habit of walking two large dogs on Glasgow Green.

His last duty was the execution of Hugh Kennedy at Glasgow in September 1834. When called twelve months later for the murderer George Campbell, he was too weak. From March 1837 he never left his house.

What became of his widow and three young children is not recorded except that they were left in very destitute circumstances.

The hope expressed in *The Scots Times* obituary, that Young would be the last such functionary in Glasgow was partly fulfilled, for although his successor, John Murdoch, was based in the city he was not in its employment.

5

Capital Crime and Culprits

Although English Law could at one point in its history boast of over 200 capital crimes, Scotland, in practice, had a mere 16.

The following brief definitions are taken from;

> *A Practical Treatise on the Criminal Law of Scotland* by Sir J H A MacDonald, pub. W Green & Son Ltd, 1929, and,
> *Principles of the Criminal law of Scotland* by Archibald Alison, Advocate, pub. Wm Blackwood, 1832.

Each definition is followed by a list of the culprits for that crime.

Attempt to Murder

Whilst Attempt to Murder is a crime at common law, certain forms were made capital under the Statute 10 Geo IV c 38 (1829), and commonly referred to as Lord Ellenborough's Act (Edward Law, 1st Earl of Ellenborough, 1790-1871).

Section 2 of the Act states:

> 'That if any person ... wilfully, maliciously, and unlawfully throw at or otherwise apply to any of his Majesty's subjects any sulphuric acid, or other corrosive substance calculated to injure the human frame ... such person being thereof lawfully found guilty actor, or art and part, shall be held guilty of a capital crime, and receive sentence of death accordingly'.

Kennedy, the only person in Scotland condemned and executed under the statute, had thrown a mixture of sand and sulphuric acid on the face of his victim.

The section was amended by the Homicide Act, 1957.

20th January 1834	HUGH KENNEDY	Glasgow

Bestiality

The unnatural carnal connexion with any of the lower animals. Geddes was the last of many capital prosecutions for the crime. On 1st March 1675 James Mitchell was drowned in the North Loch of Edinburgh between the hours of four and five in the morning; 'that the public eye might not be offended by the spectacle of the death of so vile a criminal'.

Geddes too was executed at an early hour and his body thereafter burnt.

It remained a capital crime until the passing of the Criminal Procedure (Scotland) Act 1887.

25th June 1751	ALEXANDER GEDDES	Aberdeen

Forgery

In his *Principles of the Criminal Law of Scotland* (pub. 1882), Archibald Alison considered Forgery as, 'one of the most dangerous crimes which can be committed. Its prosecution and punishment, therefore, constitute an important part in every system of criminal jurisprudence'.

He defined it as, 'the fabrication of false and obligatory writs to the prejudice of another, with intent to defraud'.

Although Gillespie was the last culprit hanged for the crime it was capital until, 'An Act to abolish the Punishment of Death in Cases of Forgery' was passed in 1837.

19th December 1750	JOHN YOUNG	Edinburgh
24th February 1768	JOHN RAYBOULD	Edinburgh
30th May 1770	WILLIAM HARRIS	Edinburgh
11th September 1780	DAVID REID	Edinburgh
8th January 1782	JOHN McAFFEE	Edinburgh
1st June 1785	NEIL McLEAN	Glasgow
28th March 1788	GEORGE McKERRACHER	Stirling
16th May 1788	JOHN SMART	Stirling
9th June 1790	JOHN BROWN	Glasgow
3rd September 1800	SAMUEL BELL	Edinburgh
5th June 1805	DAVID SCOTT & HUGH ADAMSON	Glasgow
11th June 1813	JAMES MERRY	Ayr
10th August 1814	JAMES McDOUGALL	Edinburgh
31st May 1816	WILLIAM EVANS	Ayr
28th May 1817	WILLIAM McKAY	Glasgow
11th May 1821	JOHN FLEMING	Stirling
16th May 1821	WILLIAM LEONARD SWAN	Glasgow
14th May 1823	JOHN McKANA & JOSEPH RICHARDSON	Dumfries
19th May 1824	WILLIAM McTEAGUE	Glasgow
16th November 1827	MALCOLM GILLESPIE	Aberdeen

Hamesucken

A common law crime, Hamesucken is, 'the felonious seeking and invasion of a person in his dwellinghouse'. It being essential that breaking into the house is combined with personal violence. The word is derived from the Old English 'hamsocn' (ham - home, socn - seeking, attack), and the German 'heimsuchung'.

It was made non-capital by the Criminal Procedure (Scotland) Act 1887.

11th June 1800	PETER GRAY	Glasgow
5th January 1820	BRINE JUDD & THOMAS CLAPPERTON	Edinburgh

Murder

'The greatest crime known in the law', Murder consists in the act which produces death, in consequence either of a deliberate intention to kill, or to inflict a minor injury of such a kind as indicates an utter recklessness as to the life of the sufferer, whether he live or die.

With an increasing murder rate at the opening of the 1750s parliament enacted, 'An Act for better preventing the horrid Crime of Murder', effective from the 1st day of the Easter Term 1752.

Adding, 'a further Terror and peculiar Mark of Infamy ... to the Punishment of Death', it also introduced a number of measures which would survive the life of the Act itself. It was repealed piecemeal between 1867 and 1967.

In the seventeenth century the punishment for murder was changed from beheading to hanging, and the crime made noncapital by the Murder (Abolition of Death Penalty) Act 1965.

15th June 1750	ALEXANDER McCOWAN	Perth
10th January 1752	NORMAND ROSS	Edinburgh
18th March 1752	HELEN TORRANCE & JEAN WALDIE	Edinburgh
8th November 1752	JAMES STEWART	Appin
24th November 1752	CHRISTIAN PHREN & WILLIAM WAST	Aberdeen
22nd May 1753	MARGARET MINNA	Jedburgh
23rd November 1753	JOHN DUBH CAMERON	Perth
18th September 1754	NICHOLAS COCKBURN	Edinburgh
23rd April 1755	NICOL BROWN	Edinburgh
13th June 1755	WILLIAM DOIG	Perth
7th September 1756	AGNES CROCKAT	Edinburgh
15th July 1757	HECTOR McLEAN	Perth
22nd October 1757	WILLIAM STEWART & DONALD McILROY	Inverness
30th June 1758	DAVID EDWARDS	Ayr
7th March 1759	ANN MORRISON	Edinburgh
29th June 1759	JAMES RUSSEL	Perth
2nd July 1760	ROBERT KEITH	Perth
22nd April 1761	JANET HEATLY	Edinburgh
19th October 1764	JEAN CAMERON	Perth
2nd November 1764	CHRISTIAN McKENZIE & MARGARET DOUGLAS	Inverness
7th November 1765	ALEXANDER PROVAN	Paisley
13th November 1765	PATRICK OGILVIE	Edinburgh
19th June 1767	DUNCAN CAMPBELL & JOHN CHAPEL	Perth
4th November 1767	AGNES DOUGAL	Glasgow
25th October 1769	ANDREW MARSHALL	Glasgow
29th June 1770	THOMAS STEWART	Aberdeen
15th September 1773	JAMES WILSON & JOHN BROWN	Edinburgh
19th November 1773	ALEXANDER McNAUGHTON	Perth
2nd March 1774	MARGARET ADAMS	Edinburgh
11th September 1776	ANNE MACKIE or MATHER	Edinburgh
1st November 1776	ALEXANDER MORISON	Aberdeen
21st September 1777	MARION WHITE	Stirling
25th June 1779	JAMES McLAUCHLANE	Ayr
13th October 1780	MATTHEW HAY	Ayr
29th October 1784	SARAH CAMERON	Stirling
8th June 1785	DAVID STEVEN	Glasgow
2nd June 1786	JAMES MOIR	Stirling
21st March 1787	JOHN REID	Edinburgh
30th June 1787	WILLIAM RICHARDSON	Dumfries
8th February 1790	BARTHOLEMEW COLLINS	Edinburgh
20th October 1790	JAMES DAY	Glasgow
29th October 1790	JAMES HENDERSON	Aberdeen
16th May 1792	JAMES DICK	Glasgow

7th November 1792	MORTIMER COLLINS	Glasgow
22nd May 1793	AGNES WHITE	Glasgow
13th November 1795	DONALD McCRAW	Perth
25th January 1797	JAMES McKEAN	Glasgow
16th May 1798	JOHN McMILLAN	Glasgow
12th March 1800	GRIFFITH WILLIAMS	Edinburgh
11th December 1801	JOHN YOUNG	Aberdeen
7th April 1802	GEORGE LINDSAY	Edinburgh
20th January 1804	JOHN COWIE	Edinburgh
21st June 1806	JOHN WESTWATER	Kinghorn
11th July 1806	DONALD McCRAW	Perth
7th January 1807	MARGARET CUNNINGHAM	Edinburgh
10th June 1807	ADAM COX	Glasgow
21st October 1807	MAITLAND SMITH	Dumfries
28th November 1807	PETER McDOUGALL	Inveraray
10th February 1808	BARBARA MALCOLM	Edinburgh
20th July 1808	JAMES GILCHRIST	Glasgow
25th May 1810	JOHN McMILLAN	Ayr
18th November 1810	ALEXANDER GILLAN	Spey
22nd April 1812	HUGH McINTOSH	Edinburgh
13th November 1812	ROBERT FERGUSON	Inverness
14th July 1813	JOHN McDONALD &	Edinburgh
	JAMES WILLIAMSON BLACK	
29th December 1813	CHRISTIAN SINCLAIR	Edinburgh
12th May 1814	JOHN GIBSON	Hawick
27th May 1814	JOHN McMANUS	Ayr
29th March 1815	JOHN MURDOCH	Edinburgh
4th November 1818	MATTHEW CLYDESDALE	Glasgow
17th November 1819	JOHN BUCHANAN	Glasgow
14th January 1821	JOHN DEMPSEY	Edinburgh
6th June 1821	JAMES GORDON	Dumfries
18th July 1821	DAVID HAGGART	Edinburgh
16th November 1821	GEORGE THOM	Aberdeen
7th December 1821	MARGARET TYNDALL or	Montrose
	SHUTTLEWORTH	
31st May 1822	WILLIAM GORDON &	Aberdeen
	ROBERT McINTOSH	
16th April 1823	MARY McKINNON	Edinburgh
23rd October 1823	ROBERT SCOTT	Fans Farm
12th December 1823	JAMES ANDERSON &	Ayr
	DAVID GLEN	
7th April 1824	CHARLES McEWEN	Edinburgh
21st July 1824	WILLIAM DEVAN	Glasgow
10th February 1826	WILLIAM ALLAN	Aberdeen
2nd June 1826	DAVID BALFOUR	Dundee
28th July 1826	PETER MOFFAT	Stirling
6th June 1827	JOHN KERR	Greenock
16th June 1827	MARGARET WISHART	Forfar
12th December 1827	JAMES GLEN	Glasgow
8th May 1828	FRANCIS COCKBURN	Falkirk
28th January 1829	WILLIAM BURKE	Edinburgh
20th May 1829	EDWARD MOORE	Glasgow
19th August 1829	JOHN STEWART &	Edinburgh
	CATHERINE WRIGHT	

17th March 1830	ROBERT EMOND	Edinburgh
18th August 1830	JOHN THOMSON & DAVID DOBBIE	Edinburgh
29th September 1830	WILLIAM McFEAT	Glasgow
30th September 1830	JOHN HENDERSON	Cupar
8th October 1830	CATHERINE DAVIDSON	Aberdeen
6th October 1831	JAMES BYERS & MARY STEEL	Glasgow
19th October 1831	THOMAS ROGERS	Jedburgh
24th October 1831	HUGH McLEOD	Inverness
2nd December 1831	JAMES GOW & THOMAS BEVERIDGE	Edinburgh
19th December 1831	JOHN McCOURT	Edinburgh
18th January 1832	WILLIAM LINDSAY	Glasgow
19th January 1832	SAMUEL WAUGH	Ayr
21st January 1832	JOHN HOWISON	Edinburgh
31st October 1832	JOHN CHISHOLM	Perth
7th November 1832	GEORGE DOFFY	Glasgow
2nd October 1833	ROBERT TENNANT	Stirling
31st May 1834	WILLIAM NOBLE	Elgin
23rd October 1834	JOHN BOYD	Greenock
13th July 1835	JAMES BELL	Edinburgh
3rd August 1835	ELIZABETH BANKS	Edinburgh
29th September 1835	GEORGE CAMPBELL	Glasgow
10th October 1835	JOHN ADAM	Inverness
4th April 1836	CHARLES DONALDSON	Edinburgh
8th April 1837	ALEXANDER MILLER	Stirling
18th October 1837	WILLIAM PERRIE	Paisley
21st May 1838	ELIZABETH JEFFREY	Glasgow
25th March 1839	ARTHUR WOOD	Dundee
16th April 1840	JAMES WEMYSS	Edinburgh
27th May 1840	THOMAS TEMPLETON	Glasgow
14th May 1841	DENNIS DOOLAN & PATRICK REDDING	Bishopbriggs
18th May 1843	CHARLES MACKAY	Glasgow
4th October 1843	ALLAN MAIR	Stirling
3rd April 1844	JAMES BRYCE	Edinburgh
5th October 1847	THOMAS LEITH	Dundee
19th May 1848	JAMES ROBERTSON	Forfar
26th October 1848	JAMES McWHEELAN	Ayr
22nd May 1849	JAMES BURNETT	Aberdeen
29th May 1849	JOHN KELLOCHER	Perth
16th October 1849	JAMES ROBB	Aberdeen
25th October 1849	THOMAS WILSON	Jedburgh
31st January 1850	MARGT LENNOX or HAMILTON	Glasgow
16th August 1850	WILLIAM BENNISON	Edinburgh
24th October 1851	ARCHIBALD HARE	Glasgow
5th July 1852	MICHAEL SCANLANE & PETER SCANLANE	Cupar
13th January 1853	GEORGE CHRISTIE	Aberdeen
14th March 1853	JOHN WILLIAMS	Greenlaw
11th August 1853	HANS SMITH McFARLANE & HELEN BLACKWOOD	Glasgow

25th January 1854	WILLIAM CUMMING	Edinburgh
11th May 1854	ALEXANDER CUNNINGHAM	Ayr
23rd May 1855	ALEXANDER STEWART	Glasgow
2nd February 1857	PETER McLEAN	Linlithgow
21st October 1857	JOHN BOOTH	Aberdeen
14th January 1858	JOHN THOMSON	Paisley
18th January 1861	PATRICK LUNNAY	Dumbarton
29th April 1862	MARY REID or TIMNEY	Dumfries
16th May 1864	JOHN RILEY	Glasgow
21st June 1864	GEORGE BRYCE	Edinburgh
28th July 1865	EDWARD WILLIAM PRITCHARD	Glasgow
31st January 1866	ANDREW BROWN	Montrose
22nd May 1866	JOSEPH BELL	Perth
12th May 1868	ROBERT SMITH	Dumfries
4th October 1870	GEORGE CHALMERS	Perth
5th October 1875	PATRICK DOCHERTY	Glasgow
19th October 1875	DAVID WARDLAW	Dumbarton
31st May 1876	THOMAS BARR	Glasgow
31st May 1878	EUGENE MARIE CHANTRELLE	Edinburgh
3rd October 1878	WILLIAM McDONALD	Cupar
23rd May 1883	HENRY MULLEN & MARTIN SCOTT	Glasgow
31st March 1884	ROBERT FLOCKHART VICKERS & WILLIAM INNES	Edinburgh
11th March 1889	JESSIE KING	Edinburgh
24th April 1889	WILLIAM HENRY BURY	Dundee
23rd September 1890	HENRY DEVLIN	Glasgow
11th January 1892	FREDERICK THOMAS STOREY	Greenock
18th January 1893	WILLIAM McKEOWN	Glasgow
7th June 1897	GEORGE PATERSON	Glasgow
12th March 1898	JOHN HERDMAN	Edinburgh
12th November 1902	PATRICK LEGGETT	Glasgow
26th July 1904	THOMAS GUNNING	Glasgow
14th November 1905	PASHA LIFFEY	Glasgow
5th March 1908	JOSEPH HUME	Inverness
19th August 1908	EDWARD JOHNSTONE	Perth
6th July 1909	ALEXANDER EDMONSTONE	Perth
2nd October 1913	PATRICK HIGGINS	Edinburgh
16th May 1917	THOMAS McGUINNESS	Glasgow
11th November 1919	JAMES ADAMS	Glasgow
26th May 1920	ALBERT JAMES FRASER & JAMES ROLLINS	Glasgow
21st February 1922	JAMES HARKNESS	Glasgow
11th June 1923	JOHN HENRY SAVAGE	Edinburgh
10th October 1923	SUSAN McALLISTER or NEWELL	Glasgow
30th October 1923	PHILIP MURRAY	Edinburgh
24th September 1925	JOHN KEEN	Glasgow
24th January 1928	JAMES McKAY	Glasgow
3rd August 1928	GEORGE REYNOLDS	Glasgow
13th August 1928	ALAN WALES	Edinburgh
8th February 1946	JOHN LYON	Glasgow
6th April 1946	PATRICK CARRAHER	Glasgow
10th August 1946	JOHN CALDWELL	Glasgow

6th February 1948	STANISLAW MYSZKA	Perth
30th October 1950	PAUL CHRISTOPHER HARRIS	Glasgow
16th December 1950	JAMES RONALD ROBERTSON	Glasgow
1st September 1951	ROBERT DOBIE SMITH	Edinburgh
12th April 1952	JAMES SMITH	Glasgow
29th May 1952	PETER GALLAGHER DEVENEY	Glasgow
26th January 1953	GEORGE FRANCIS SHAW	Glasgow
23rd April 1954	JOHN LYNCH	Edinburgh
23rd June 1954	GEORGE ALEXANDER ROBERTSON	Edinburgh
11th July 1958	PETER THOMAS ANTHONY MANUEL	Glasgow
22nd December 1960	ANTHONY JOSEPH MILLER	Glasgow
15th August 1963	HENRY JOHN BURNETT	Aberdeen

Piracy

Defined as, 'Hostile depredations committed on the seas, without a commission from any state to authorise them', Piracy was dealt with by the Admiralty Court until its abolition in 1829.

The Criminal Procedure Act 1887 made it non-capital.

9th January 1822	PETER HEAMAN & FRANCOIS GAUTIEZ	Leith

Rape

The carnal knowledge of a woman forcibly and against her will, or of a girl below twelve, whether by force or not.

It was capital until the passing of the Criminal Proceedure (Scotland) Act 1887.

13th January 1762	WILLIAM RIPLEY	Edinburgh
10th October 1809	CHARLES STEWART MERCER	Jedburgh
28th June 1811	HANS REGELSON	Kinghorn
20th December 1822	JAMES BURTNAY	Ayr
30th May 1835	MARK DEVLIN	Dundee

Robbery

The violent and forcible taking away of the property of another, robbery is so closely allied to stouthrief, that there is no real difference between them. It is essential that the property was seized and carried off by violence.

Within the list of culprits will be found street robbers and the more romantic sounding highway robbers. The Criminal Proceedure (Scotland) Act 1887 made it non capital.

12th July 1751	JAMES ROBERTSON	Perth
25th October 1751	EWAN McPHERSON & DUNCAN KENNEDY	Inverness
22nd June 1753	ROBERT DAVIDSON & GEORGE BRUCE	Perth
1st May 1754	HUGH LUNDIE	Edinburgh
10th July 1765	HUGH BILSLAND	Glasgow
11th July 1766	JAMES TAYLOR	Inverness
25th March 1767	ROBERT HAY	Edinburgh

25th April 1770	ANDREW McGHIE	Edinburgh
25th September 1771	WILLIAM PICKWITH	Edinburgh
2nd July 1773	WILLIAM McINTOSH	Inverness
7th July 1773	KENNETH LEAL	Janet Innes's Cairn
17th November 1773	WILLIAM MITCHELL &	Glasgow
	CHRISTOPHER JARDYNE	
10th May 1780	DAVID DALGLEISH	Edinburgh
23rd November 1781	ROBERT DUN	Ayr
4th February 1784	JAMES ANDREW	Edinburgh
7th July 1784	JAMES JACK	Glasgow
17th May 1785	ADAM HISLOP &	Jedburgh
	WILLIAM WALLACE	
9th November 1785	THOMAS VERNON	Glasgow
17th January 1787	DANIEL DAVOREN	Edinburgh
23rd May 1787	JOHN McAULAY &	Glasgow
	THOMAS VEITCH	
22nd October 1788	WILLIAM McINTOSH	Glasgow
23rd February 1791	WILLIAM GADESBY	Edinburgh
27th July 1791	JOHN PAUL &	Edinburgh
	JAMES STEWART	
11th January 1792	JAMES PLUNKET	Glasgow
22nd May 1793	JAMES McKENZIE	Glasgow
31st May 1793	JAMES DORMAND	Perth
21st June 1793	ROBERT ROGERS	Perth
15th June 1810	ANDREW HOSACK	Aberdeen
27th March 1811	ADAM LYALL	Edinburgh
26th December 1811	THOMAS McNAIR	Falkirk
21st February 1812	ALEXANDER O'KAIN	Stirling
22nd April 1812	HUGH McDONALD &	Edinburgh
	NEIL SUTHERLAND	
26th May 1813	JAMES FERGUSON	Glasgow
18th November 1813	WILLIAM MUIR &	Glasgow
	WILLIAM MOODIE	
27th May 1814	ROBERT GIBSON	Ayr
19th October 1814	WILLIAM HIGGINS &	Glasgow
	THOMAS HAROLD	
25th January 1815	THOMAS KELLY &	Edinburgh
	HENRY O'NEIL	
17th February 1815	JOHN WORTHINGTON	Symington Toll
1st November 1815	JOHN SHERRY	Glasgow
11th December 1816	JOHN BLACK	Edinburgh
17th October 1817	JOSEPH CAIRNS &	Ayr
	WILLIAM ROBERTSON	
29th October 1817	FREEBAIRN WHITEHILL	Glasgow
3rd June 1818	WILLIAM BAIRD &	Glasgow
	WALTER BLAIR	
30th December 1818	ROBERT JOHNSTON	Edinburgh
8th October 1820	EDWARD McRORY	Dumfries
8th November 1820	DANIEL GRANT	Glasgow
	PETER CROSBIE	
	JOHN CONNOR	
	THOMAS McCOLGAN	
17th January 1821	SAMUEL MAXWELL	Edinburgh
29th October 1823	FRANCIS CAIN	Glasgow

1st June 1825	JAMES STEVENSON	Glasgow
7th June 1826	JAMES DOLLAN	Glasgow
18th October 1826	JAMES McMANUS	Dumfries
1st November 1826	ANDREW STEWART & EDWARD KELLY	Glasgow
1st March 1827	WILLIAM THOMSON	Dalkeith
22nd October 1828	THOMAS CONNOR & ISABELLA McMENEMY	Glasgow
29th October 1829	JOHN CRAIG & JAMES BROWN	Paisley
6th January 1830	WILLIAM ADAMS	Edinburgh
12th May 1830	JOHN HILL & WILLIAM PORTER	Glasgow
11th August 1831	GEORGE GILCHRIST	Edinburgh
7th February 1833	HENRY BURNETT	Glasgow
2nd April 1834	MANNES SWINEY	Greenlaw

Stouthrief

Formerly used for every species of theft involving violence to the person, it was synonymous with Robbery. Latterly it was used, 'for forcible and masterful depridation within or near a dwellinghouse'.

17th August 1797	THOMAS POTTS	Paisley
28th February 1817	JOHN LARG & JAMES MITCHELL	Perth
31st October 1817	MALCOLM CLARK	Perth
10th March 1820	WILLIAM McGHEER & CHARLES BRITTEN	Ayr
23rd May 1823	THOMAS DONALDSON & WILLIAM BUCHANAN	Aberdeen
2nd June 1824	JOHN McCREEVIE	Glasgow
27th January 1831	DAVID LITTLE	Glasgow

Theft

At its simplest, Theft is the felonious taking and appropriation of property without the consent of the owner or custodier.

Amongst its many aggravations are Theft by Housebreaking, Cattle-stealing, Horse-stealing and Sheep-stealing.

It was made non-capital by the Criminal Procedure (Scotland) Act 1887

Simple Theft

6th July 1750	HENRY GREIG	Kirkcudbright
8th January 1752	JAMES WILSON & JOHN McDONALD	Edinburgh
7th August 1753	DONALD BANE LEANE CAMERON	Rannoch
2nd November 1753	ANN CAMPBELL SARAH GRAHAM	Inveraray
27th December 1753	ROBERT LYLE	Paisley
1st November 1780	WILLIAM JOHNSTON	Dumfries
31st October 1783	WILLIAM BURNETT	Aberdeen
25th July 1784	JEAN CRAIG	Aberdeen

14th January 1785	ELSPET REID	Aberdeen
19th April 1786	WALTER ROSS	Edinburgh
29th January 1787	CHARLES JAMIESON &	Edinburgh
	JAMES JAMIESON	
23rd May 1787	THOMAS GENTLES	Glasgow
25th May 1787	JAMES HACKET	Perth
1st June 1787	WILLIAM WEBSTER	Aberdeen
27th June 1788	JAMES GRANT	Aberdeen
9th June 1789	WILLIAM MURRAY	Jedburgh
3rd July 1789	JOHN MONRO	Aberdeen
6th March 1799	JAMES STEWART	Edinburgh
11th February 1801	RICHARD BROXUP	Edinburgh
8th June 1803	WILLIAM CUNNINGHAM	Glasgow
14th April 1819	GEORGE WARDEN	Edinburgh
29th October 1823	GEORGE LAIDLAW	Glasgow
27th August 1824	ALEXANDER MARTIN	Aberdeen

Theft by Housebreaking

16th November 1753	JAMES MILLER	Aberdeen
27th February 1754	RICHARD MUIR	Edinburgh
14th June 1754	MURDOCH CURRY	Dumbarton
29th June 1763	THOMAS PRICE	Dumfries
28th June 1765	JOHN HUTCHEON	Aberdeen
21st September 1770	ALEXANDER McDONALD &	Linlithgow
	CHARLES JAMIESON	
19th November 1773	THOMAS McLATCHIE	Stirling
17th June 1774	FRANCIS THORNILOE	Perth
10th May 1780	WILLIAM DONALDSON	Edinburgh
6th June 1781	ROBERT HISLOP	Glasgow
3rd November 1784	JAMES BRODIE	Glasgow
	WILLIAM BRODIE &	
	JEAN SCOTT	
19th March 1785	ANDREW LOW	Forfar
20th May 1785	WILLIAM MOSSMAN	Ayr
	BERNARD MEANS &	
	JOHN BARNS	
21st September 1785	WILLIAM MILLS	Edinburgh
22nd March 1786	JOHN HAUGH	Edinburgh
7th June 1786	JAMES SPENCE	Glasgow
25th October 1786	ELIZABETH PAUL	Glasgow
4th July 1787	WILLIAM HAUGH	Edinburgh
2nd July 1788	PETER YOUNG	Edinburgh
1st October 1788	WILLIAM BRODIE &	Edinburgh
	GEORGE SMITH	
17th October 1788	WILLIAM CORMACK	Inverness
3rd December 1788	WILLIAM SCOTT	Glasgow
24th December 1788	PETER BRUCE &	Edinburgh
	JAMES FALCONER	
27th May 1789	JOHN CARMICHAEL	Dumfries
9th June 1790	PATRICK FITZPATRICK	Dumfries
12th October 1791	WILLIAM SMITH	Edinburgh
12th June 1801	JOHN WATT	Dundee
22nd February 1809	ROBERT STEWART	Edinburgh

26th May 1809	WILLIAM DORNAN & ROBERT SMITH	Ayr
8th November 1809	JOHN GORDON McINTOSH & GEORGE STEWART	Glasgow
17th January 1810	JOHN ARMSTRONG	Edinburgh
11th October 1811	ROBERT BROWN ANDERSON & JAMES MENZIES	Stirling
5th June 1812	MOSES McDONALD	Greenock
13th March 1816	DAVID THOMSON	Edinburgh
10th October 1817	BERNARD McILVOGUE HUGH McILVOGUE & PATRICK McCRYSTAL	Greenock
29th October 1817	WILLIAM McKECHNIE & JAMES McCORMACK	Glasgow
4th November 1818	SIMON ROSS	Glasgow
6th November 1818	JOHN BARNETT	Aberdeen
7th April 1819	ALEXANDER ROBERTSON	Glasgow
28th May 1819	JOHN McNEIL	Ayr
27th August 1819	RALPH WOODNESS	Linlithgow
3rd November 1819	ROBERT McKINLEY WILLIAM BUCHANAN ROBERT GUTHRIE & ALEXANDER FORBES	Glasgow
21st May 1820	RICHARD SMITH	Glasgow
25th October 1821	MICHAEL McINTYRE WILLIAM PATERSON & WARDROP DYER	Glasgow
28th May 1822	WILLIAM ROBISON	Jedburgh
29th May 1822	WILLIAM CAMPBELL	Glasgow
5th June 1822	THOMAS DONACHY	Glasgow
26th February 1823	WILLIAM McINTYRE	Edinburgh
23 May 1823	WILLIAM McLEOD	Aberdeen
4th June 1823	JOHN McDONALD & JAMES WILSON	Glasgow
12th November 1823	DAVID WYLIE	Glasgow
14th May 1824	JOHN CAMPBELL	Stirling
26th May 1826	JOHN McGRADDY	Stirling
16th May 1831	JAMES CAMPBELL	Glasgow
20th October 1831	WILLIAM HEATH	Glasgow

Cattle Stealing

9th July 1750	KENNETH DOW KENNEDY	Inverness
6th December 1751	HUGH FRASER	Inverness
26th June 1752	DONALD McILIOG	Old Castle of Inverlochy
21st July 1753	JOHN BRECK KENNEDY	Perth
27th November 1772	ALEXANDER McDONALD	Perth

Horse Stealing

12th July 1751	HUGH KNOX	Perth
31st October 1753	ROBERT McILYMONT	Dumfries
11th June 1773	WILLIAM BROWN	Perth
31st October 1786	JOHN CLARK	Jedburgh
19th October 1787	JAMES McNAB	Ayr

21st January 1807	THOMAS SMITH & GEORGE STEPHENSON	Edinburgh
7th June 1811	GEORGE WATSON	Ayr

Sheep Stealing

5th June 1770	JOHN BROWN	Jedburgh
5th June 1818	JOHN RITCHIE	Aberdeen

High Treason

At the Treaty of Union in 1707, Scottish Law regarding High Treason was replaced by that of England, which made the following acts treasonable; Compassing the death of the king, his queen or his eldest son and heir; violating the king's companion or eldest unmarried daughter; levying war against the king; adhering to the king's enemies; or counterfeiting the great or privy seal;

15th October 1794	ROBERT WATT	Edinburgh
30th August 1820	JAMES WILSON	Glasgow
8th September 1820	ANDREW HARDIE & JOHN BAIRD	Stirling

Wilful Fire-raising

The wilfully setting fire to any house, store, barn, or other building, or to growing or stored corn, or to growing wood, or to coalheughs, the crime was capital until the Criminal Proceedure (Scotland) Act 1887.

26th January 1750	CHARLES GRANT	Aberdeen
4th November 1785	JOHN McDONALD	Aberdeen
17th October 1817	MARGARET CROSSAN	Ayr

Summary

CRIME	Last Execution	Male	Female	Total
Att to Murder	1834	1		1
Bestiality	1751	1		1
Forgery	1827	22		22
Hamesucken	1820	3		3
Murder	1963	187	33	220
Piracy	1822	2		2
Rape	1822	4		4
Robbery	1834	76	1	77
Stouthrief	1831	11		11
Theft	1824	24	4	28
Theft by Housebreaking	1831	71	2	73
Cattle Stealing	1772	5		5
Horse Stealing	1811	8		8
Sheep Stealing	1818	2		2
Treason	1820	4		4
Wilful Fire-Raising	1817	2	1	3
Total		**423**	**41**	**464**

6

Alphabetic List of Culprits

Surname	Forename	Place	Crime	Date
ADAM	John	Inverness	Murder	10/10/1835
ADAMS	James	Glasgow	Murder	11/11/1919
ADAMS	Margaret	Edinburgh	Murder	02/03/1774
ADAMS	William	Edinburgh	Robbery	06/01/1830
ADAMSON	Hugh	Glasgow	Forgery	05/06/1805
ALLAN	William	Aberdeen	Murder	10/02/1826
ANDERSON	James	Ayr	Murder	12/12/1823
ANDERSON	Robert Brown	Stirling	Theft by Housebreaking	11/10/1811
ANDREW	James	Edinburgh	Robbery	04/02/1784
ARMSTRONG	John	Edinburgh	Theft by Housebreaking	17/01/1810
BAIRD	James	Stirling	Treason	08/09/1820
BAIRD	William	Glasgow	Robbery	03/06/1818
BALFOUR	David	Dundee	Murder	02/06/1826
BANKS	Elizabeth	Edinburgh	Murder	03/08/1835
BARNET	John	Aberdeen	Theft by Housebreaking	06/11/1818
BARNS	John	Ayr	Theft by Housebreaking	20/05/1785
BARR	Thomas	Glasgow	Murder	31/05/1876
BELL	James	Edinburgh	Murder	13/07/1835
BELL	Joseph	Perth	Murder	22/05/1866
BELL	Samuel	Edinburgh	Forgery	03/09/1800
BENNISON	William	Edinburgh	Murder	16/08/1850
BEVERIDGE	Thomas	Edinburgh	Murder	02/12/1831
BILSLAND	Hugh	Glasgow	Robbery	10/07/1765
BLACK	James Williamson	Edinburgh	Murder	14/07/1813
BLACK	John	Edinburgh	Robbery	11/12/1816
BLACKWOOD	Helen	Glasgow	Murder	11/08/1853
BLAIR	Walter	Glasgow	Robbery	03/06/1818
BOOTH	John	Aberdeen	Murder	21/10/1857
BOYD	John	Greenock	Murder	23/10/1834
BRITTEN	Charles	Ayr	Stouthrief	10/03/1820

BRODIE	James	Glasgow	Theft by Housebreaking	03/11/1784
BRODIE	William	Glasgow	Theft by Housebreaking	03/11/1784
BRODIE	William	Edinburgh	Theft by Housebreaking	01/10/1788
BROWN	Andrew	Montrose	Murder	31/01/1866
BROWN	James	Paisley	Robbery	29/10/1829
BROWN	John	Glasgow	Forgery	09/06/1790
BROWN	John	Edinburgh	Murder	15/09/1773
BROWN	John	Jedburgh	Sheep Stealing	05/06/1770
BROWN	Nicol	Edinburgh	Murder	23/04/1755
BROWN	William	Perth	Horse Stealing	11/06/1773
BROXUP	Richard	Edinburgh	Theft	11/02/1801
BRUCE	George	Perth	Robbery	22/06/1753
BRUCE	Peter	Edinburgh	Theft by Housebreaking	24/12/1788
BRYCE	George	Edinburgh	Murder	21/06/1864
BRYCE	James	Edinburgh	Murder	03/04/1844
BUCHANAN	John	Glasgow	Murder	17/11/1819
BUCHANAN	William	Glasgow	Theft by Housebreaking	03/11/1819
BUCHANAN	William	Aberdeen	Stouthrief	23/05/1823
BURKE	William	Edinburgh	Murder	28/01/1829
BURNETT	Henry	Glasgow	Robbery	07/02/1833
BURNETT	Henry John	Aberdeen	Murder	15/08/1963
BURNETT	James	Aberdeen	Murder	22/05/1849
BURNETT	William	Aberdeen	Theft	31/10/1783
BURTNAY	James	Ayr	Rape	20/12/1822
BURY	William Henry	Dundee	Murder	24/04/1889
BYERS	James	Glasgow	Murder	06/10/1831
CAIN	Francis	Glasgow	Robbery	29/10/1823
CAIRNS	Joseph	Ayr	Theft by Housebreaking	17/10/1817
CALDWELL	John	Glasgow	Murder	10/08/1946
CAMERON	Donald Bane Leane	Rannoch	Theft	07/08/1753
CAMERON	Jean	Perth	Murder	19/10/1764
CAMERON	John Dubh	Perth	Murder	23/11/1753
CAMERON	Sarah	Stirling	Murder	29/10/1784
CAMPBELL	Anne	Inveraray	Theft	02/11/1753
CAMPBELL	Duncan	Perth	Murder	19/06/1767
CAMPBELL	George	Glasgow	Murder	29/09/1835
CAMPBELL	James	Glasgow	Theft by Housebreaking	16/05/1831
CAMPBELL	John	Stirling	Theft by Housebreaking	14/05/1824
CAMPBELL	William	Glasgow	Theft by Housebreaking	29/05/1822
CARMICHAEL	John	Dumfries	Theft by Housebreaking	27/05/1789
CARRAHER	Patrick	Glasgow	Murder	06/04/1946
CHALMERS	George	Perth	Murder	04/10/1870
CHANTRELLE	Eugene Marie	Edinburgh	Murder	31/05/1878
CHAPEL	John	Perth	Murder	19/06/1767
CHISHOLM	John	Perth	Murder	31/10/1832

CHRISTIE	George	Aberdeen	Murder	13/01/1853
CLAPPERTON	Thomas	Edinburgh	Hamesucken	05/01/1820
CLARK	John	Jedburgh	Horse Stealing	31/10/1786
CLARK	Malcolm	Perth	Stouthrief	31/10/1817
CLYDESDALE	Matthew	Glasgow	Murder	04/11/1818
COCKBURN	Francis	Falkirk	Murder	08/05/1828
COCKBURN	Nicholas	Edinburgh	Murder	18/09/1754
COLLINS	Bartholomew	Edinburgh	Murder	03/02/1790
COLLINS	Mortimer	Glasgow	Murder	07/11/1792
CONNOR	John	Glasgow	Robbery	08/11/1820
CONNOR	Thomas	Glasgow	Robbery	22/10/1828
CORMACK	William	Inverness	Theft by Housebreaking	17/10/1788
COWIE	John	Edinburgh	Murder	20/01/1804
COX	Adam	Glasgow	Murder	10/06/1807
CRAIG	Jean	Aberdeen	Theft	25/07/1784
CRAIG	John	Paisley	Robbery	29/10/1829
CROCKAT	Agnes	Edinburgh	Murder	07/09/1756
CROSBIE	Peter	Glasgow	Robbery	08/11/1820
CROSSAN	Margaret	Ayr	Wilful Fire-Raising	17/10/1817
CUMMING	William	Edinburgh	Murder	25/01/1854
CUNNINGHAM	Alexander	Ayr	Murder	11/05/1854
CUNNINGHAM	Margaret	Edinburgh	Murder	07/01/1807
CUNNINGHAM	William	Glasgow	Theft	08/06/1803
CURRY	Murdoch	Dumbarton	Theft by Housebreaking	14/06/1754
DALGLEISH	David	Edinburgh	Robbery	10/05/1780
DAVIDSON	Catherine	Aberdeen	Murder	08/10/1830
DAVIDSON	Robert	Perth	Robbery	22/06/1753
DAVOREN	Daniel	Edinburgh	Robbery	17/01/1787
DAY	James	Glasgow	Murder	20/10/1790
DEMPSEY	John	Edinburgh	Murder	14/01/1821
DEVAN	William	Glasgow	Murder	21/07/1824
DEVENEY	Patrick Gallagher	Glasgow	Murder	29/05/1952
DEVLIN	Henry	Glasgow	Murder	23/09/1890
DEVLIN	Mark	Dundee	Rape	30/05/1835
DICK	James	Glasgow	Murder	16/05/1792
DOBIE	David	Edinburgh	Murder	18/08/1830
DOCHERTY	Patrick	Glasgow	Murder	05/10/1875
DOFFY	George	Glasgow	Murder	07/11/1832
DOIG	William	Perth	Murder	13/06/1755
DOLLAN	James	Glasgow	Robbery	07/06/1826
DONACHY	Thomas	Glasgow	Theft by Housebreaking	05/06/1822
DONALDSON	Charles	Edinburgh	Murder	04/04/1836
DONALDSON	Thomas	Aberdeen	Stouthrief	23/05/1823
DONALDSON	William	Edinburgh	Theft by Housebreaking	10/05/1780
DOOLAN	Dennis	Bishopbriggs	Murder	14/05/1841

DORMAND	James	Perth	Robbery	31/05/1793
DORNAN	William	Ayr	Theft by Housebreaking	26/05/1809
DOUGAL	Agnes	Glasgow	Murder	04/11/1767
DOUGLAS	Margaret	Inverness	Murder	02/11/1764
DUN	Robert	Ayr	Robbery	23/11/1781
DYER	Wardrop	Glasgow	Theft by Housebreaking	25/10/1821
EDMONSTONE	Alexander	Perth	Murder	06/07/1909
EDWARDS	David	Ayr	Murder	30/06/1758
EMOND	Robert	Edinburgh	Murder	17/03/1830
EVANS	William	Ayr	Forgery	31/05/1816
FALCONER	James	Edinburgh	Theft by Housebreaking	24/12/1788
FERGUSON	James	Glasgow	Robbery	26/05/1813
FERGUSON	Robert	Inverness	Murder	13/11/1812
FITZPATRICK	Patrick	Dumfries	Theft by Housebreaking	09/06/1790
FLEMING	John	Stirling	Forgery	11/05/1821
FORBES	Alexander	Glasgow	Theft by Housebreaking	03/11/1819
FRASER	Albert James	Glasgow	Murder	26/05/1920
FRASER	Hugh	Inverness	Cattle Stealing	06/12/1751
GADESBY	William	Edinburgh	Robbery	23/02/1791
GAUTIEZ	Francois	Leith	Piracy	09/01/1822
GEDDES	Alexander	Aberdeen	Bestiality	25/06/1751
GENTLES	Thomas	Glasgow	Theft	23/05/1787
GIBSON	John	Hawick	Murder	12/05/1814
GIBSON	Robert	Ayr	Robbery	27/05/1814
GILCHRIST	George	Edinburgh	Robbery	11/08/1831
GILCHRIST	James	Glasgow	Murder	20/07/1808
GILLAN	Alexander	Speyside	Murder	18/11/1810
GILLESPIE	Malcolm	Aberdeen	Forgery	16/11/1827
GLEN	David	Ayr	Murder	12/12/1823
GLEN	James	Glasgow	Murder	12/12/1827
GORDON	James	Dumfries	Murder	06/06/1821
GORDON	William	Aberdeen	Murder	31/05/1822
GOW	James	Edinburgh	Murder	02/12/1831
GRAHAM	Sarah	Inveraray	Theft	02/11/1753
GRANT	Charles	Aberdeen	Wilful Fire-Raising	26/01/1750
GRANT	Daniel	Glasgow	Robbery	08/11/1820
GRANT	James	Aberdeen	Theft	27/06/1788
GRAY	Peter	Glasgow	Hamesucken	11/06/1800
GREIG	Henry	Kirkcudbright	Theft	06/07/1750
GUNNING	Thomas	Glasgow	Murder	26/07/1904
GUTHRIE	Robert	Glasgow	Theft by Housebreaking	03/11/1819
HACKET	James	Perth	Theft	25/05/1787
HAGGART	David	Edinburgh	Murder	18/07/1821
HAMILTON	Margaret Lennox or	Glasgow	Murder	31/01/1850
HARDIE	Andrew	Stirling	Treason	08/09/1820

HARE	Archibald	Glasgow	Murder	24/10/1851
HARKNESS	William	Glasgow	Murder	21/02/1922
HAROLD	Thomas	Glasgow	Robbery	19/10/1814
HARRIS	Paul Christopher	Glasgow	Murder	30/10/1950
HARRIS	William	Edinburgh	Forgery	30/05/1770
HAUGH	John	Edinburgh	Theft by Housebreaking	22/03/1786
HAUGH	William	Edinburgh	Theft by Housebreaking	04/07/1787
HAY	Matthew	Ayr	Murder	13/10/1780
HAY	Robert	Edinburgh	Robbery	25/03/1767
HEAMAN	Peter	Leith	Piracy	09/01/1822
HEATH	William	Glasgow	Theft by Housebreaking	20/10/1831
HEATLY	Janet	Edinburgh	Murder	22/04/1761
HENDERSON	James	Aberdeen	Murder	29/10/1790
HENDERSON	John	Cupar	Murder	30/09/1830
HERDMAN	John	Edinburgh	Murder	12/03/1898
HIGGINS	Patrick	Edinburgh	Murder	02/10/1913
HIGGINS	William	Glasgow	Robbery	19/10/1814
HILL	John	Glasgow	Robbery	12/05/1830
HISLOP	Adam	Jedburgh	Robbery	17/05/1785
HISLOP	Robert	Glasgow	Theft by Housebreaking	06/06/1781
HOSACK	Andrew	Aberdeen	Robbery	15/06/1810
HOWISON	John	Edinburgh	Murder	21/01/1832
HUME	Joseph	Inverness	Murder	05/03/1908
HUTCHEON	John	Aberdeen	Theft by Housebreaking	28/06/1765
INNES	William	Edinburgh	Murder	31/03/1884
JACK	James	Glasgow	Robbery	07/07/1784
JAMIESON	Charles	Linlithgow	Theft by Housebreaking	21/09/1770
JAMIESON	Charles	Edinburgh	Theft	29/01/1787
JAMIESON	James	Edinburgh	Theft	29/01/1787
JARDYNE	Christopher	Glasgow	Robbery	17/11/1773
JEFFREY	Elizabeth	Glasgow	Murder	21/05/1838
JOHNSTON	Robert	Edinburgh	Robbery	30/12/1818
JOHNSTON	William	Dumfries	Theft	01/11/1780
JOHNSTONE	Edward	Perth	Murder	19/08/1908
JUDD	Brine	Edinburgh	Hamesucken	05/01/1820
KEEN	John	Glasgow	Murder	24/09/1925
KEITH	Robert	Perth	Murder	02/07/1760
KELLOCHER	John	Perth	Murder	29/05/1849
KELLY	Edward	Glasgow	Robbery	01/11/1826
KELLY	Thomas	Edinburgh	Robbery	25/01/1815
KENNEDY	Duncan	Inverness	Robbery	25/10/1751
KENNEDY	Hugh	Glasgow	Attempt to Murder	20/01/1834
KENNEDY	John Breck	Perth	Cattle Stealing	21/07/1753
KENNEDY	Kenneth Dow	Inverness	Cattle Stealing	09/07/1750
KERR	John	Greenock	Murder	06/06/1827

KING	Jessie	Edinburgh	Murder	11/03/1889
KNOX	Hugh	Perth	Horse Stealing	12/07/1751
LAIDLAW	George	Glasgow	Theft	29/10/1823
LARG	John	Perth	Stouthrief	28/02/1817
LEAL	Kenneth	Janet Innes's Cairn	Robbery	07/07/1773
LEGGETT	Patrick	Glasgow	Murder	12/11/1902
LEITH	Thomas	Dundee	Murder	05/10/1847
LIFFEY	Pasha	Glasgow	Murder	14/11/1905
LINDSAY	George	Edinburgh	Murder	07/04/1802
LINDSAY	William	Glasgow	Murder	18/01/1832
LITTLE	David	Glasgow	Stouthrief	27/01/1831
LOW	Andrew	Forfar	Theft by Housebreaking	19/03/1785
LUNDIE	Hugh	Edinburgh	Robbery	01/05/1754
LUNNAY	Patrick	Dumbarton	Murder	18/01/1861
LYALL	Adam	Edinburgh	Robbery	27/03/1811
LYLE	Robert	Paisley	Theft	27/12/1753
LYNCH	John	Edinburgh	Murder	23/04/1954
LYON	John	Glasgow	Murder	08/02/1946
MACKAY	Charles	Glasgow	Murder	18/05/1843
MAIR	Allan	Stirling	Murder	04/10/1843
MALCOLM	Barbara	Edinburgh	Murder	10/02/1808
MANUEL	Peter Thomas Anthony	Glasgow	Murder	11/07/1958
MARSHALL	Andrew	Glasgow	Murder	25/10/1769
MARTIN	Alexander	Aberdeen	Theft	27/08/1824
MATHER	Anne Mackie or	Edinburgh	Murder	11/09/1776
MAXWELL	Samuel	Edinburgh	Robbery	17/01/1821
McAFFEE	John	Edinburgh	Forgery	08/01/1782
McAULAY	John	Glasgow	Robbery	23/05/1787
McCOLGAN	Thomas	Glasgow	Robbery	08/11/1820
McCORMICK	James	Glasgow	Theft by Housebreaking	29/10/1817
McCOURT	John	Edinburgh	Murder	19/12/1831
McCOWAN	Alexander	Perth	Murder	15/06/1750
McCRAW	Donald	Perth	Murder	13/11/1795
McCRAW	Donald	Perth	Murder	11/07/1806
McCREEVIE	John	Glasgow	Stouthrief	02/06/1824
McCRYSTAL	Patrick	Greenock	Theft by Housebreaking	10/10/1817
McDONALD	Alexander	Linlithgow	Theft by Housebreaking	21/09/1770
McDONALD	Alexander	Perth	Cattle Stealing	27/11/1772
McDONALD	Hugh	Edinburgh	Robbery	22/04/1812
McDONALD	John	Edinburgh	Murder	14/07/1813
McDONALD	John	Glasgow	Theft by Housebreaking	04/06/1823
McDONALD	John	Edinburgh	Theft	08/01/1752
McDONALD	John	Aberdeen	Wilful Fire-raising	04/11/1785
McDONALD	Moses	Greenock	Theft by Housebreaking	05/06/1812

McDONALD	William	Cupar	Murder	03/10/1878
McDOUGALL	James	Edinburgh	Forgery	10/08/1814
McDOUGALL	Peter	Inveraray	Murder	28/11/1807
McEWEN	Charles	Edinburgh	Murder	07/04/1824
McFARLANE	Hans Smith	Glasgow	Murder	11/08/1853
McFEAT	William	Glasgow	Murder	29/09/1830
McGHEER	William	Ayr	Stouthrief	10/03/1820
McGHIE	Andrew	Edinburgh	Robbery	25/04/1770
McGRADDY	John	Stirling	Theft by Housebreaking	26/05/1826
McGUINNESS	Thomas	Glasgow	Murder	16/05/1917
McILIOG	Donald	Inverlochy	Cattle Stealing	26/06/1752
McILROY	Donald	Inverness	Murder	22/10/1757
McILVOGUE	Bernard	Greenock	Theft by Housebreaking	10/10/1817
McILVOGUE	Hugh	Greenock	Theft by Housebreaking	10/10/1817
McILYMONT	Robert	Dumfries	Horse Stealing	31/10/1753
McINTOSH	Hugh	Edinburgh	Murder	22/04/1812
McINTOSH	John Gordon	Glasgow	Theft by Housebreaking	08/11/1809
McINTOSH	Robert	Aberdeen	Murder	31/05/1822
McINTOSH	William	Glasgow	Robbery	22/10/1788
McINTOSH	William	Inverness	Robbery	02/07/1773
McINTYRE	Michael	Glasgow	Theft by Housebreaking	25/10/1821
McINTYRE	William	Edinburgh	Theft by Housebreaking	26/02/1823
McKANA	John	Dumfries	Forgery	14/05/1823
McKAY	James	Glasgow	Murder	24/01/1928
McKAY	William	Glasgow	Forgery	28/05/1817
McKEAN	James	Glasgow	Murder	25/01/1797
McKECHNIE	William	Glasgow	Theft by Housebreaking	29/10/1817
McKENZIE	Christian	Inverness	Murder	02/11/1764
McKENZIE	James	Glasgow	Robbery	22/05/1793
McKEOWN	William	Glasgow	Murder	18/01/1893
McKERRACHER	George	Stirling	Forgery	28/03/1788
McKINLAY	Robert	Glasgow	Theft by Housebreaking	03/11/1819
McKINNON	Mary	Edinburgh	Murder	16/04/1823
McLATCHIE	Thomas	Stirling	Theft by Housebreaking	19/11/1773
McLAUCHLANE	James	Ayr	Murder	25/06/1779
McLEAN	Hector	Perth	Murder	15/07/1757
McLEAN	Neil	Glasgow	Forgery	01/06/1785
McLEAN	Peter	Linlithgow	Murder	02/02/1857
McLEOD	Hugh	Inverness	Murder	24/10/1831
McLEOD	William	Aberdeen	Theft by Housebreaking	23/05/1823
McMANUS	James	Dumfries	Robbery	18/10/1826
McMANUS	John	Ayr	Murder	27/05/1814
McMENEMY	Isabella	Glasgow	Robbery	22/10/1828
McMILLAN	John	Glasgow	Murder	16/05/1798
McMILLAN	John	Ayr	Murder	25/05/1810

McNAB	James	Ayr	Horse Stealing	19/10/1787
McNAIR	Thomas	Falkirk	Robbery	26/12/1811
McNAUGHTON	Alexander	Perth	Murder	19/11/1773
McNEIL	John	Ayr	Theft by Housebreaking	28/05/1819
McPHERSON	Ewan	Inverness	Robbery	25/10/1751
McRORY	Edward	Dumfries	Robbery	08/10/1820
McTEAGUE	William	Glasgow	Forgery	19/05/1824
McWHEELAN	James	Ayr	Murder	26/10/1848
MEANS	Bernard	Ayr	Theft by Housebreaking	20/05/1785
MENZIES	James	Stirling	Theft by Housebreaking	11/10/1811
MERCER	Charles Stewart	Jedburgh	Rape	10/10/1809
MERRY	James	Ayr	Forgery	11/06/1813
MILLER	Alexander	Stirling	Murder	08/04/1837
MILLER	Anthony Joseph	Glasgow	Murder	22/12/1960
MILLER	James	Aberdeen	Theft by Housebreaking	16/11/1753
MILLS	William	Edinburgh	Theft by Housebreaking	21/09/1785
MINNA	Margaret	Jedburgh	Murder	22/05/1753
MITCHELL	James	Perth	Stouthrief	28/02/1817
MITCHELL	William	Glasgow	Robbery	17/11/1773
MOFFAT	Peter	Stirling	Murder	28/07/1826
MOIR	James	Stirling	Murder	02/06/1786
MONRO	John	Aberdeen	Theft	03/07/1789
MOORE	Edward	Glasgow	Murder	20/05/1829
MORISON	Alexander	Aberdeen	Murder	01/11/1776
MORRISON	Ann	Edinburgh	Murder	07/03/1759
MOSSMAN	William	Ayr	Theft by Housebreaking	20/05/1785
MOODIE	William	Glasgow	Robbery	18/11/1813
MUIR	Richard	Edinburgh	Theft by Housebreaking	27/02/1754
MUIR	William	Glasgow	Robbery	18/11/1813
MULLEN	Henry	Glasgow	Murder	23/05/1883
MURDOCH	John	Edinburgh	Murder	29/03/1815
MURRAY	Philip	Edinburgh	Murder	30/10/1923
MURRAY	William	Jedburgh	Theft	09/06/1789
MYSZKA	Stanislaw	Perth	Murder	06/02/1948
NEWELL	Susan McAllister or	Glasgow	Murder	10/10/1923
NOBLE	William	Elgin	Murder	31/05/1834
O'KAIN	Alexander	Stirling	Robbery	21/02/1812
O'NEIL	Henry	Edinburgh	Robbery	25/01/1815
OGILVIE	Patrick	Edinburgh	Murder	13/11/1765
PATERSON	George	Glasgow	Murder	07/06/1897
PATERSON	William	Glasgow	Theft by Housebreaking	25/10/1821
PAUL	Elizabeth	Glasgow	Theft by Housebreaking	25/10/1786
PAUL	John	Edinburgh	Robbery	27/07/1791
PERRIE	William	Paisley	Murder	18/10/1837
PHREN	Christian	Aberdeen	Murder	24/11/1752

PICKWITH	William	Edinburgh	Robbery	25/09/1771
PLUNKET	James	Glasgow	Robbery	11/01/1792
PORTER	William	Glasgow	Robbery	12/05/1830
POTTS	Thomas	Paisley	Stouthrief	17/08/1797
PRICE	Thomas	Dumfries	Theft by Housebreaking	29/06/1763
PRITCHARD	Edward William	Glasgow	Murder	28/07/1865
PROVAN	Alexander	Paisley	Murder	07/11/1765
RAYBOULD	John	Edinburgh	Forgery	24/02/1768
REDDING	Patrick	Bishopbriggs	Murder	14/05/1841
REGELSEN	Hans	Kinghorn	Rape	28/06/1811
REID	David	Edinburgh	Forgery	11/09/1780
REID	Elspet	Aberdeen	Theft	14/01/1785
REID	John	Edinburgh	Murder	21/03/1787
REYNOLDS	George	Glasgow	Murder	03/08/1928
RICHARDSON	Joseph	Dumfries	Forgery	14/05/1823
RICHARDSON	William	Dumfries	Murder	30/06/1787
RILEY	John	Glasgow	Murder	16/05/1864
RIPLEY	William	Edinburgh	Rape	13/01/1762
RITCHIE	John	Aberdeen	Sheep Stealing	05/06/1818
ROBB	James	Aberdeen	Murder	16/10/1849
ROBERTSON	Alexander	Glasgow	Theft by Housebreaking	07/04/1819
ROBERTSON	George Alexander	Edinburgh	Murder	23/06/1954
ROBERTSON	James	Forfar	Murder	19/05/1848
ROBERTSON	James	Perth	Robbery	12/07/1751
ROBERTSON	James Ronald	Glasgow	Murder	16/12/1950
ROBERTSON	William	Ayr	Theft by Housebreaking	17/10/1817
ROBISON	William	Jedburgh	Theft by Housebreaking	29/05/1822
ROGERS	Robert	Perth	Robbery	21/06/1793
ROGERS	Thomas	Jedburgh	Murder	19/10/1831
ROLLINS	James	Glasgow	Murder	26/05/1920
ROSS	Normand	Edinburgh	Murder	10/01/1752
ROSS	Simon	Glasgow	Theft by Housebreaking	04/11/1818
ROSS	Walter	Edinburgh	Theft	19/04/1786
RUSSEL	James	Perth	Murder	29/06/1759
SAVAGE	John Henry	Edinburgh	Murder	11/06/1923
SCANLANE	Michael	Cupar	Murder	05/07/1852
SCANLANE	Peter	Cupar	Murder	05/07/1852
SCOTT	David	Glasgow	Forgery	05/06/1805
SCOTT	Jean	Glasgow	Theft by Housebreaking	03/11/1784
SCOTT	Martin	Glasgow	Murder	23/05/1883
SCOTT	Robert	Fans Farm	Murder	23/10/1823
SCOTT	William	Glasgow	Theft by Housebreaking	03/12/1788
SHAW	George Francis	Glasgow	Murder	26/01/1953
SHERRY	John	Glasgow	Robbery	01/11/1815
SHUTTLEWORTH	Margaret Tyndall or	Montrose	Murder	07/12/1821

SINCLAIR	Christian	Edinburgh	Murder	29/12/1813
SMART	John	Stirling	Forgery	16/05/1788
SMITH	George	Edinburgh	Theft by Housebreaking	01/10/1788
SMITH	James	Glasgow	Murder	12/04/1952
SMITH	Maitland	Dumfries	Murder	21/10/1807
SMITH	Richard	Glasgow	Theft by Housebreaking	21/05/1820
SMITH	Robert	Ayr	Theft by Housebreaking	26/05/1809
SMITH	Robert	Dumfries	Murder	12/05/1868
SMITH	Robert Dobie	Edinburgh	Murder	16/09/1951
SMITH	Thomas	Edinburgh	Horse Stealing	21/01/1807
SMITH	William	Edinburgh	Theft by Housebreaking	12/10/1791
SPENCE	James	Glasgow	Theft by Housebreaking	07/06/1786
STEEL	Mary	Glasgow	Murder	06/10/1831
STEPHENSON	George	Edinburgh	Horse Stealing	21/01/1807
STEVEN	David	Glasgow	Murder	08/06/1785
STEVENSON	James	Glasgow	Robbery	01/06/1825
STEWART	Alexander	Glasgow	Murder	23/05/1855
STEWART	Andrew	Glasgow	Robbery	01/11/1826
STEWART	George	Glasgow	Theft by Housebreaking	08/11/1809
STEWART	James	Appin	Murder	08/11/1752
STEWART	James	Edinburgh	Robbery	27/07/1791
STEWART	James	Edinburgh	Theft	06/03/1799
STEWART	John	Edinburgh	Murder	19/08/1829
STEWART	Robert	Edinburgh	Theft by Housebreaking	22/02/1809
STEWART	Thomas	Aberdeen	Murder	29/06/1770
STEWART	William	Inverness	Murder	22/10/1757
STOREY	Frederick Thomas	Greenock	Murder	11/01/1892
SUTHERLAND	Neil	Edinburgh	Robbery	22/04/1812
SWAN	William Leonard	Glasgow	Forgery	16/05/1821
SWINEY	Mannes	Greenlaw	Robbery	02/04/1834
TAYLOR	James	Inverness	Robbery	11/07/1766
TEMPLETON	Thomas	Glasgow	Murder	27/05/1840
TENNANT	Robert	Stirling	Murder	02/10/1833
THOM	George	Aberdeen	Murder	16/11/1821
THOMSON	David	Edinburgh	Theft by Housebreaking	13/03/1816
THOMSON	John	Edinburgh	Murder	18/08/1830
THOMSON	John	Paisley	Murder	14/01/1858
THOMSON	William	Dalkeith	Robbery	01/03/1827
THORNILOE	Francis	Perth	Theft by Housebreaking	17/06/1774
TIMNEY	Mary Reid or	Dumfries	Murder	29/04/1862
TORRANCE	Helen	Edinburgh	Murder	18/03/1752
VEITCH	Thomas	Glasgow	Robbery	23/05/1787
VERNON	Thomas	Glasgow	Robbery	09/11/1785
VICKERS	Robert Flockhart	Edinburgh	Murder	31/03/1884
WALDIE	Jean	Edinburgh	Murder	18/03/1752

WALES	Alan	Edinburgh	Murder	13/08/1928
WALLACE	William	Jedburgh	Robbery	17/05/1785
WARDEN	George	Edinburgh	Theft	14/04/1819
WARDLAW	David	Dumbarton	Murder	19/10/1875
WAST	William	Aberdeen	Murder	24/11/1752
WATSON	George	Ayr	Horse Stealing	07/06/1811
WATT	John	Dundee	Theft by Housebreaking	12/06/1801
WATT	Robert	Edinburgh	Treason	15/10/1794
WAUGH	Samuel	Ayr	Murder	19/01/1832
WEBSTER	William	Aberdeen	Theft	01/06/1787
WEMYSS	James	Edinburgh	Murder	16/04/1840
WESTWATER	John	Kinghorn	Murder	21/06/1806
WHITE	Agnes	Glasgow	Murder	22/05/1793
WHITE	Marion	Stirling	Murder	21/09/1777
WHITEHILL	Freebairn	Glasgow	Robbery	29/10/1817
WILLIAMS	Griffith	Edinburgh	Murder	12/03/1800
WILLIAMS	John	Greenlaw	Murder	14/03/1853
WILSON	James	Glasgow	Treason	30/08/1820
WILSON	James	Glasgow	Theft by Housebreaking	04/06/1823
WILSON	James	Edinburgh	Theft	08/01/1752
WILSON	James	Edinburgh	Murder	15/09/1773
WILSON	Thomas	Jedburgh	Murder	25/10/1849
WISHART	Margaret	Forfar	Murder	16/06/1827
WOOD	Arthur	Dundee	Murder	25/03/1839
WOODNESS	Ralph	Linlithgow	Theft by Housebreaking	27/08/1819
WORTHINGTON	John	Symington	Robbery	17/02/1815
WRIGHT	Catherine	Edinburgh	Murder	19/08/1829
WYLIE	David	Glasgow	Theft by Housebreaking	12/11/1823
YOUNG	John	Aberdeen	Murder	11/12/1801
YOUNG	John	Edinburgh	Forgery	19/12/1750
YOUNG	Peter	Edinburgh	Theft by Housebreaking	02/07/1788

7
Bibliography

The following excludes archival references and contemporary newspapers.

General

Beattie, J.M.; Crime and the Courts in England. (Oxford, 1986).
Berry, James; My Experiences as an Executioner. (Percy Lund & Co., Bradford and London, 1892).
Bland, James; The Common Hangman. (Hornchurch, 1984).
Chambers' Edinburgh Journal, No. 105, Saturday 1st February 1834.
Cockburn, Lord; Circuit Journeys. (Byway Books, 1983).
Gordon, Anne; Death Is For The Living. (Edinburgh, 1984).
Tod, T.M.; The Scots Black Kalendar. (Perth, 1938).

Aberdeen

Adams, Norman; Hangman's Brae. (Banchory, 1993).
Anderson, James; The Black Book of Kincardineshire. (Stonehaven, 1843).
Anon; The Black Kalendar of Aberdeen 1746 - 1867. (Aberdeen, 1871).
Anon; Report of the Trial of Malcolm Gillespie for Forgery. (Aberdeen 1827).

Appin

Carney, Seamus; The Killing of the Red Fox. (Lochar Publishing, 1989)

Ayr

Blair, Anna; Tales of Ayrshire. (Sheapherd Walwyn, 1983).
Hunter, John Kelso; The Retrospect of an Artist's Life. (Greenock, 1868).
Paterson, James; Report on the Prison of Ayr. (Quarter Sessions, 1812).

Dumfries

McDowall, William; History of the Burgh of Dumfries. (4th ed. 1986).

Dundee

Millar, A.H.; Haunted Dundee, 1923.
Strange Tales of Tayside. (Lang Syne Publishers Ltd, 1978).

Edinburgh

Catford, E.F; Edinburgh, The Story of a City. (Hutchison, 1975).
Chambers, Robert; Traditions of Edinburgh. (W & R Chambers Ltd, Edinburgh).
Gibson, John Sibbald; Deacon Brodie - Father of Jekyll & Hyde. (The Saltire Society, 1993).

Glasgow

Gordon, J.F.S.; Glasghu Facies, A View of the City of Glasgow. (pub. John Tweed, Glasgow)
McDowall, John K; The People's History of Glasgow.
Senex Reid, Robert; Glasgow, Past and Present.
McKenzie, Peter; Reminiscences of Glasgow and the West of Scotland. (John Tweed, Glasgow, 1866).

Inverness

Pollitt, A Gerald; Historic Inverness. (The Melvin Press, 1981).
Anon; The Life and Trial of John Adam. (John Noble, 1888).
Anon; The Life of Hugh McLeod, Assynt. (John Noble, 1889).

Kirkcudbright

The Trial and Execution of Henry Greig. (The Stewartry Museum ref. 2144).
McKenzie, Rev W; The History of Galloway. 1841.

Montrose

Lowson, Alexander; Tales, Legends and Traditions of Forfarshire. (pub John MacDonald, Forfar, 1891)

Paisley

Brown, Robert; The History of Paisley. (J & J Cook, Paisley, 1886).

Perth

Penny, George; Traditions of Perth. 1836.

Rannoch

Cunningham, A D; Tales of Rannoch. (A D Cunningham and Perth & Kinross Libraries 1989).
Cunningham, A D; A History of Rannoch. (A D Cunningham 1989).

Stirling

Drysdale, William; Old Faces, Old Places and Old Stories of Stirling. (Eneas Mackay, Stirling, 1898 & 1899).

Appendix 1
The Indictment

The following indictment was served on Eugene Marie Chantrelle (executed 31st May 1878 at Edinburgh) for the murder of his wife. It was followed by a list of productions or articles referred to in the case, and a list of the witness for the prosecution.

EUGENE MARIE CHANTRELLE, now or lately prisoner in the prison of Edinburgh, you are indicted and accused at the instance of the Right Honourable William Watson, Her Majesty's Advocate for Her Majesty's interest; That albeit, by the laws of this and every well-governed realm, murder is a crime of an heinous nature, and severely punishable; yet true it is and of verity, that you, the said Eugene Marie Chantrelle, are guilty of the said crime, actor, or art and part; in so far, as on the 1st or 2nd day of January, 1878, or on one or other of the days of December immediately preceding, within the dwellinghouse in or near George Street, Edinburgh, then occupied by you, the said Eugene Marie Chantrelle, you did wickedly and feloniously administer to, or cause to be taken by, Elizabeth Cullen Dyer or Chantrelle, your wife, now deceased, then residing with you, in an orange, or part or parts thereof, and in lemonade, or in one or other of those articles, or in some other article of food or drink to the prosecutor unknown, or in some other manner to the prosecutor unknown, a quantity or quantities of opium or other poison to the prosecutor unknown; and the said Elizabeth Cullen Dyer or Chantrelle, having taken the said opium or other poison by you administered or caused to be taken as aforesaid, did in consequence thereof, die on the said 2nd day of January, 1878, and was thus murdered by you the said Eugene Marie Chantrelle; And you the said Eugene Marie Chantrelle had previously evinced malice and ill-will towards the said Elizabeth Cullen Dyer or Chantrelle, and on many occasions between the time of your marriage with her in the month of August 1868, and the date of her death aforesaid, had falsely accused her to other persons of adultery and of incest, and struck and otherwise maltreated and abused her, and threatened to shoot her and to poison her, and by your violence and your threatenings put her in fear of losing her life; And you the said Eugene Marie Chantrelle having been apprehended and taken before Thomas Rowatt, Esquire, one of the magistrates of the city of Edinburgh, did in his presence at Edinburgh, on each of the 8th and 9th days of January 1878, emit and subscribe a declaration; Which declarations; as also the reports, letters, books, prints, and other articles enumerated in an inventory thereof, hereunto annexed and referred to, being to be used in evidence against you the said Eugene Marie Chantrelle at your trial, will, for that purpose be in due time lodged in the hands of the Clerk of the High Court of Justiciary, before which you are to be tried, and that you may have an opportunity of seeing the same; All which, or part thereof, being found proven by the verdict of an assize, or admitted by the judicial confession of you the said Eugene Marie Chantrelle, before the Lord Justice-General, Lord Justice-Clerk, and Lords Commissioners of Justiciary, you the said Eugene Marie Chantrelle ought to be punished with the pains of law, to deter others from committing the like crimes in all time coming.

Jas. Muirhead, A.D.

Appendix 2 – The Death Warrant

As the following examples show, the essence of the Death or Dead Warrant changed little over the years. Latterly, however, long hand gave way to the pre-printed form.

MATTHEW HAY
Executed; Ayr, 13th October 1780

'The Lords Kames and Braxfield having considered the verdict against Matthew Hay, Pannel, whereby the Assize by a great Plurality of Voices have Found the Pannel Guilty, In respect of the said Verdict Decern and Adjudge the said Matthew Hay to be carried from the Bar back to the Tolbooth of Ayr, therein to be detained, and in terms of the Act of Parliament of the Twenty fifth year of the Reign of His late Majesty King George the Second, intitled An Act for better preventing the horrid Crime of Murder, to be fed on bread and water only untill Friday the Thirteenth day of October next to come - And upon that day to taken furth of the said Tolbooth to the place of Execution on the Common Muir of Ayr, and there betwixt the hours of two and four afternoon to be hanged by the neck by the hands of the Common Hangman upon a Gibbet untill he be dead, and thereafter his body to be delivered to George Charles, Surgeon in Ayr, to be by him dissected and anatomised in terms of the foresaid Act, for an Example to others; And ordain all his Moveable Goods and Gear to be Escheat and Inbrought to His Majesty's use; which is pronounced for Doom.'

EDWARD WILLIAM PRITCHARD
Executed; Glasgow, 28th July 1865

'In respect of the verdict before recorded, the Lord Justice-Clerk and Lords Commissioners of Justiciary decern and adjudge the panel, Edward William Pritchard, to be carried from the bar back to the prison of Edinburgh, and from thence forthwith to be transmitted under a sure guard till brought to and incarcerated in the prison of Glasgow, therein to be detained, and fed on bread and water only, until the 28th day of July current; and upon that day between the hours of eight and ten o'clock forenoon, ordain the the said Edward William Pritchard to be taken furth of said prison to the common place of execution of the burgh of Glasgow, or to such place as the magistrates of Glasgow shall appoint as a place of execution, and there, by the hands of the common executioner, be hanged by the neck upon a gibbet till he be dead, and ordain that his body thereafter be buried within the precincts of the prison of Glasgow; and further ordain his whole moveable goods and gear to be escheat and inbrought to Her Majesty's use. Which is pronounced for doom, and may God Almighty have mercy upon your soul'.

HENRY JOHN BURNETT
Executed; Aberdeen 15th August 1963

'In respect of the foregoing Verdict of GUILTY of CAPITAL MURDER as libelled, LORD WHEATLEY sentences the said HENRY JOHN BURNETT, Pannel, to be taken from this place to the Prison of ABERDEEN, therein to be detained till the fifteenth day August next and upon that day within the said Prison of ABERDEEN between the hours of eight and ten o'clock forenoon to suffer death by hanging; Which is pronounced for Doom.